JUST
BOW

Amy Wilson Billingsley

COVENANT
Counseling & Consulting

Hendersonville NC

Just Bow: Re-orienting the soul to a place where love can grow.
Copyright © 2019 by Amy Billingsley, Covenant Counseling and
Consulting
ISBN 978-0-578-51222-8
Publication date: 2019-06-20

Classifications:
FAM030000 FAMILY & RELATIONSHIPS / Marriage & Long-Term
Relationships

REL050000 RELIGION / Christian Ministry / Counseling & Recovery

REL012160 RELIGION / Christian Living / Parenting Family &
relationships: advice & issues Religion & beliefs

Distribution by Ingram Book Group

Cover & Interior Content Design by Nathan Billingsley:
BillingsleyConcepts.com, bconcept@bellsouth.net

Dedication

To my husband, Nathan, who has helped me learn to say, "It is finished," and to our five children, Wilson, Grant, Bennett, Allana Belle and Canaan. Thank you for your kind hearted confidence in this project. A special thank you to Bennett for the expression "Just Bow." Family, you all are the right ones for me! I love bowing to these terms and having the privilege of being a wife and mother. I'll love you forever.

Table of Contents:

To the reader,

In my own personal experience with the material presented here, I have been put to the test. True change comes only through grace. We may see a need and make an attempt, and we may see a solution and taste the possibility... but sustaining it into real change is a miracle. This is a book of miracle stories. We need to see a handful of miracles to build faith in this kind of grace, and then we have to wrestle with the foundations and the strength of this grace to hold us, because trust takes time. Some could find these accounts provocative, but I've included/integrated some timely pieces for breathing room and to draw activity from both sides of the brain.

I studied family systems in the late 80's, graduated and then worked with crisis for a decade. In the early 2000's I was introduced to a german slant on family work from the perspective of facilitators who necessarily had an intense view on family, given their country's role in WWII. Their own need for reconciliation among themselves and the Jews was and is intense. What exactly do you do when you learn that your own grandparents played a part in atrocities? The need for generational healing is hefty there. No one offers the germans a book celebrating "The Greatest Generation." Clearly, the off-spring have symptoms. So how does reconciliation even happen in such families? What do we do with guilt, and how does one even begin to reconcile all parts when the faith route was so exploited by Hitler? If a group of facilitators had found solutions, I wanted to see and take notes. So I took a few trips to Germany to study. The old adage, "The truth will set you free, but first it will make you miserable," applied.

It was half-way through the first week of an intensive training workshop that I saw the generosity of Jesus—even though His blessed name was never mentioned. Overwhelmed by His presence, I bolted from the room, sat down in the hall and started mentally packing my bags simply because my small view of Christ's love was shattered and I was undone. Literally, the thoughts that overwhelmed my mind were, "This Love will never fly in my church/family." I felt shoved out of my small box and was forced "outside" to look at the gardens and the waterways of benevolent mercy. I've been getting used to Him on these terms. It's not so easy, as Love has His own say about things.

Love is our eternal subject and thankfully, sometimes painfully, we are also His. There is a blessed rhyme and reason to things that have happened. This book will help a reader venture into seeing things as they are. It's a challenge to see. Love Himself ruins life as we know it. But, blessed riddance! All real change comes from grace, so I welcome readers to the fields of grace in the pages that follow. I trust the eyes of your heart will open to a new way to see, to pray, to walk in love, to reconcile with others and God, and of course to Just Bow.

A. W. Billingsley
May 12, 2019

Introduction

"It is a serious thing to live in a society of possible gods and goddesses, to remember that the dullest most uninteresting person you can talk to may one day be a creature which, if you saw it now, you would be strongly tempted to worship, or else a horror and a corruption such as you now meet, if at all, only in a nightmare. All day long we are, in some degree helping each other to one or the other of these destinations. It is in the light of these overwhelming possibilities, it is with the awe and the circumspection proper to them, that we should conduct all of our dealings with one another, all friendships, all loves, all play, all politics. There are no ordinary people. You have never talked to a mere mortal. Nations, cultures, arts, civilizations - these are mortal, and their life is to ours as the life of a gnat. But it is immortals whom we joke with, work with, marry, snub, and exploit - immortal horrors or everlasting splendors." C.S. Lewis The Weight of Glory.

Welcome to fields of grace where we learn to Just Bow and come out from under the burden of symptoms of love lost, and bow into awareness of love present. The stories and navigational tools presented here demonstrate powerful transformations. JUST BOW will teach the reader how to effectively puzzle out key strongholds that present themselves both in family lines as well as in Biblical contexts that prohibit or release healing Love.

The book has two parts. Part one presents accounts from counseling, workshops and embodied Bible studies, as well as Biblical accounts which demonstrate divine order, disorder, and how transformation becomes activated. On all fronts of family life be it spousal, parental, small and adult children, each station will be examined for wholeness, and resolution of the disorder that sets up displacement and unfinished business. In part one the reader will discover the keys to unlock the miracle they need in all their family relationships.

In part two, we move straightway into the heart and art of reconciliation especially when faced with impossible destruction. In the main section of part two we leave the study of graphs and settle into a teaching novella which lays out the cosmic scope of the matters at hand. Through the use of the larger story, all the previous tools of dynamics are applied to the greatest trauma and injustice known to history, Calvary. Inclusion, exclusion, crisis, trauma, forgiveness and healing are reconsidered through the ultimate cosmic frame. Together, part one which deals with the soul, prepares us for part two which heals us spiritually. This part of the book in indispensable when we consider that "unless the Lord builds the house, we labor in vain." Psalm 127:1.

One final introductory note is almost an aside in the respect that this thought will not be further developed beyond these few paragraphs. This note is in regards to the seriousness of that which is allowed to inform our identities. When we discuss the definitions of Love and Life, and the impact of those definitions on personal identity — and their consequent actions — I take definitions from scripture, not popular psychology. Sounds simple, except that many times cultural definitions have crossed over and clouded our understanding of the Word, and thus our identity. This book will help us take our Bibles out with greater enthusiasm having rinsed off the mud.

Example: Throughout this book there are interchangeable references made to 'self' and 'soul.' Although 'self' may be used occasionally for ease of reading, the intent is still the 'soul.' The difference is foundational. Stay with me here. As a branch of study, psychology roots go back thousands of years ago to ancient Greece as a study in philosophy/religion. But in the recent hundreds of years the subject of psychology was reassigned in our education to the branch of soft sciences during the late 1800s, and is now moving into hard sciences via high tech study tools of brain scans. Today, in a post-modern field of faith, psychology has a place in both arenas of science and philosophy/religion. However there is a slippery slope to which I'd like to speak regarding the first point of reassignment into science.

The tension between science and faith began in the enlightenment era five hundred years ago when Galileo and Copernicus determined that the way we saw the relationship between the sun and earth departed from scripture's testimony. The divide reached a crescendo in 1859 when Darwin published his book on species and identified man as an animal. Recategorized as an animal, man was theoretically reduced to navigating life by the power of instincts. This justified a new ethic called the 'survival of the fittest.' Every identity, survivalist or otherwise, has it's behavior and consequences.

Scientific survivalists' identities were soon applied to business, education, politics, war, the sum of which became the justification for Hitler's dream of an Aryan race. The survivalist's ethic was expensive for the competition between world powers but particularly so for the Jewish people. Although Adam's race, or the human race if you prefer, never required a good reason for dismissing God, science offered an intellectual reason and in doing so temporarily assuaged a genocidal conscience. The boast of the mind of this 'manimal' species is naturally hostile toward God. Scientific survivalists unwittingly sanctioned atrocities.

The soul of man was discarded in preference to a self. But what was not so easily dismissed at the top of the food chain in the animal kingdom were the manimal troubles. With his deep need to talk and reflect and find meaning in life, the competitive survivalist still suffered heartache from war, economic troubles, and communication problems between the so called sexes common to people seeking power over connection. The broken heart was still a plague for the upgraded ape, but now he had no one smart enough to talk to — thus psychiatrist were needed — preferably to dispensed medication for the addled brain.

Whatever it meant to be afraid, real concerns or not, became scientifically diagnosed as an anxiety disorder. How to go about mending a broken heart—be it loss, death, divorce, or war— became a medical issue recategorized as clinical depression. These weaker physiologies would be treated by doctors, not the clergy, nor the elder. Thus the stigma of counseling was real because people who were in need were deemed constitutionally weak. They were unlikely leaders in the survival of the fittest with certainly nothing to offer us in terms of communal healing. Doctors would try to help contain the body's stress response but could not "see" the soul or spirit since they didn't exist in that medical science world view. One could hardly speak of a spiritual experience without being diagnosed as psychotic.

In a material only world view partnered with enlightened rationale, faith was excluded and science enthroned as if the two were mutually exclusive. In trading a 'soul' for a 'self' whose 'cognitions' needed to be reshaped with pharmaceuticals and a cognitive/behavioral theories we lost touch with many soul connections. Ironically therapy discussions centered around the self and the automatic negative thoughts — minus context, minus a plumb line for larger reality— often entrenched a person into more lonely negative meditations. Counseling easily makes matters worse when we regurgitate pain without setting a new course; that would be too close to something called repentance which has no solid place in a survivalists view. The role of conscience is clearly compromised in a survivalist's ethic.

We might ask, who establishes conscience in a survival of the fittest slant? Hitler or another political guru? How could others significantly matter except in slavery for the sake of the top of the food chain? There is no conscience in mass, just control and loss of freedom. Psychology, the cure for the weak, addressed manimals as a self — without God or very many others in mind. The product was an untethered focus on self-esteem, self-empowerment, and a free floating idea of self-actualization. Where these ideas are predicated upon the ethics of the survival-of-the-fittest paradigm, it is a recipe for becoming ego-centric, self-serving, and ultimately self-destructive in the name of liberation. The relativity of truth was the battle cry against anyone who might contradict someone on their way to the top.

Today, there is a deep social reaction demanding utter inclusivity for the marginalized but still without any notion as to how people actually fit together in a survivalists framework. Survivalists by definition have to exclude. Without a God whose heart was to make a place for us in Eden, and still is to make a place for us directly with Himself, there is no ethic that has room for others. Only God makes a place for the marginalized... in His own house. Scientifically speaking now, what if quantum physics includes a God particle? Identity matters, what kind of God exists? What's He like?

If we identify ourselves as living souls, made in God's image, not Him made in our image, we will reconsider ourselves as having an embodied experience. We agree that we are inherently something more than a physical being. Viewing ourselves as a living soul we make room for God and life beyond the body but clearly we have another reference beside "self," and competition between earthly powers. There is a subtle shift toward community with God in mind.

When we think self, we think achievement. When we think soul, we think of connection. Selves and souls relate by a different kind of conscience, one leans into power, the other inclines toward the spiritual. One answers to no one, the other listens to a higher One with others in mind.

We can not love well as survivalists when we lean into power struggles for control in a relationship. A survivalist may want to mate and call it love, but their ethic reduces an 'other' as an object for mastery which is defined by getting a "catch" who agrees to stay sexy and prop up the ego. Societally trying to sort this out in law making is hard without a shared world view.

More importantly when we accidentally mix the two consciences as a compromise, Christians end up playing one of two games. Either we become legalists, power hungry for dominance and control, as if there is no God of sovereign grace, or we shed legalism for relevance/relativity, and have little serious use for scripture at all. Either way, we imagine God in our image.

The good news though, beneath all the surface tension and confusion about the designer of life, there remains a divine order in Love that is personally testable regardless of world views, and once tested, it demonstrates that the nature of love is that of a soul bonded to other souls all pointing towards an undeniable beautiful spiritual door (with a name written on it.) When divine orders are tested and proven helpful, the orders draw a soul upwards toward God, who comes to our aid. "Unless the Lord builds the house, the laborers labor in vain." Psalm 127:1.

Test cases are included throughout this book. The tools are available for the reader to try out individually as well as in groups. No degrees are needed, no diagnosis is prohibitive, and no one loses by venturing a new "look" at an old family story.

We know there is something wrong at home and at church. Christians believe it is the fall of Adam and perhaps assume it always will be distorted. Deliverance and inner healing are important but not widely sought. But for the sake of a Biblical soul mandate, imagine, very seriously imagine just for a moment, a world where Adam actually fulfilled his original commission given by God. What exactly was that commission? Adam was commissioned to represent God on earth by cultivating the garden, expanding it, and having dominion over the animals... this included the animal described as the wild crafty serpent. Together with Eve they were to be fruitful and multiply. Daily Adam — living soul — walked with God — connected in Spirit — in the cool of the day. What if Adam had maintained his place of spiritual hierarchy? What if instead of taking his cues from an animal, he fulfilled his commission by giving nature the directive to just bow? Adam might have grown into his true identity as an offspring of God. "But why," people ask, "why did God allow the serpent?" It was a gift, an opportunity for Adam to know himself IN God and take his place in the world as a servant of God, a kind keeper of His work, a shepherd taming wild things.

That offer has been put back on the table by Christ. We are still commissioned to represent Love. The animal instinct, feeds the survivalist identity with an urge to usurp power. This instinct is still within us and our systems, but so is the other option of the Spirit. There is a designer and He has His kind eye of Love on us and has committed Himself to our becoming like Him.

Chapter One: The Art of Wishing Well

*"Most of us miss the presence of others
because we are too preoccupied with
observing, listening, and confirming preconceptions."
Presence and Encounter: David G. Benner, Ph.D.*

Finding a good place to start requires we find a good place to end. Destination must be in mind before we purchase a ticket out of the place we want to leave. What exactly do you want in a particular relationship? Name the outcome you want, given what you are facing? Notice that this is not a description of a problem. That is a complaint, not a solution. Exactly how we get to the solution is also another matter for pages ahead. Creativity helps us engage with hope by allowing ourselves to dream about outcomes.

Identifying what we would like to move toward is a part of the basic order as heirs of Christ. In the Kingdom, with God as Father, we identify as His children, and in childlikeness, or something we call faith, we are appointed to "ask." What we ask for says something about what grace God is working into our lives. In our souls we are entangled in many broken places. We aren't just asking for trinkets and whatnots to set on some shelf. We ask for things that reflect our relationship coming to peace, on earth as it is in Heaven. It seems easy enough to ask, but it is actually a challenge. Consider the following odd tale.

Johnny's Unlist:
"Johnny, have you been good?" Santa asked as he made room for a small boy on his lap.

"Yes, sir, I have. I didn't cheat on any of my spelling tests this year — or math."

Half-way listening, given the long line of children waiting, Santa chuckled his rote "Ho, ho, ho," and continued, "Well then my good boy, tell me what you would like for Christmas."

Worried and annoyed little guy that he was, Johnny whispered, "Santa, I think you should know that in-line skates are out now."

"Oh?"

"Yes, sir."

"Did I give those to you last year?" Santa asked while casting a quizzical look at the boy's mom.

"No, sir, but someone else did, and I didn't like them. I don't like chocolate covered cherries either."

"Oh! Ho, ho." He winked at the mom. "Well, then, speak up now, loud and clear: what would you like for Christmas?"

"I don't like reading, so I don't want books, and I'm the only boy I know who doesn't play video games; both give me a headache."

Santa replied loudly for the child's mother to hear him say, "Well, would you like a pair of glasses, which might take away your headaches?"

"No, sir. I don't want to be a dork."

Sliding his own glasses up the bridge of his nose, Santa continued, chuckling now, and glanced over at the other parents, "Well, son, what would you like, then?"

"I'm not done yet. I don't like getting clothes, and I also don't want a musical instrument of any kind. Please, no more harmonicas, flutes, or horns, and I don't know what the use was in a guitar without lessons. And, really, Santa— a banjo?"

Santa said loudly, "Sorry, folks; I'm getting an un-list at the moment. Elves, take notes!" Johnny's mom turned red. "What would you like, then, Johnny?"

"I don't want new shoes because me and Jesus both have birthdays in December, so I already get new shoes. And I don't want a new suit because I would only wear it for Christmas Eve services. At Easter I wear shorts, and by next year—the suit wouldn't fit, so I would have to get another one! It would be too big this year and too small next year."

Now, having vented his frustration, Johnny was nearly in tears. His head was weighed down, and Santa could feel him starting to quiver.

"Even red suits?" Santa said genuinely, offering a little joke.

"Santa, I really don't want to dress up like you. I'm just a kid."

Santa stroked the boy's back and patted his little leg. Something about the sense of exhaustion seemed clearer now and the real man in the suit paused to ask, "Are you just a kid?"

Feeling suddenly seen beneath his outpour of un-wishing, Johnny let his tears flow freely while the Christmas music played eerily cheerfully and out of place in his little heart.

Santa saw the boy and whispered, "Son, you really are just a kid. The burdens in life are supposed to go in big sacks on big people's backs because they are strong enough to carry them. Now, I wonder if you could be a little boy-brave and tell me the truthful wish: do you have any idea at all about what you really would like for Christmas, Johnny?"

Johnny lifted his eyes to read the eyes of the old man, glanced at his mom and then couldn't bear to speak his wish out loud. But then Santa cupped his hand beside his ear as if it might be their secret, and the little boy joined his small hand in the secret and whispered something in Santa's ear that turned the old face red and moistened his eyes like the real the Santa might feel rising up in him.

The photographer snapped the picture of Johnny's guarded confession.

They both sniffled. "Well, then. That is a good boy. I understand your wish. And it's a good wish." And with that small hope, Johnny dried his eyes and jumped down while Santa dried his own. Santa asked the "elf" if he got it, while directing a curious look at Johnny's mother. Santa then said he would do his best and wished Johnny's mother a "good luck" to go with her "Merry Christmas."

"The picture is on the house," said the Elf.

Santa and his crew hoped the free picture would prompt Johnny to tell his mom what he really wished for—soon and before Christmas.

We will return to Johnny's wish shortly.

Breaking Trance

It seems like a simple thing to say what you want. But a version of Johnny's conversation happens regularly in counseling offices and in prayer meetings. We are more aware and inclined to say what we do not want: depression, cancer, divorce—than to describe what we do want— joy, reconciliation, peace, health, strong business, etc. And in saying those things that we do not want repeatedly, "I have a bad this or that," these things become a meditation, not a context clue. And as a meditation, the un-wanted is neither a solace nor a route to something else. The un-wanted easily becomes our only focus. We have to learn to think and pray like we are souls on mission to reconciling things on earth.

But our first Johnny-glitch is fearing trouble, due to a divided loyalty. Fear keeps us silent. We don't easily own our wish which is the first part of our Life's power for union. In fear, we think that if someone else will figure out what we "should want" or suggest it, or give it to us without our asking, then we are not "at fault" if it works out. We can get away with happiness. There is a fear of being held responsible for having what we wished for. But even Santa can't hide that. Wishing tells our secret.

There is an illegal fear trance that seeks control and is disrupted when we own up to our wish. The slave nature in man doesn't dare to ask or hope — that could lead somewhere. There is something about change that is prohibitive in the unconscious. But it might be okay to wish for the desired outcome if someone else thinks it is an okay idea. Johnny did not think his mom was a resource, but Santa was an option of hope and became a secret keeper. So Johnny whispered a wish. To state a wish outright is to own it, which is half the journey—just in naming the wish. Naming it comes from another part of the self that is more inclined toward creativity than defense mechanisms. So when we own our wish, we activate another part of our soul process. There is a lot of criticism about 'name it and claim it' theology, which does smack of selfishness. But when this is applied to the soul, not to material greed, there is an essential honesty that breaks a trance.

A clear wish breaks a spell. Owning a desire creates an interruption in the negative meditation. Stating a clear wish creates a shift—even in the midst of contradictions. It is interesting to note that ten people feeling a similar distress may wish for ten entirely different outcomes. Let's say ten people experience depression. All ten may wish for a different outcome: one wants reconciliation, others want peace, others want energy, another creativity, or health in healing. Each wish is likely related to a relationship with someone they fear is impacted perhaps negatively by their wish.

The point here is that no one can do another person's wishing: not a spouse, a parent, friend, or minister. The wish is generally related to the deep needs of the soul and are as personal as Johnny's secret. Johnny told Santa that he wanted a bow-and-arrow set. Some little boys like Johnny have to whisper their secret wish for reasons that make sense to them.

Johnny struggled to say it because his father was a champion archer; his parents were divorced, and his stepfather was a musician. Johnny was afraid of hurting someone's feelings. But he desperately missed his father and the ongoing conflicts between the adults made him feel disloyal for his desire to reach out and reconcile with his own father, even if his mother didn't want him to be closer to 'her ex.' He just couldn't love his stepfather the way she wanted him to, he couldn't forget his own father. Wishes are serious matters of a desired outcome.

If we prematurely looked at Johnny as an ungrateful child, and scolded him for taking too much of Santa's time, we'd miss the window of the heart. Symptoms are clues; patience with ourselves and others will help. Once we've broken an unconscious trance by stating a wish, we are ready to move into the depths of love. What happens when Johnny's mom finds out about her son's wish? She may in fact be surprised and glad to accommodate, or she may be angry because, to her, in her own unfinished business with Johnny's dad, she sees the man as a failure who never does his part. But Johnny just misses what is his: his own dad, with or without a bow and arrow. And this is a matter of the soul, a matter to which the arrows point.

A wish is like a harness of hope–hope that life can be seen in a new way. This is part of being made in the image of God: to think, imagine, and see it, and then speak it into our life, not as a demand, but as a matter of gentle trust, or a wish.

For an entire counseling session or more, I've watched many adult-Johnnys struggle to answer the question, "What would be a good outcome for you?" They can discuss the losses forever, but to state the wish is hard for adults. But children actually come to it quicker, though it never quite rolls right off someone's tongue.

A little guy like Johnny was in my office once, saying he was very sad. I kept myself and his mom quiet while he struggled to say what his wish was. No guessing on our part, no "helping" him. It took an eternal moment of quiet thought, but he finally said he wanted to feel like he belonged. Our jaws dropped.

Knowing how devoted his mom was, it was like the wind was knocked out of both of us. It was not at all what either his mother nor I expected him to say. How in the world did he feel he did not belong?

But his wish was solid and gave me the clue I needed to help them work through a presenting conflict. He dearly loved his parents, all of three of them. He loved his mom, he loved his stepfather very much, but he also loved his "nere-do-well" father. So we set up a family model on a table board so we could all see what he was looking at in his soul's view.

I laid the board flat on my coffee table, and I drew large circle as a space for his family in the middle of the board. I asked him to set up some small plastic figures inside or outside of this family circle so that he could show me where everyone in his family stood in relation to him and to one another. He placed the figure representing himself very close to his mom and his devoted step dad on the right side of the circle, and he placed his father at a distance on the left side of the circle. But the direction of the face of the figure for himself was pointed toward his father, though his body was with his mother in proximity. The gaze in his soul was with his father.

I asked him if there was anyone in his family that he thought also might feel like they did not belong. And he said his father. And then he started to tear up. His mom tendered.

This young "Johnny" had listened to the poverty narrative and loosened his connection with his father in order to blend well with the new father figure provided for him by his mom who was happily married again. But inside, Johnny missed his father. He didn't want to be disloyal to his mother, nor reject his stepfather who had no children of his own. Taking advantage of a sudden and rare conflict at home actually gave him an opportunity to find his wish and reconnect with his father. Once he made the connection, he found his mother to be very supportive, and they made new plans to include the "ex" as a continued family member who still belonged to the whole as the son's father. It mattered little to the son that his father was not as successful materially as his stepfather. What mattered was that Johnny connect with him, even if he had to sleep on a pallet on the floor and eat pb&js. Love loves.

Wishing is childlike by nature, not childish. It has more in common with prayer than ego because it doesn't demand—it hopes. As a child, a person small or large has an awareness of something greater. A goal is a bit more self-directed and self-determined—powerful. A wish is a nice way of opening up to that which is larger—trusting.

A child has no way to know if the toy he asked for is what he's going to receive. He has to leave it with the giver of gifts in good faith that the one greater is going to accomplish that wish, or do better. That's the energy of a wish: it is as gentle as hope. We entrust it to the angels who nudge us along, and we work with the Spirit as the process unfolds to lead to our next steps.

Pausing for practice

I like to invite folks to use their mind's eye and describe what they see in their own personal Field of Grace, whatever that looks like to the individual. Imagine a large wide open field, noticing the uniqueness of it, however it appears; then walk out into that field, and call the Lord to meet you there. Make a request. The request is for yourself in relation to yourself perhaps, but perhaps in relation to others, or God. For experiment, jot the wish down on the last page of the book. It may be that by the end of the book you'll see how it may come to pass, or you'll know your next steps towards it, or the wish may change.

"Ask, and it will be given to you; seek, and you will find; knock, and it will be opened to you. For everyone who asks receives, and the one who seeks finds, and to the one who knocks, it will be opened." (Matthew 7:7-8)

Grace reminds us of His generosity. *"Which one of you, if his son asks him for bread, will give him a stone? Or if he asks for a fish, will give him a serpent? If you, then, who are evil, know how to give good gifts to your children, how much more will your Father who is heaven give good things to those who ask him!" (Matthew 7:7-11 English Standard Version).*

Wishing with a Sore Conscience

You wouldn't think your conscience could be misleading, but it depends upon who the conscience is serving. Often the conscience is informed by family, even ancestry, or perhaps culture. It is a gate keeper of sorts. Jesus said we can't serve two masters (Matthew 6:24). Although the reference he made was about trusting God or money, the idea also includes becoming a slave to anything or anybody else due to our unmet dependency needs; these old fears make gamblers out of us.

The conscience reveals the governing rules of our loyalties without telling us whether or not our rules for life are truthful. Our struggle to make a wish is connected to the relationship we identify with, and when we are divided in loyalties, we struggle with guilt. Guilt reflects the rules and the limits they impose on us. But if the rules are unruly, our conscience can't produce a healthy kind of guilt as a fair warning.

That we even have a conscience at all is evidence that we are created by God, but the way that our conscience can be ensnared is evidence that we are divided and in need of reconciliation in higher realms that have a wider view of our human terrain.

Reconciliation is not only meant for the heavenly relationship with God, but it is also meant for all that is broken on earth. The conscience sets the limits of who we are allowed to connect with, allowing us to know the terms for community or fellowship. Whoever/whatever informs the conscience is internalized as the authority, and sometimes that is not God. The inner conflicts are gifts that ask us to examine the terms for relationships.

Just because we have a conscience does not mean we have a pure sense of right and wrong, but it does mean that we have the seed of God in us, calling us to transcend the limits of loyalties and move into the Kingdom where we can see the fuller love of God for all of us. There we can find the best place for each other.

The Kingdom view has room and placement for everyone at the table. The spirit in us sees a higher plane of love than what the mind of the flesh would naturally welcome. Seeing that space is critical to love.

Issues of conscience differ from family to family, group to group, culture to culture, nation to nation, and from age to age. Navigating relationships with only the earthly conscience creates limitations and tricks us into playing judge, not child of the Judge who is also Father.

As long as we have attachments with people who are at odds with others we love, we will have a need to clarify how Love orders the affairs of love in various relationships. If there is a place for us all, where is it?

Chapter Two: New Arrangements for Love: Seeing the Missing Siblings

"In Him we live and move and have our being."
–Apostle Paul (Acts 17:28)

We now begin the loving work of seeing. The soul has an inner image of itself in relationship to others. The following two stories demonstrate two processes. One is doing the work by proxy in a group and the other in private. Both are graphed for the reader. Every model delivers an impactful image.

In a workshop setting, unlike a general therapy session, people don't give long narratives about relationship issues. We start with the wish, gather only the facts, and then set up a model for exploration. In a proxy process we interview the representatives that are participating as stand-ins for people they've never met and gather impressions from them based on the placement they've been assigned by the wisher. It's wildly interesting, impactful and miraculous.

The Brother

A man attended a workshop and expressed his wish to be in a better relationship with his father. He could not account for why they'd not spoken in more than two years. Regarding simple profile facts, he said that his parents divorced when he was a young boy. Both parents were happily remarried, and he'd lived primarily with his mother as he grew up. He was now married. For most of his life, he and his father had had pleasant contact but couldn't understand the recent silence of two years. Choosing people from the group to represent himself and his family, he set them up as it felt like they stood in relation to himself.

In the diagram below, the larger square F and the circle M symbolize the client's father and mother who both faced the son, the smaller square. The stepparents were placed behind their spouses, as shown in the upper part of the family circle. After the set-up, he sat down to watch me facilitate the work with the representatives.

The arrangement did not seem to demonstrate any estrangement between the son and either of his parents. The representatives also seemed warm and attentive. Checking in with each one starting with the representative for the man, I asked how the placement felt for each of them. Everyone was comfortable. No one reported any sense of estrangement. Instead, they all seemed well connected to him as parents, and stepparents also had warm feelings for him. The estrangement he felt did not show up in the set up, neither in how he placed them nor how they felt as proxy family members.

That was baffling. It occurred to me to ask the man if there were any other children. He reported being an only child.

But when he said this, the representative standing in for him had a slight reaction and turned to me with a doubtful look. I asked what the matter was and the representative said he felt like someone was missing and felt like someone else belonged there beside him. To clarify, I asked the client again: "Were there any other children conceived or perhaps lost in miscarriages, abortions, or adoptions?"

He said no.

I didn't see any point in guessing or pressing against his known facts, so I dismissed the participants to sit down so we might all reflect a bit with the young man on what he saw, if anything, in that live model.

When I asked what he noticed, he said he actually agreed with the representative's sense of the presence of another person. He was curious about the representative's experience because he had always felt like someone else was there and had been with him all his life. But it was not something he would ever have put into words since it seemed like an odd thing to say out loud, so he'd always just kept that feeling to himself.

With that, a woman in the group who had observed the set up asked him if he'd ever heard of a vanishing twin. He said no, but he was interested in her thoughts and asked her to continue. She said she knew that sometimes two children are conceived, but only one makes it to term.

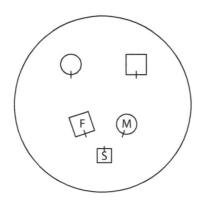

Diagram 2.1

He brightened considerably.

Seeing his energy and sensing the support of the group, I asked the representatives to each retake their places again and then we added another representative for a hypothetical lost sibling to see what it felt like to the representatives.

With this addition, not only was everyone still fine together, but now the representatives for himself and the hypothetical lost sibling felt very happy together; they seemed to belong together and both felt a strong connection. They liked the way that arrangement felt.

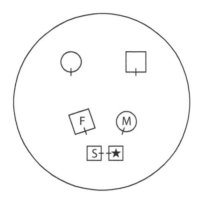

Diagram 2.2

I asked the man to take his own place and dismissed his proxy representative for him to see how it felt directly. He immediately felt comfortable and also comforted by the presence of a sibling. His new feeling shifted from estrangement with his dad to a warm connection to a lost sibling. Here, he felt whole. With the new image for consideration, we left it there with him in a good place.

Clearly, this image was only a working theory. If this new model of his family was true, and if someone was there as an "unknown" this might create a shift in the family. But how this was going to bear any fruit between the man and his father was unknown.

Three weeks later, I had a chance to speak with the referring therapist about the man and asked if there had been any feedback from him about the workshop.

Yes, there was. He reported that shortly after the workshop, his father called him out of the blue. After they caught up on life in general, he told his father about the workshop and asked if there were any other children in their family that he had not known.

Yes, there was another child who died before him. This is the report I received.

The man's parents had been married for several years when his mother became pregnant. She was unwilling to accept the child at that time. Without her husband's knowledge, she aborted their first child. The abortion was so upsetting to the father when she informed him, that she decided to become pregnant again to try to reconcile their broken relationship. She soon conceived their second child, this man.

The loss of the child explained the loss of the marriage and likely resurfaced in a timely manner as father-son estrangement at a time in life when the son approached the same age as his parents when they lost their first child. Now that the roster was complete, everyone had been seen and had a place in the whole. The symptom of parent/child estrangement belonged to the family system, he was the carrier.

The Sister

An adolescent girl was brought to a private session by her mother to address recurring bouts of depression which lasted for months at a time. This pattern had been going on for five years. Her stated wish was to be stable and happy.

Not finding any particular precipitating event, I asked her to set up the image of her family by using small figures to represent each family member. The figures varied in size. She chose three adult-sized figures to represent herself (D- Daughter) and her parents (M- Mother and F- Father), and chose a small figure for her sibling (S) two years her junior. When she arranged the figures, she placed herself between her parents and her sister beneath herself.

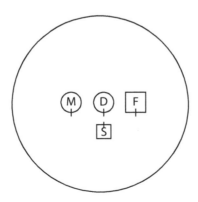

Diagram 2.3

At first glance, it was apparent that by standing between her parents instead of beside her sister, she was out of order. So I wondered how she came to see herself there and in whose place she was standing.

Children do not naturally put themselves out of place; the family soul is out of balance, perhaps missing someone of importance, and that 'hole' draws another family member in to fill it as a representative for the forgotten. Then, the representative member takes on those misplaced feelings as their own. It is an unconscious family action. At least this is the theory that bears out once resolved.

Given that she placed herself as an adult peer, I wondered if she was entangled in the place of a former partner of one of her parents, perhaps a former spouse or first love with whom a parent had unfinished business. But there was no report regarding prior significant relationships. I asked if her parents had any significant losses among their siblings, and there were none to her knowledge.

As soon as I asked if there were any other children in their family, she burst into tears, saying there were four miscarriages before her birth, adding "I'm so sorry I'm the first one to make it."

She was heavily identified with her deceased siblings. Quickly handing her the bag of small figures again, I asked her to find her siblings. She was jolted out of her tears and somewhat confused by my instruction.

I repeated, "Look in the bag and find your siblings and put them on the board where you can see them, and place them where you think they belong."

Carefully, with serious deliberate attention, she sorted through the bag for specific selections. Meanwhile, I removed the adult figure she'd chosen for herself, leaving that space open for the miscarried children should she want to place them in that station. She gingerly selected four small figures and placed them in the same spot previously held by her own adult figure. Then I chose another small figure to represent her more accurately as a child, and placed her figure with her living sibling.

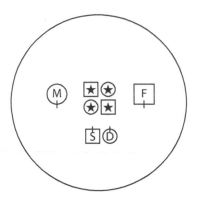

Diagram 2.4

She took a deep breath and studied the new image of her whole family of souls. We discussed the new image briefly. She could see that her place was with the living, and the losses of life that preceded her was a grief that belonged between her parents and was not for her to carry. She was already visibly less burdened.

Then I asked her to close her eyes and imagine a Field of Grace, and to describe it to me once she saw it.

People report very different things to visualize a Field of Grace. Some see wheat fields, some see green grass, others see flowers, some see a high mountain peak, shores on a lake or a beach, and some see a dark place. She said out loud, "There is a huge bright light, and they are all in it. We are all together now." With that she took another deep breath.

I paused momentarily for her to settle into her new image of her family. Then I told her to give them over to the care of Christ and honor their lives by seeing them continuing life in Him on His terms. She did so and breathed a sigh of relief.

Then, I had her and her mother stand up in the office together and had her lean back on her mother's chest and feel her support and love as a child again. She was very comfortable resting back on mother.

In a follow-up session, I learned about how dramatically she was affected by the new image and how helpful it was. She went home and for three days purged things she'd been holding onto for a long time. Mother did brief work around the losses and years later, her daughter is still happy and well adjusted.

Without a way to search out a matter and see such relief, I shudder to think about what might have happened had she gone somewhere and received a medical diagnosis and medication.

Summary Thoughts

By viewing symptoms as belonging to the system, we have a chance to honor and mourn our losses, and reconcile all members to the whole. When it frees the symptom-bearer to stand in their own place and live their own life we have healing — also for the whole.

Everyone in a family belongs. The dead still hold a place in our hearts, and we are restless until all are accounted for. In a survivalist world view, these losses would never be queried because we have a view of people as individual. If man is made in His image, as a triune whole, we are not only designed by and for union, but to be otherwise is contrary to our design. We must ask about our place and our sense of belonging and what community means. We don't do well with division. Our sense of being at home in our own skin requires us to be at home with others.

Chapter Three: Embodied Bible Studies

Let the word of Christ dwell in you richly.
(Colossians 3:16)

Embodied Bible Study

Family workshops are intense healing encounters as are private work, but there is another way to explore healing without a formal investigation. Through an embodied study of the sacred families, parables, and teachings in the Scriptures we can study by proxy. This is another way to encounter the mystery that heals us by doing so according to God's wish. Not only does the Lord reach people with spontaneous reconciliations, but He builds fellowship as well. This encounter is very user-friendly.

The Bible is a rich encyclopedia of thin-space experiences between God and humanity chronicling over a period of five thousand years. Scripture records the patterns and revelations of God and his relations with people and their relations with one another. These book collections celebrate family arrangements that are consistent with the movements of Love, and record the aches and pains of life out of order.

Encountering the sacred texts as representatives by proxy offer endless opportunities for healing and reconciliation. Embodying the text allows us to see the layers of story in-depth as the representatives place themselves in various stations and positions that provide a landscape for the participants. The Holy Spirit, who was promised to teach us, shows up. Representatives begin to identify their own projections and prior blocks to understanding a text by working together and participants often notice the difference between what they previously thought about the story and its meaning and what "came" into their awareness through the representation.

We all have blind spots by nature in life, so it is easy to project those onto a text without noticing the blurring. Not only do we bring personal projections, but also we bring a variety of well-developed and underdeveloped inherited teachings to a text. But in an embodied reading we can catch our errors by working together. Often the 'a-ha' experience unsettles an old false belief and encourages freedom in a person. By seeing events or people of scripture in a new light we see God's grace in a fuller way. It is inspiring, especially when the youngest of the participants in a group are able to deliver the strongest message of encouragement. Examples of representing scripture will follow in this chapter. But first I want to explain the process.

In embodied Bible studies, everything in a text is an option for representing. God, the Lord of Hosts, the Spirit, human characters, their emotions, the angels, demons, Satan, and any physical thing like bread, water, fish, land, blood, and so on. Every word in the Word can have a voice through a representative and enrich our experience of the logic of God.

In contrast to family set-ups, there are only so many family models a person needs to build to put their own house in order. But the opportunities to build up the Spirit through the scriptures are endless.

Biblical models set up a little differently than a family model. In the family work, a wish is declared by the wisher. The God of Scriptures also has a wish which we don't see going into the set-up but it is revealed in the reading. Family work mends the soul, this work heals the spirit. We are spiritual in nature and are spiritually discerning when we open ourselves to God's wish by embodying His Word. This is where the work gets amazing because God's wishes suit us all.

Participants have experiences in the parts they represent that are impactful in their own lives in highly specific issues, some of which they were not always mindful of as a need or wish. In this way, many receive an unexpected wish fulfilled without asking.

How to

The protocol is simple. To begin, we gather, we pray simply asking the Spirit to teach us. Then we have a short round of feedback as an icebreaker — some lingering take away feedback from the previous week's study, or introducing a friend, or a bit of news. Then we read through a selected biblical text.

During the reading participants notice the parts of the text that stand out to them with interest. We make a list of all those points of interest on a board: for example: Jesus, Peter, disciples, a boat, water, wind, fear, and so on. Participants then study the list and choose the part(s) that they want to represent and we cross that option off. Each person receives a name tag identifying who or what they are representing in the story. The players then stand in a circle to see one another and they state their proxy name. As we go around the circle each settles into their part and takes notice of the other parts and which ones their part is relating to most.

When the circle breaks, the representatives slowly move to a place in the room that suits their part as they see it, each becoming more aware of the significances of the part they are representing, as well as aware of their place in relation to others. This is how they all become oriented as one part in relation to the whole.

If there is some restlessness in someone's part, the facilitator checks to see if participants are having second thoughts about their part or if they would prefer to make a change perhaps to add some part or switch with someone. We generally can catch a mis-pick and find the right part for each participant.

Once representatives move out into their spaces in the room, they get a new sense of the whole story as it begins to come into view all around them. A new picture of an old story immediately emerges and continues to move through the reading. We gather a few initial impressions of the parts and how participants have found their places. Then we re-read the passage slowly verse by verse pausing to notice changes in direction, positions or thoughts in the participants as they happen. When the text moves someone to another place, we get feedback as the story unfolds in the representatives' experiences.

In terms of housekeeping rules, there are only a few and they are useful else where. First, no one directs others as to where they need to go; each person only finds his or her own best place among all others. Second, although there is a place for everyone, not everyone is in their best place in the initial set-up. Representatives may have to discover their place in a story as it unfolds which is another good rule for life.

If a station in the space seems to be "owned" by two people, they make room for both, knowing the reading will naturally move people around. As the story unfolds, a testimony of God emerges—every time. We can trust the representatives and their sense of movements: another rule for life. God can tell His story through all of us.

In terms of interpreting stations and places, what we've seen over time is that 'places exist,' and stations in the room represent meaning. Orders are a legitimate and living part of the universe, and, by being in the right place, a person comes into the right sense of ownership and authority for that placement. A right place has authority and boundaries. Again, this is an important life lesson. Boundaries only work in the right station.

There is a dynamic of presence that shows up in each placement and moves people into alignment in a story, a sense of connection with a placement is common. There is a trust that each person is being lead by the story. This movement in the Spirit is very encouraging to developing faith.

Those who sense that they are representing a person in a position of authority may go to a space we've come to notice as the top of the room, others go the bottom, some take one particular side of the room or the other for some reason, which unfolds in the story. Some stand on furniture, go beneath something, or lay on the ground. There is permission to find what works that allows a story to unfold in greater depth.

In a practical manner of speaking, it is important for participants as persons to notice how it is to bring their full attention to their own inner movements and to learn to register their own places in a larger story going on around them. In a room full of moving parts and people, learning to dial into one's interior is essential to setting up an image that will bring hidden themes to light. Good life lesson—dial in.

Often, two things are happening. One is that the theme of God's wish in a text is better understood by the group resonance. Secondly, participants also notice what is touched within their own soul that may be a personal issue which drew them to choose their part. Both are points of discernment as to what belongs to the universal story and what belongs to them personally. Training one's eye of the heart to take in more parts while staying in touch with their own part, is a great practice of holding one's own place while making room for all other places. All parts matter. We practice being in union with the greater soul of a story.

In these practices, people not only become comforted that the Spirit's reasoning is trackable, but also folks feel confident that the Spirit moves in others, and, together, we are in the service of His great story. As participants practice dialing into resonance, we learn the beauty of interdependence in the body. We cannot afford to lose touch with each other. Unity is a universal need. We are all parts of the whole.

After the reading is complete, participants de-role and briefly report their favorite "take-aways" from the text, whether it came from their own part or another's. We keep it brief so everyone has a chance to give a sacred piece.

Sometimes we may begin with a quiet moment to present a need to God before reading. Then afterwards, also people have time to check privately with that need and how it may have been touched or better understood in the experience. Occasionally we share communion, and always we pray the Lord's Prayer on bended knee together.

Below are some excerpts from studies. I trust the reader to reference the Biblical texts to familiarize themselves with the passages as needed. If something presented here conflicts with the reader's previous study or understanding in previous learning, I suggest the reader sketch out the story for themselves, and also do a word search for clearer definitions in original language which is easily done from the website blueletterbible. org. This resource is indispensable in searching out the meaning of a text when doing a private study.

There have been times when a representative experienced a text differently than the translation's interpretation. But upon further study into the language, the representative is generally supported in what they have experienced. An embodied Bibles study experience is complimentary not substitutionary of other important forms of Biblical hermeneutics.

Genesis 3: Through Eden and Beyond:

In Genesis 3, the root-of-life events in the Garden of Eden have been interpreted in many ways for thousands of years. When participants embodied this story, they came to some new insights, even though some of the participants considered themselves to be seasoned Christians.

The group initially only chose to represent the following parts of the story: God, Adam, Eve, and the serpent. More parts were taken up by observers who spontaneously chose them during the reading: Enmity, a Skin Covering, and Angels with flaming swords.

No one chose to represent the Tree of Life, nor the Tree of the Knowledge of Good and Evil. These key parts of the story seemed to be passed over at first. And yet, they found expression just the same.

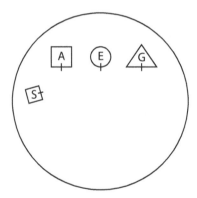

Diagram 3.1

Representatives for Adam and Eve positioned themselves at the topmost part of the room at the right hand of 'God.' God was in support of them and had given them their charge as representatives of Him on Earth. The set-up in terms of station and position is the original order and right place for humanity in our beginnings. In the New Testament, we find this is the placement of Christ who is seated at the right hand of God. The 'serpent' set up as stationed beneath mankind, off-centered to the left. The whole action took up the top most part of the room.

During the group's early days of study, we hadn't yet discussed the stations as holding a sense of authority. But this was the start of the participants' beginning to take notice of the positions as meaning-filled stations in the story.

The first tasks were to govern the animals, care for the garden, and pass life on to fill the earth. All these tasks were resourced by God. Seeing God as a support role in this image—stationed as their helper—'looked' to some like the presence of the Holy Spirit at hand and in communion. The Holy Spirit was "helping" them to fulfill their call, filling them with authority.

Man's place of authority was tested by a wild animal, the 'serpent.' The couple's first test presented itself as a wild animal and made an accusation to Eve against God, and—inadvertently—Adam.

Adam did not over-rule the wild animal, though he and Eve were stationed above it. Eve followed an animal; Adam followed them both, and, immediately, they were sin-conscious. They embodied the will of the animal they were called to subdue instead of the Life that created them.

In this picture, the tester of authority was beneath them and, interestingly, continued to be so throughout the reading of Genesis 3:1-24. Interestingly the couple didn't move, indicating Adam even in his following had passively lead by his agreement.

The major movements we saw in this story were as follows:

1) When the serpent deceived Eve, and Adam agreed to follow the animal's way, Enmity spontaneously came out of the group of observers and stood in-between the couple. Where Adam had previously 'seen' and identified Eve as part of himself, now there was a presence of division between them. They hid from God. When we can't see God, we can't see ourselves or others very well.

2) Although the conflict was severe, God's attention and station beside the couple was never altered. God never moved away. This surprised the participants.

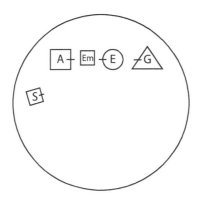

Diagram 3.2

Seeing the presence of the division of Enmity was a powerful movement for the group as well. The marriage connection itself was now poisoned and did not reflect the union of identification between Adam and Eve.

When God sought them and found them per the text, He assisted their confession of the main events, and He rearranged them. He removed Enmity from standing between them as a couple and placed it between the woman and the serpent.

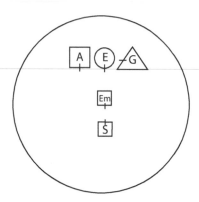

Diagram 3.3

It was a point of insight for the group to witness and discover that there is a wish or intent on the part of the animal-energy to divide humans from one another through disorder. In contrast to being enemies, Adam and Eve demonstrate that marriage evidently was designed to jointly host and to honor the presence of God's union with them. God's wish was lovely in preservation.

3) After Enmity was re-ordered, God added a protection for the couple and covered them with 'Skin.' An observer in our group bounced up off the floor where she'd been sitting at the bottom of the room, and took a place standing in front of the now-reconciled couple as if to act as a shield—feet spread apart, hands on hips, Skin intervened, and Enmity moved to stand between the woman and the serpent. Skin laughed at the Serpent and at Enmity and declared, "I feel like a Superman kind of skin; I am awesome and protective!"

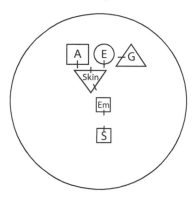

Diagram 3.4

God's attention was constantly there with focus and support to mankind, periodically saying things like, "I'm right here; I'm still right here," and "I haven't left." That constancy and intervention was a new reflection for many in the group who previously feared that God had rejected mankind. The new image of the story was comforting. Some discussed that they had expected to see God move away and be separated entirely but in this image, God stayed near throughout the ordeal, particularly in the gift of a new covering.

4) When God covered them with Skin, He made a promise to send His seed through the woman to crush the serpent's head. At that point, seeing the new image, an observer seated in the group reacted with an outburst. Her feet popped up off the floor, and she squealed, "Oh, oh, oh! I know Who that is! That Skin is Jesus! He was there in the very beginning! How did I ever miss that? I've read this story a hundred times; how did I not see him there from the very beginning? He's our covering, y'all! He's the promise represented in the Skin. He's the Lamb!" Her thrill and discovery of a promise that brought about faith and assurance gave her new joy. Her spontaneous declaration was a breakthrough of security.

Others then puzzled it out with her that in order for a skin covering to be there, an animal had to have been offered—as a representative—for the couple—to "die that day," in their place. In Genesis, God said, "In the day you eat of that fruit, you will die," but in the sacrifice that provided skin, God represented man in the offering. Providing a representative was God's initiative. In the offering, man's representative mediated a covering for a time.

5) In the Skin, we come into contact with the natural law of representing. Because the deepest order is union, that which is lost, divided, cut off, forgotten, hidden, or in any way missing is going to have to be re-presented for the sake of wholeness.

6) With enmity re-stationed, God restored order in the couple by giving Eve a desire for her husband. He also restored Adam's over-rule of dominion. He re-assigned leadership to mankind by faith in a promised future seed that would crush the enmity between the woman and the serpent. But there were still consequences of the injury in nature which could not be undone. As nature represented them in death, death had become a hard part of nature. Adam's work became more difficult, and Eve's work in childbirth was also slated to become labor-intensive.

7) As the story moved forward, the couple left the upper part of the room, the Garden, and moved to the lower part of the room. Then an angel stood up to represent protection and centered himself in the room. He barred their re-entry into the garden. According to the text he guarded (Genesis 3:24) the way to the Tree of Life as if it was now a hazard. The direct access to the Tree of Life became protected by guardian angels. The representative for the angel said a few interesting things while in his stationed position.

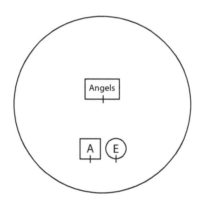

Diagram 3.5

"I am here so they don't get in more trouble by eating from the Tree of Life just yet." Then he added, "I was also later at the Garden Tomb, at the resurrection of Christ."

That statement is impossible for anyone to prove. But it gave people a sense of wonder of the larger context of the cosmos. The statement directly connected one garden to another, and one lamb's skin to Jesus crucified. That was the representative's immediate experience.

Discussion that followed:

After the participants de-roled, the group sat in a circle and discussed the text. The participants wondered if Adam and Eve being exiled from the garden was not perhaps a rejection by God as much a protection, given their now mortal standing. Their terms for life had changed.

Though we did not have representatives for the two most notable trees— the Tree of Life and the Tree of the Knowledge of Good and Evil— it occurred to the group that humans must have originally been designed for immortality, and immortality was interrupted. Still eternity was set in their hearts.

They pondered together the 'what-ifs' of partaking from the Tree of Life in the new state of mortality with enmity in the mix. The unwholesome mix of eternal life enmeshed a state of enmity as eternal would be a living hell. They felt protected from having a captivity of disorder and conflict without end. From that potential hell, man was spared by way of a mediator. By the intervening presence of God, Skin, and Faith, the Angels protected them from that eternal dead mortality—a zombie existence with no exit. They discussed mortality and death in new terms as a door to a new life: not an end, but a new beginning.

Those who have watched a loved one suffer and perhaps prayed for the peace of the death of suffering appreciate the doorway out of a tormented mortality. So the group was able to give a place to death—as hard terms — but also as having lost its sting in the presence of the Skin (Jesus) with the promise of hope. Earth is a place of exile until the promise is complete.

Interestingly, after we dismissed for the night, the man who had participated as the representative of the snake spoke to me privately saying, "I'm glad I got to be the snake tonight. I didn't notice it until I was representing, that I had harbored an irrational thought in the back of my mind that God and the devil were somehow equals in strength. But tonight, as I was the snake, it seemed that God was much larger than me, and there was actually no contest. I might not have ever caught that thought in the back of my mind unless I had a chance to be the serpent. I'm glad to have gotten that sense of size right in my mind. God is bigger and greater than all."

Personally I still wondered about God's station with man as it set up in the room. But when I looked at the very first verse of the Bible, Genesis 1:1, I saw something new — something whole. "In the beginning God created the heavens and the earth. Now the earth was formless and empty, darkness was over the surface of the deep, and the Spirit of God was hovering over the waters. . . . I reflected back to the Lord's prayer, "thy will be done on earth as it was in heaven." Then it all fit. He is doing something on Earth to mirror the fullness of Heaven. Heaven was not empty it was being created on the Earth — still. Then I saw the whole.

The Great Representative

Having now briefly demonstrated the function of a representative both in a family and as a process tool in the study of a sacred text, we should discuss the question of definition. The fact that a law of representation exists, which permits one person to step into another's place to resonate with that person's station in some degree, is a part of the mystery of reconciliation. To be clear, representing is not a role play. It is resonant connection. A representative is in the service of reconciliation. In sacred text we see a natural order that calls for unity. When enmity creates division, a representative is needed until unity is restored. In family work, the function of symptoms is to reveal a divide for someone in need of reconciliation. When we view symptoms with an eye for the whole we can find the divide a soul is trying to bridge.

To notice this work of reconciliation directly in the Gospel, I refer to the scriptures that speak of two Adams, the first and the last Adam, the alpha and the omega: both are noticed by Paul in the book of Romans, and Apostle John in the book of Revelation. Jesus stood in the gap for Adam's race. Successfully so, according to the resurrection. There is no divide on God's part, only a bridge called mercy.

In Eden, the first Adam was tested in his leadership, and by falling from his place brought the entire race into a wilderness of mortality. The second Adam is Christ, the seed promised to Eve, who was conceived thousands of years later in Mary. The Word promised became the Word incarnate, the Word with skin on, and in whose skin we were all covered: Jesus, the great representative, came. God lived an ordinary human life for three decades as one of us.

At his baptism, He fully identified with our state, and immediately was driven into the wilderness to also be tested, as Adam was. He had to finish Adam's unfinished assignment and demonstrate whether or not He believed God. He had to demonstrate that he knew who God was. Would He concede to getting out of order by seeking to dominate the kingdoms of the world, or would he serve them?

Jesus, the second Adam, passed every test the first Adam failed. The similarities are clear: in Mark's Gospel 1:12, Jesus "was tempted by Satan for 40 days. He was there with the wild animals, and the angels took care of him." In the wilderness test, He, as a man of authority, demonstrated his Vice Regency, declaring His deep hunger for the Word of His Father. He came to fulfill his Father's Words as the purpose for His life. The Living Word—the logos or logic of God—unkept by Adam, was embodied and fully represented in Jesus. Whereas Adam disowned the Word of God, Jesus fully embodied the Word, and He quoted the Word as His deepest being. He believed God to be in His identity. 'I and the Father are one' (John 14). Perfect union: no separation. In His resurrection, He reintroduced God as His and our Father.

The invitation to Salvation is an invitation to right orientation with God as Father. This is known as a bow: God is bigger; I am smaller, Father gives, child receives. God's logic is what hangs in the balance in a man's soul. Do we listen to the natural nature, or do we listen to the logic of God in the Spirit?

Thin Space through Communion Symbols

In family work, we orient ours souls rightly in earthly relationships through an honest roster, (is everyone accounted for,) and authentic placement, (is everyone in their own place.) In Biblical processes, we reorient our spirits to God's Spirit. Both are needed. To be clear, Jesus prayed that God's will would be done on earth as it is in heaven. We are trying to bring our lives into alignment with His. There are a variety of representations we see in scripture and there are also several that we practice in our faith already. An embodied study is an extension of these encounters.

If we accept Paul's identification of Christ as the last Adam, we notice too that we share the call to be reconciled, and He gives us ways to connect in the identification—or better said, how to wear the Skin of Christ.

In baptism, communion and more, we represent a higher reality through participating in the symbols. Through them, our physical connects with the spiritual by way of the soul. We may enter in as if we are only role playing while we learn to yield, but there comes a point of revelation where the role-playing gives way to the presence of being, and we find we too are representing or hosting His Life in us. We re-member-ship Christ in our lives through the symbols He has given us for seeing Him in ourselves as one of us.

Every time we take part in these divine rites or ordinances, we are embodying a spiritual reality when we allow these teachings to touch our hearts. These gifts aren't present to us as strategies but as a live happening.

We refer to communion in several synonyms: a ceremony, a religious rite, an ordinance or sacrament. We have a common ground for the reenactment of reconnection.

A Roman Catholic describes the Eucharist as a sacrament seeing Christ present in the mystery; He is the wine which is the blood, and in it, grace is conveyed. The protestant branch is part of the same vine. Be it grape juice or wine, the mystery escorts us to a higher awareness of the is-ness of the Kingdom of Heaven.

Many people encounter God in communion. Some do not, but it happens. Once upon a time, I entered a Protestant church and saw that the table was set for the Lord's Supper, as it is called there, and my heart leapt since the habit there was to observe the ordinance only once a quarter.

After the sermon was over and the elements were being served, the pianist began a solo. I closed my eyes and prayed. I asked—wished—for the Lord to come. And in my mind's eye, I imagined my spirit released above the congregation in that higher open space. And for the first time, I asked the Lord to dance with me. In my mind's eye, I began to dance with the Spirit. We danced and twirled together and spun to the music of the piano.

The serving trays of elements came my way, and I partook of the wafer and resumed the dance of my spirit. Then the music changed as the pianist finished his song and gave way to the organist who began to play his solo.

Just then, a memory surfaced. I was a little girl of ten, in my childhood church, kneeling and praying at the altar. I saw it all again from the perspective of the top of the church wall. The roof was off, and Christ sat next to me. We weren't dancing now; I was seeing myself from his point of view. I knew the image exactly. I knew the prayer I'd pray over and over and over every single week for a period of two months time during a hard period in my young life.

By now though in the live service, the cup passed, and I took the small juice cup, drank, and then returned to the scene of my old memory.

I recalled the childhood prayer I'd offered, which was, "Dear God, thank you for forgiving me of all my sins. But could you also forgive me of all my future sins because I just don't think I can behave for the whole rest of my life."

It was a simple child's prayer, but that deep fear of separation was a worry. Seeing that old scene unfold, I heard the Lord say "Amy, I've loved you for all of my life."

Misunderstanding the words, I felt a correction was in order. I wasn't quite aware that my imagination had become a thin space in communion. I had supposed the voice of the Lord was reminiscing like a parent recalling something special to Him, and so I replied, "You mean you've loved me for all of my life."

"No," came the clear response of correction, "I've loved you for all of my life."

That communion thin space brought an answer to my childhood prayer.

I gasped when I understood the unsearchable mercy and said, "Lord, that is a long, long time." That answer was a mystery I was not able to fathom.

An eruption of deep weeping commenced and left me in quite a spell for a while. I could not explain to my husband nor any of the people around me for about twenty minutes what had happened.

During communion, Jesus came.

Does it always happen like that in communion? No. And some folks do not know that God is willing to break bread with us whenever we are so vulnerable as to invite him to dance. He will not say no. Nor will He be out-loved. Thin space exists. Representation opens a door to communion. That was a thin space encounter. That was communion. That was Skin. That was protection, and that was Love.

Two Pictures of One Story: Key Revelation of Representation

In the Upper Room, Jesus took bread and wine, broke it, and said, 'Take and eat. This is my body; this is my blood. Do this in re-member-ance of me.' He represented himself in solid elements and assigned them power to represent His own Spirit embodied in His body of disciples. He presented Himself as something we could ingest, assimilate, and integrate like the manna of old, and the forfeited Tree of Life in Eden. His disciples partook of those elements as a mystery at first, but they understood Him better thereafter. Mystery invites us to grow into something that is over our heads.

Jesus gave this teaching as The New Covenant. He was celebrating it as fulfilling the Old Covenant of the passover lamb with them — the Skin. "This is my body, broken for you." He was about to unveil Himself as the Lamb of God and the scapegoat of humanity in less than twelve hours.

The first time he explained his body and blood were edible, it caused such a stir that he lost a following, but Peter declared that he would stay saying, "Where would we go? You have the Words of life." Now though, the skin of Eden, the Lamb of Passover, was about to bring God's testimony to its real conclusion, God was always man's life.

In the Upper Room record, Jesus added another expression to the new covenant, which only John reports. We've not done nearly as much with this sign of the covenant as we have with the Lord's supper. Of the four

Gospel records, not only does John report this as 'the sign' of the New Covenant, he also omits the bread and wine sign. The new treaty was not only what we ate; it was how we served by washing each other's dirty feet. To what is this sign of foot-washing referring?

Foot-washing is related to how the community would learn to take care of each other when they needed reconciliation with one another. This was given as a command to love each other this way. They were to approach one another in a bow, in humility, in the service of God and to fully engage in washing the filth off of each other. The whole person may be otherwise clean, but it will take a humble Kingdom-family member to tend to the feet with gentleness and, in doing so, re-present Christ's mercy.

The family work of representing by proxy is one way of cleansing and reconciliation. When we set up a wish, we may have to see where we or a beloved member has been. With kindness, we see where the holes are, and where we've lost touch with someone. Then we have the privilege of reorganizing around an injury so that love has another chance. We are in the service of love.

Communion represents the heavenly reconciliation between us and God. Foot-washing represents the earthly reconciliation between us and other people. Each offers orders of reconciliation to re-member-ing God in our relationships, and re-ordering humility between one another.

The Second Garden

After the ministry in the Upper Room, Jesus then led the disciples out to the Garden of Gethsemane to pray. This is why He came. This is the hour He would glorify God — embodying man's judgment in God's glorious mercy. These passages are well-known, but Luke 22:39-46, Mark 14:37 and Matthew 26: 36-46 all report key things for us about the representative transaction that took place in the space of one hour.

In one of our Tuesday Bible studies, we "embodied" this story. The diagram below is not a complete roster of the participants in our study. What is not shown here are angels, drops of blood, and several other parts of the whole which may be hidden to the surface reader but present to the searcher.

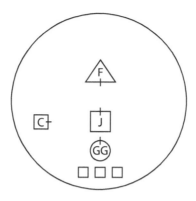

Diagram 3.6

Key: F is The Father God, J is the son Jesus, C is the cup of wrath, GG is the Garden of Gethsemane, and the three smaller squares are the disciples.

When we embodied this story in our study, more than two years after the earlier Eden set-up, the representative for the Garden of Gethsemane said, "I feel like I'm representing a representation. I feel like I'm a symbol here. Why is that?" she asked.

I asked her to give more consideration to find an answer to her own question.

Perplexed she said, "I think I'm a representative for Eden."

That was a reasonable connection since they were both gardens where transactions for humanity took place. The first was a shadow, and the second, the reality.

In our study of Eden, the representative for Skin had declared, "I am awesome and protective." In our Gethsemane, the representative for the Cup of Wrath said, "I feel like I am turning into a slithering serpent. I want to take off this scarf I have around my neck and wind it around Jesus."

I told her to follow her movement. She wrapped her scarf around the neck of the representative for Jesus.

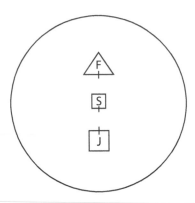

Diagram 3.7

This diagram shows how the representative for the Cup of wrath from the previous diagram has now become the serpent, and repositioned to stand between Jesus and His father God.

The representative for the Father remained attentive, present, supportive, and proud of His Son's trust through the entire ordeal. In this garden, we could see the Greater Soul of Jesus actively become the Representative of all of Adam's race. This is the hour where He embodied the sin of humanity. "Watch and pray," He told the disciples (Mark 14:34), "and He saith to them, 'Exceeding sorrowful is my soul—to death; remain here, and watch." (Young's Literal Translation).

Follow the sequence of events:

He gave the disciples a physical representation of Himself in the cup of communion, which they accepted. He washed their feet. He then went to the garden to pray through a different cup, one of wrath—the sentence of man's judgment—man's rejection of God for an hour. And then Jesus began to sweat great drops of blood. Humanity bled-through. Transaction complete. He became our sin and marched enmity toward its death.

Jesus, as our representative of mankind, drank in and embodied our humanity in order to enter mankind's death as our scapegoat. Genuinely representing us in Himself to die our death, He fulfilled the promise made in Eden. Behold—see—the Lamb of God who takes away the sin of the world.

That image, though reported in all the Gospels in earthly detail, was recorded again in heavenly detail by John when Christ gave him the Revelation of Himself representing us in the courts of heaven. He sent the cosmic Revelation to the Apostle John to given to the seven churches in Ephesus. Reading the book of Revelation is challenging unless one acknowledges the lens of the Lamb, about whom it is written. In Revelation 5, the scribe, John, details the heavenly court's reception of Jesus hailed as a Lamb slain and therefore worthy to open the scroll of human destiny. He owns the scroll of destiny. He purchased us. John saw it in Gethsemane, and, later, he saw it in a window into eternity.

If a person can SEE what Jesus did in this Garden to represent us in those High Courts, not only will he approach the mystery, but he will begin to better understand Redemption as his deep security. It's the Miracle we all look for. It's the second Garden. Life began in the Garden of Eden, was redeemed in the Garden of Gethsemane, and was resurrected in the Garden Tomb, preparing us for the Garden of Life yet to come on earth as it is in heaven.

When the disciples arrived in Gethsemane, Jesus told them,
"Watch and pray so that you don't enter into temptation."
What were they watching? What did they see?
And who else was there to tempt them?
This was the moment of crushing the serpent's head which was promised and prophesied in Eden. (Gen 3:15) This was the moment the prophet Isaiah foresaw and foretold in Isaiah 53.

Look at the foresight and explanation from the prophet Isaiah, five hundreds of years before Jesus was born.

Isaiah 53: 7-12 – He was oppressed, and he was afflicted, yet he opened not his mouth; like a lamb that is led to the slaughter, and like a sheep that before its shearers is silent. So he opened not his mouth. By oppression and judgment he was taken away; and as for his generation, who considered that he was cut off out of the land of the living, stricken for the transgressions of my people. And they made his grave with the wicked and with a rich man in his death, although he had done no violence, and there was no deceit in his mouth. Yet it was the will of the Lord to crush him; he has put him to grief; when his soul makes an offering for guilt, he shall see his offspring; he shall prolong his days; the will of the Lord shall prosper in his hand. Out of the anguish of his soul he shall see and be satisfied; by his knowledge shall the righteous one, my servant make many to be accounted righteous, and he shall bear their iniquities. Therefore I will divide him a portion with the many, and he shall divide the spoil with the strong, because he poured out his soul to death and was numbered with the transgressors; yet he bore the sin of many, and makes intercession for the transgressors.

It wasn't just the body in anguish; it was the soul of Jesus representing the souls of men. In the Garden of Gethsemane, we can SEE it literally in the record: He sweated great drops of blood as God laid on Him the sins of the world.

It's important to notice that the first drop of blood did not fall from a physical blow. Jesus bled before he was arrested, before his mock trial, before he was hit, before his trial by Pilate where he was spit upon, flogged, crowned with thorns, and before he was executed on a stake. His first drop of blood was in the Garden, out of the travail of His soul for ours. We bled through in our representative. Our suffering came through.

Sometimes we need to embody the story to get inside the skin of this redemption and such great a revelation of our salvation. The disciples watched Jesus embody us. It is entirely central. He promised to separate our sin as far as the east is from the west and this is how he did it.

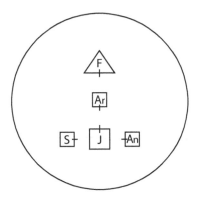

Diagram 3.8

Key: Father, Adam's race, serpent, Jesus, Adam now redeemed.

Jesus prayed three times to be spared. In doing so he agreed and thereby drank three times to partake of the full cup. Jesus prayed through the cup as He, also representing the wishes of all three parts of the Trinity—sacrificially, intentionally, and in passion—drank us all in. The reason we drink His cup is because we know He drank ours.

Jesus bowed.

Jesus bowed.

Jesus bowed.

We have a brief transcript of our earthly trial, but we can only imagine the heavenly dialogue. I imagine the double-representative's trial this way:

"Dearly Beloved Son, in whom I am still well pleased, rise up now and carry them through their trial as I cast their judgment out through you. As they determine to judge God-in-man as criminal, their rebellion will be absorbed without retaliation and expose our mercy for them."

The Father and Son in perfect agreement mediated a great judgment on our sin, crushing the serpent's head, striping enmity of any power to veil His love for us. And the problem of judgment became the solution to it.

The Trinity did this in re-member-ance of Adam's race to God. We celebrate the Lord's Table to re-member-ship the Godhead in our humanity. He was baptized into our death and rose to justify us.

Who hung on the tree?

The great representative of humanity carried us through. He entered into our death and owned the keys to death and hell. And in the Sabbath to which all other Sabbaths pointed, there we were put to rest. And in His perfection, salvaging our acquittal, He—still representing man—was raised by an indestructible life. He who knew no sin became sin so that we might become the righteousness of God (2 Corinthians 5:21). This is God's testimony offered to us to become ours. A receiving heir has no way to boast in an inheritance received by another's death, we just wear the skin. Any boast is in Him alone.

To Represent

Representing, as a service of reconciliation, is a gift. The earlier family stories of representing an earthly missing person show us where the burden rests. Serving families is serving God. We cannot represent the way Jesus did. We can only represent in a small ministry of reconciliation as students of the Lord and as His foot-washers. We cannot add to His work; we are supported by His work so that we may participate in His rule of mercy. Now ascended in our Skin, He still lives and reigns and sits on a throne called the mercy seat, the right hand of God, the second Adam sits representing the second Eve, His bride.

Seeing the tasks of intentionally representing for the sake of healing a family soul is a sacred ministry. It is an honor to be asked to represent so that a troubled family might gently move through a tangle with the hope of finding the path that lets Love have a chance to set a soul free. It is a kindness and is a gift of intercession. But sometimes a family burden in need of resolution can unfold as a gift in an embodied sacred text. The story below is a miracle from an embodied Bible study.

Healing in Study: The Late Christmas Gift

The Bible study group had been doing a six-week series on the Christmas stories of Jesus's infancy. Two weeks after Christmas, in January, we arrived at our final infancy story. In this passage, King Herod killed all the baby boys under two years of age in an effort to kill the Christ child whose reality had been reported by the foreign dignitaries. These men, according to their own artful study of stars, discovered a King had been born. They came to worship. Herod was alarmed, and all of Jerusalem was as well.

After reading the passage in Matthew 2, the roster of parts that participants selected were Bethlehem, Star, Magi, Herod, Soldiers, Mary, Joseph, and Baby Jesus. One person chose to represent all the slaughtered babies, and one person chose to represent all the bereaved mothers.

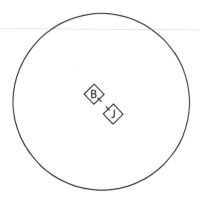

Diagram 3.9

What was at first striking was that the representative for the babies slated for death and the representative for Baby Jesus both sat down cross legged in the center of the room and stared at each other for a long time. The room became very still. They looked at each other face-to-face: baby Jesus facing the babies slated for death. The innocent children were born into an environment on Earth that was not hospitable to any of them.

Slowly the rest of the representatives quietly found their places in relation to the babies. Then we read through the story line by line.

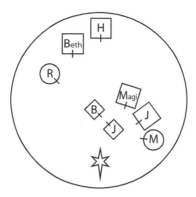

Diagram 3.10

Key: H is Herod, Beth is Bethlehem, R is for Rachel or the weeping mothers whose children were killed, B is babies, small J is Jesus, Magi, J is Joseph, M is Mary, and the star was the Guiding star.

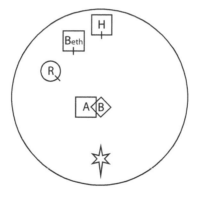

Diagram 3.11

Key: A is Angel

After Herod's soldiers carried through with his order, the representative for the babies laid dead on the floor and repeatedly said, "I'm okay."

A person who'd been an angel in a previous study spontaneously engaged. She'd said she only wanted to observe that night, but as soon as the babies were dead, she spontaneously represented as an angel, though no mention was made of angels in this text. She came over to the dead, and covered the 'babies' as if they were under her wings for a brief time. We stopped our reading for what was happening in that movement.

The representative for the babies said again, "The babies are okay."

The angel said she just wanted to cover them with comfort.

And there they remained for a sweet moment in time.

Everyone was still.

Next, the angel escorted the babies out from the center of the room to a nearby seat, saying, "I'm taking them over here to be in heaven."

Then the 'angel' came back across the room and sat down beside the representative for the bereaved mothers. The representing mother was frozen in speechless, inconsolable grief and was unresponsive.

The now heavenly babies' representative said she was 'conscious' and reported that they were okay with their short time and with God's bigger plan for them and the story of Jesus.

The story continued to unfold as we read, and other representatives provided feedback for their experiences. Intermittently, the babies in heaven interjected. The representative for the babies wanted to let us know that she could see the mothers seated across the room. Placement wise, she was now in a position to stare directly across at the woman representing the bereaved mothers.

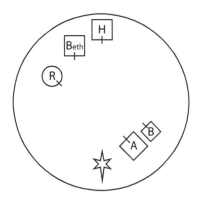

Diagram 3.12

The babies stared at the mothers for a long time, while we continued reading parts of the story and others reflected. Slowly, there came over the heavenly baby's face a look of innocence, peace and sweetness. Visibly, the heavenly baby looked as if a fret eraser moved over her expressions and smoothed out all worry and concern.

We continued reading, and again, intermittently, the heavenly baby interjected, saying to the mother as she pointed her finger gently, "I just want you to know that I can see you." The bereaved mother was still not responsive. She was in a cold stare with no ability to do much in revolt to Herod's edict.

Again, we continued to read, and again the baby offered intermittently, "I'm not trying to get off track here, but I just want the mothers to know that I can see you." No response from representing mother: just speechlessness.

We finished the reading: participants de-roled, sat down in the round circle, and began debriefing the experience with notable takeaways.

Herod had been a very difficult part to represent, and the gentleman carrying that part was aware of a certain weight of corruption that surrounded that role. He was glad it was over. In fact, he said weeks later that it had been a difficult role to represent and his thoughts about the nature of a depraved king taken over by evil had been something for him to consider for a period of time.

When we arrived at the woman who represented the babies, she had this to say.

"I know we don't talk much in here about our own lives since we are doing Bible studies, but I want everyone to know how much this story has meant for me tonight." She kept her head down and wiped the tears that began to roll down her cheeks.

"I've had five miscarriages. The last time I did a personal set-up at a family workshop was two years ago: that was when I had to face the reality of my lost children. I had to lay down with the representative of those babies and just decide whether I wanted to stay there. I acknowledged how much I really wished to move toward death. I had to notice whether I was going to get up in my soul and stay here in life — or not. I had no idea how much I'd been wanting to die until I laid there with them in that set-up and felt relief from the sense of separation I'd had."

"But when the representative of one of my babies had told me I didn't belong there, it sort of snapped me out of my gaze in that direction. Suddenly, I knew that I had to get back up, even though I didn't want to live. I feel like I've been trying my best to live hanging on by my fingernails. But tonight, by representing the dead babies, I realized they can see me. I felt that for myself. I felt them inside me. They can see me, and they are okay, and I know now that we are only separated in the body but not in the Spirit. It feels like I have my babies now, even though the terms are unwelcome. I can carry them in my heart, and it feels so good to know that we are together. We're reconciled on some level. It's all okay. And it's all going to be okay, ultimately."

That was a beautiful Christmas gift, full of wonder and mystery.

Chapter Four: Giving God His Place: Macro Ages to Micro Marriage

If history and dates have previously seemed irrelevant, the next two chapters will change that. There are some surprising findings that will likely give a reader a bit of pause when the implications dawn on the reader. Just as families have patterns and ways of being with each other which we will examine closely here and again in chapters ahead, God has patterns as well. God's ways of engagement in relationship with families are visible to us through both a micro and macro lens.

500 Hundred Year Leaps

Historically speaking, there is a pattern whereby earth reaches a point of chaos and moral collapse about every 500 years, at which point, God intervenes with a reset button of sorts with a major prophet that leads His people back into fellowship with Him. The chaos/recovery pattern is consistent beyond the close of the Biblical record and continues well into the church age. The reader may easily fact check this pattern by looking at a time line common in the back of a study bible. The great prophets each had their say about 500 years apart.

I'm going to come back to a pre-flood curiosity in the next chapter, but I want to say here that the record states that prior to the flood men had lifespans pushing one thousand years. Impossible? If true, then during those years we can imagine that what we call oral history was reliable. Given the long lifespans, what was passed on to Noah was common knowledge existing within one four-generational family system.

At the time of the flood an intervention was needed since there was no end to the evil man plotted. Thereafter, God set His own boundary for how long He would struggle with a man. When he reset the time frames, He assigned man a general life span of seventy years, and also shortened how long he would deal with man before he intervened. The reset of the record shows this.

At God's first intervention, the flood, mankind was around 1500 years old. After Noah, He gave mankind a span of 500 years before He would again step in through a major prophet. Clearly no one can assert that God just needs to give man more time, since He did that first. Time is not our issue and a 500 year epoch demonstrates it.

A 500-year epochs lies between each of the following prophets:

500 years after Noah, the land of Canaan was cluttered with war and debauchery. God chose Abraham to know Him by faith.

500 years later, the descendants Israel was enslaved to Egypt. God raised up Moses.

500 years later, the land settled by the tribes of Israel was in worse shape than when God brought Abraham to it. God raised up Samuel and soon David.

500 years later, Israel went into exile for rebellion. A remnant returned and the rest were scattered throughout what became the Roman Empire.

500 years later, God embodied man in Jesus. Christianity was born in the Jews first. It was the dispersion of the Jews throughout the Roman Empire that laid track for the gospel to Jews first and then the Gentiles. The Gospel spread, synagogue by synagogue by synagogue, throughout the empire. As it spread, western civilization was established as Christian.

Still the spiral-down/reset pattern continued through the church age with timely 500-year schisms and splits, the last one being on October 31, 1519 with Martin Luther. We are due and in need of a reset, because once again, everyone does what is right in his own eyes.

God knows exactly what time it is in history. And He has established a pattern of movement and shaking the earth to set people free to know Him.

In the book of Genesis, although the entire time line covers a span of almost 2000 years in 50 short chapters, 40 of those chapters are about one four-generational family system, which covers only a time-span of around 200+ years. Genesis gives us a snap shot of the fallout from the first Adam's lineage, and then a longer narrative about Abraham, the man who believed God.

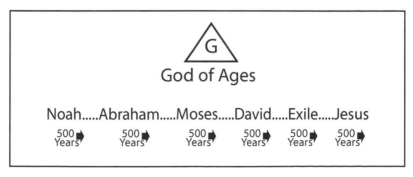

Diagram 4.1

Time lines speak. It takes a few hundred years for the sin of a nation's apostasy to morally collapse its people through idolatry. But God faithfully raises up another representative of Himself to realign man with His ways of approaching life from the higher spiritual plane.

On May 14, 2018, Israel was seventy years old as a nation again, and their own return in mass and growing revival has been rising since 1948. We may wonder what God has in mind and take Paul's treaty to the Romans serious regarding God's dealings with Israel. By all the signs it seems we must be near the close of the Church age, and the threshold of the awakening of Israel. It is time.

Things seem to be shifting. The United States of America has honored Jerusalem as the City of David and moved the embassy to affirm that the capital of the nation is what it is and what it has always been since the time of David.

Two thousand years before Christ, God established a Hebrew people to be a light, a testimony people for the world. For the 2,000 years after Jesus's ascension, God moved that testimony of Jesus throughout the nations via the Church. Billy Graham, the prophet of the Gospel, having preached to 215 million souls, has gone home. The wish and the prayer is the same as it has been since Eden: Thy will be done on earth as it is in heaven.

King David remembered that the sacred hill He established as Zion was first anointed by Melchizedek, the priest and king of Salem in the days of Abraham. Perhaps Paul's prophetic anticipation of Israel's awakening to Christ is at hand.

The testimony of God at work in heaven and earth is an encouragement, that this is His story and the one in which ours is unfolding. Looking up for redemption is a delightful contemplation and one that calls us all to get our own house in order.

What does the macro family of God mean for the micro families of God? How do we get our houses in order? Let's return to Genesis for the pattern to learn about intergenerational patterns.

Micro Family Patterns: Four Generational Leaps

In an embodied Bible study, I once asked a representative what he meant when he said he had been 'set apart.'

He answered, "Oh. That just means that I understand I'm not God."

There has been a long running joke among Jewish people that it would be nicer for them if God would "choose" another people to set apart since being the "chosen" was such a hazard. But God works within the mess, be it inward or outward, and Joseph, the great-grandson of Abraham, is a case in point. To explore this story, we will read the chronicle backwards.

Why should I start at the end of the family system? I start here because it is where we all start in our own investigation of patterns. In our own stories, we come in last and then add more pages for our children. But if we want to understand what happened in our story we go backwards and glean information about people, places and significant events that preceded us. If we test this on Joseph's story, the whole thing reads differently than when we read it forward.

Let us imagine that I had Joseph as a client and he attended a family workshop and set up a wish. His wish is to have peace with his brothers. We learn that his brothers sold him as a slave to Egypt where he rose in favor to vice president and saved the world from famine, including his family of origin who came to him for food and reconciled. But now that their father is dead, the brothers are terrified he will kill them. He wants peace and new trust. (Kinda like what's about to happen with Israel and Christ—but I digress)

Joseph has a gallery of people from whom he may choose representatives. Use your mind's eye. To avoid a huge crowd, he takes a representative for himself and three brothers and places them at the bottom of the room on the left. He places himself higher up at the top of the circle. As soon as his brothers' representatives look at him "way up there" the three turn away and face outside the circle. The reps say that they are afraid and can't look at him.

So I might ask about other family events, or things that happened among his siblings before or during enslavement.

He might say he had a sister who was raped when he was a little boy, and his brothers executed vengeance on the entire town of Shechem. So we may find a representative for Dinah and some for the town of Shechem and let them find a place that suits them. She may go outside the circle with those of Shechem on the left. How would that be for Joseph?

This may remind him of how unjustly he had been jailed when he was falsely accused of raping the wife of Potiphar. Hearing that, Dinah may turn and look at her brother with sympathy and the representatives for Shechem.

When asked about other significant events in his generation, Joseph mentions the grief in his elder brother Judah's life: deaths of his childless sons, death of his half wife, and the severity of a law to give his remaining son to a barren daughter-in-law. When he broke the law, she, pretending to be a prostitute, conceived twins with Judah. Not knowing better, he tried to have her killed. Upon learning that they were his, he took her and the twins to raise.

"Twins? So, in addition to rivalry, there are hard events around marriage, sex and children. Are there other twins?" I ask Joseph.

Joseph recalled that his father was in a serious rivalry with his own twin brother Esau and that was the cause of his leaving the homeland initially. "Okay, so you moved before?"

Joseph answered, "Father left home because Esau was angry over the birthright, and we were all born in mother and grandmother's homeland."

So, we would add a representative for Esau and Jacob and place them in the center at a distance. And we added grandmother Rebekah above them. "So, rivalry didn't start with the children."

"What about before your parents, any rivalry back there?"

We learn that their grandfather Isaac also had an estranged and disinherited elder brother, Ishmael. Representatives for both Ishmael and Issac are added to stand above Jacob and Essau. They all stood behind their parents.

"Are there any other forgotten siblings?"

"Yes, Isaac also has six younger brothers." Several representatives stand up outside the circle to the upper right.

"Let's keep going backward. Did any special events occur in the generation before Isaac?"

"Yes," Joseph answers. "Actually, Great-Grandfather Abraham immigrated to Canaan after his brother died. He married his half-sister, Sarah. She couldn't conceive. In an encounter with God, Abraham was promised a new land and later a child. He followed God by faith to Canaan but a famine took place, and he and Sarah came down here to Egypt for food. Pharaoh took Sarah into his own harem, and then the whole country became as barren as she was. When it was discovered that she was married to Abraham, Pharaoh sent them away—and among their payments to leave was an Egyptian slave, Hagar. Sarah later gave her to Abraham as a surrogate mother. Sarah wanted to take Hagar's child as her own. Later when she had her own child, she excluded Hagar and Ishmael from the family.

Representatives for Hagar, Sarah and Abraham stand next to Joseph.

I ask what is going on for the representatives for Joseph's brothers. One says, "This is very repetitive."

I ask Joseph what's happening when he looks at it. "My representative is up there with them. And when my brothers sold me, they sold me to the Ishmaelites, who sold me to Egypt. While there, I married an Egyptian. I agree, this is a repetition of Hagar's rejection on an earthly plane."

It looks like you, Judah and Dinah have borne similar sufferings of previous generations. I switch out the representative for Joseph for the real man and he bows to the representative for Hagar who then blesses him. He looks up and says, "You're one of us." Hagar's representative replies, "And you're one of us."

How is this for the representatives of the brothers?

"It's true. It is an old story. He has carried a heavy load. We have greater respect for the outsiders in our family and their loss and pain. Everyone belongs."

The Genesis family system story reads one way forward, and it reads another way when we read it backwards. How might Dinah and Judah look at Hagar?

In light of her, how does Joseph look at his Egyptian wife, Asenath?

How do we understand the blessing Jacob gave to Joseph's son half Hebrew half Egyptian sons Ephraim and Mannasah when he intentionally reversed the blessing of the firstborn?

Perhaps the whole story of sibling rivals was pattern code for how to remember Hagar and Ishmael and help them find their place in the whole family.

Perhaps they all bow to Abraham and agree, "We will honor all the covenants God made with you: the land, the circumcision, which included Ishmael, the ram that represented Issac. We are all here because you believed."

And Father Abraham blesses the entire house of reconciled insiders and outsiders.

Abraham's family is the micro system in a larger context of the fallen earthly system, the macro. Everyone comes from a family system. If we go farther back, we might add someone to represent Adam and God and realize what happens when anyone plays God. Perhaps then we see the greater whole and we reconcile ourselves to just bow and pray:

Our Father, who art in heaven, hallowed by thy name.
Thy Kingdom come, thy will be done on earth as it is in heaven.
Give us this day our daily bread, and forgive us our trespasses as we forgive
those who trespass against us, and lead us not into temptation, but deliver
us from evil, for thine is the Kingdom, the power,
and the glory forever and ever. Amen.

The book of Genesis is rich. God is always in the story; it all belongs to Him. He is the Kingdom we are calling home.

Establishing A place for God to make a marriage safe: a micro story.

We were near the end of a family workshop where we had used a representative for God, the True Father, in all of our family work all day. The process had been very helpful. Honoring the presence of God as a member made all the difference in reconciling differences and relieving burdens.

We had time to set up one more wish when a woman said she was ready to set up. Heart racing, she came to sit beside me to state her wish and set-up her work.

"What is your wish?" I asked.

Quite suddenly, she became confused and disowned her wish. So startled by the sudden loss of her wish, she said, "I don't know now. When I was sitting over there, I thought I knew, but now that I am here and ready to set it up, it's like I don't even know it. How weird is that? I thought I knew what I wanted to wish. Now, I'm not so sure."

Her wish had been snatched, it seemed. Baffled, she scratched her head and exhaled in wonder of how her thoughts could suddenly shift within seconds of making what she thought was a firm decision.

The group had already seen me send a few people back to their seats to rethink their wish when they made a wish concerning someone else. Those are prayer requests, but not wishes for the soul's work. Remember, the Johnny in us all has to make a wish and own it. It is not unusual to hit a glitch from time to time when someone has not landed firmly on their wish.

Going back to watch and pray is part of the step of ownership at times. It's awkward for a moment, but it helps. The facilitator should not suggest a wish for a client; that would be out of place. With this in mind, I proceeded carefully. She thought she had it straight, and in the course of less than ten steps to come sit beside me in the circle to work, she'd lost it. Something was happening, and I needed to pause with her, slow everything down, and wait for it.

Maybe a movement was already shifting things for her beneath the surface. She'd already gone into the depths of so much work that day in the service of others, I trusted she was already in a process where that deeper wish would surface. Hopefully we only needed to catch the swell rising up in her like a new ocean wave coming into shore and ride the wave with her as the Spirit drew her into His wish.

After all that I've stressed thus far about owning wishes, this example demonstrates how to hold guidelines loosely to be able to move sensitively with the Spirit. I needed to do a little checking to be sure it was the Spirit redirecting her and not her shrinking from a wish out of fear.

To better understand, I like to figure out what "size" the person is who is sitting next to me. I wondered if she suddenly felt too small for her life before God, or perhaps she was becoming a child to me and asking for my permission, or asking me to do her wishing, which would shift responsibility from herself onto me for her life and would not help her at all since I'm just a child of God too.

She didn't feel smaller than me. So I assumed it was the Lord intervening in her attention. So I offered a little prompt.

"Okay," I said. "Something may already be shifting from all the work today. Tell me what you were going to wish."

"I was going to say that I wanted to look at my marriage, but now I'm not so sure. As soon as I sat down I changed my mind; I thought, 'No,' I don't know if I even want that anymore. He's not safe."

She was conflicted about not wanting the marriage in the shape it was in. It is no one's responsibility to direct another person to stay or leave a relationship, but it is important to support a person fully owning their choice and acknowledging the costs in either case. But we weren't solidly working on the marriage wish.

"What do you want for yourself in these circumstances?"

"Oh, I don't know. He's not safe. I don't know if I want that. I want to be safe, and I'm not safe when I am with him."

Safety was sounding more like her wish, but I needed to check for some energy behind that.

"So, you would like to feel safe? Is that your wish for yourself?"

Her answers came in spurts of recognition, growing in volume as her wish came into her awareness. Verbally now, she said, "Ah… yes. Okay. Yes. Yes! Yes, that is what I want." Again, as if she'd just seen land from the top of a wave on the sea, she declared, "Oh, my gosh, yes! I want to be safe."

Now there was a lot of energy in her wish.

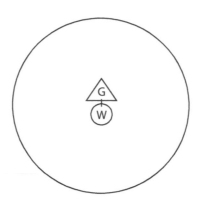

Diagram 4.2

Key: G is God/Safety, W is her as a "wife"

It made sense then for her to go ahead and choose a representative for Safety and one for herself as a wife, and to only set up those two parts to begin with. Safety was her wish. We'd been seeing God represented all day as resource and healer with immediate help, and it was clear to her what would likely happen. She said, "We all know Safety is going to turn out to be God, so let's name the representative for Safety "God."

She chose and arranged the representatives so that the wife leaned back onto God for support. She took her seat again and I started working with the set-up.

"How's it going for the wife?" I asked the representative for the woman. By referencing her as a 'wife,' I automatically referenced her relationship to her husband without him being represented yet. She wanted a resource for herself in regard to that part of her life. So he was in my mind to bring in eventually.

The representative for wife replied, "It's good; this feels nice. It's a comfort."

"How's it going for God-Safety?" I asked the representative.

"I'm good." God's arms wrapped around the wife securely and the wife leaned back against God like a child in her Father's arms and rested comfortably.

We watched the resting for a moment and shortly the representing wife straightened up and said, "I can do that for a little while, but I can't lean back on God for very long. I think I'm a burden. I feel like I'm too heavy."

God-Safety rolled his eyes. I checked with the woman to see if that reflected her experience, and she smiled sheepishly in agreement and said,

"I do feel like that."

"How's God?" I asked again.

"I'm fine! I'm planted. I'm not going anywhere, and she's not too heavy."

I instructed the representative for the wife to lean back again saying, "See if you can get comfortable or even get used to being at rest." She consented and allowed herself to do so. Then I looked at her and said, "Now I will test your resolve to rest in a storm."

I found someone in the group circle to represent what she had referred to in the past as her 'hot mess' of a husband. I asked this representative to set himself up by feeling his own way into the space and seeing where he felt his body needed to go in this field as the husband of this woman. Slowly he moved into the space and took a station to stand behind God to the left side. I checked in with the woman who was seated watching her story unfold, to see if it fit, and she nodded in agreement.

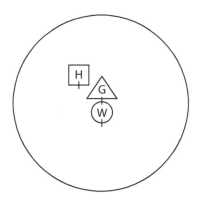

Diagram 4.3

"How's that for the husband?"

"I'm good here. I know where my place is. I'm supporting my family."

At that I noticed that God-Safety's head twitched in annoyance.

"How's that for the wife representative?" I asked.

The representative said, "I can't see him back there." But neither his presence nor his placement had an effect to move her out of her rest.

So it seemed it was a good place for the husband, but not for Safety nor the wife in terms of seeing him.

I looked at it curiously. God-Safety wasn't happy, and it was an odd placement to be behind God-Safety and out of view of his wife. This is what Adam's race does.

Suddenly, the words for the picture came to me, and I said to the representing husband, "Tell your wife that she and her God are beneath you." It was a literal statement.

The representing husband let out a quick gut check as if he'd been punched in the stomach. "Amy," he said softly, "those are hard words to say." However, the reaction of the wife and her representative agreed with the words by a nod of their heads.

I spoke directly to the man himself who was representing the husband and said, "I know. They are hard words. And it's a hard position to find yourself in as a representative. But this is her soul's work." Maybe it was his too, as these things are common ailments, but that was for him to explore privately since we often get the parts we may need to experience healing for ourselves. "Go ahead and say the words, and let's see what happens."

"You and your God are beneath me," he repeated.

The representatives for God and the wife nodded their heads. "I know," she said in agreement. So, from the disordered stations, God-Safety was now a block between them, or so it seemed.

I looked at the woman seated, and she was in agreement with the picture.

I said, "I guess that's why you don't feel safe in the relationship. If you imagine he trumps God or judges your God, then he is not accountable to anyone." She agreed.

"How is that placement working for the husband?" I asked the representative.

"Not sure it's working for me all that well," he said.

"You can find another place if you like," I said.

He moved slowly to join her in resting back on God."

She made room for him but after a bit she said, "I don't believe it."

"Okay, let's test it," I said. I brought in another representative to introduce an "other" option for him to pursue outside of their marriage as a resource or comfort apart from God. This resource represents a rival of sorts, or some company to keep other than God or his wife. Without giving their personal details, I simply gave a place in their shared family soul for what it was that the wife found unsafe or threatening in her husband.

The representative for this new option-of-interest was focused on him with full attention. She said, "I can wait on him to come back around." She seemed to be a part of their situation, a presence that was waiting and available.

I worked with those two representatives to bring some ownership and closure to this option, but for this book, I'm omitting the details of the movements we made through those parts of the work.

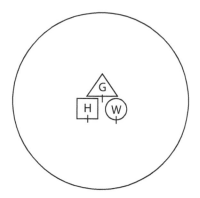

Diagram 4.4

After it was addressed in the field of grace, the husband was also able to come back and rest in God as a Safety for himself and then the husband and the wife representatives both became still, leaning on God as their safety. At that point, I dismissed the representative for the wife and asked the woman herself to step into her own place to sense the new arrangement.

She stood in her own place and said, "I still don't trust him," meaning her husband.

"Of course not," I said, "so turn around now, and look at God-Safety and say, 'I'm sorry. I've been unfaithful.'" I was remembering the initial interview where she'd changed her wish and was looking at her issues with God-Safety, instead of her marriage. This spiritual relationship had trumped her marriage wish as soon as she had taken a seat. She had a crisis with her husband, but it was a secondary issue to God as her resource in her spirit.

She spun around at me sharply and said, "What? Me? I've been unfaithful?"

"Okay, hard words again. If those words don't suit you, then just look at your husband and say, "You are not the right God for me.""

Her pause was palpable perfection. She had to tease out the differences in her soul in regard to resources, relationships, and their right places in her heart. She was disentangling beautifully, and the whole room with her was walking over the same incredible bridge over troubled waters; she was escorting everyone. She thought carefully about the words and repeated them inwardly as tears rolled down her cheeks.

She looked at the husband representative and repeated tenderly, "You are not the right God for me."

"Ugh," she said as if she'd felt that same punch in the gut as the representative for her husband had earlier, and she began again, her words now making perfect sense, "Oh, okay," she said with deeper conviction. "You are really not the right God for me." It was she who'd placed her husband above her God. This was her constellation.

A visible burden lifted from him, and he relaxed more deeply in God-safety. He leaned back on God and closed his eyes, free to be as needy for rest as she was.

The woman looked at God-Safety and began to tear up, saying. "I have. I have been unfaithful to you. It's true. He's not the right God for me. I can't find my safety in him." And she transferred her dependency needs upon the only One strong enough to hold anyone up.

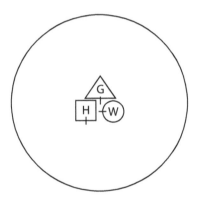

Diagram 4.5

She spontaneously went down to the floor in a bow. And there she stayed and there she let herself cry her heart out for all the hidden falls in her life and her family. I knelt with her in support.

It was a sober moment for every single soul in the room. Who in the world has not walked that thin line in an upshot of disaster of idolizing a person to their own harm?

Shortly I looked up and asked the husband, "What's happening for you?"

"This is all very humbling," he said quietly.

When she finished her bow, she got up. She gratefully dismissed all the representatives and sat down again with me, collecting her thoughts. When she looked around at the group, she saw several people deeply moved by her piece of work. Several thanked her for doing "their work" too.

Discussion of basic placements

Our micro stories have many patterns from our own histories, and those are important to identify and then to transcend them into allegiance to Our Father. He is our life and our spiritual resource for all the relationships we steward as a representative of Christ who has placed His priestly blessing and name on our heads. We will discuss that blessing further in the last chapter.

Marriage is a stewardship relationship, as all our relationships are. Stewarding changes ownership. We don't own people; God does. We love one another in His name. If love will begin to satisfy, it has to be on His terms.

We have multiple roles and stations in life. In each one we steward the Christ life differently. We are children of parents, spouses in marriages, and parents of children; we are siblings to others, peers among peers in organizations, and in all of these stations or positions, we function as ambassadors of love in alignment with Christ who is our real Life.

These stations are our basic trinities of relationships. Every twosome is a spiritual threesome where we learn to see God in us, and with us. We can trust Him and His fairness and generosity to move within the dynamics of the particularities of the relationships.

In other words, how do I "daughter" with God or my parents and not act like a daughter with my spouse? How do I parent my child and not act like a daughter or sibling to that child? These distortions hinder the flow of Love. If a wish was stated on the back page of this book, draw a circle and sketch out a place for you (the wisher) and the person(s) involved in the wish as they feel spatially related to you. Leave it for now and see how things may change.

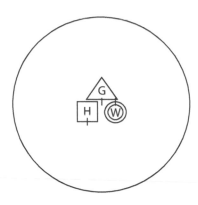

Diagram 4.6

Key: In the wife's story demonstrated above, the imbalances as seen in the "rival option" had roots as patterns in their family tree and had been addressed in prior work. Her fear of fully entering back into the union required her to find safety that supported her unmet dependency needs from her own family.

Neither her parents nor her spouse had been in good order nor fully capable of following the orders of Love in their own early patterns. She needed to find some spiritual resource to sustain her healing in order for Love to have a new chance in establishing a new order for them. When we act out of role confusion, we trespass and injure love. In a later chapter we will further detail the stations of love in each relationship in family life to be thorough about the Spirit of love. Below is a small treatment regarding the injury of misplacements.

Trespasses

What does trespassing mean? It means that in a relationship we stand in a station that is not our own, and we absorb the patterns from events that belong to another person, such as their responsibilities or hurts, and act out as if we can impact something we cannot touch, as if we are someone we are not. It happens deep in our consciousness as a loyalty to a hurt person.

To act as a rescuer to a parent is rather to act superior to them. But a child will do it out of deep sympathy. And being aware of a loss, they may try to help. Sometimes, the whole system entanglement just repeats in the next generation, seeking a resolution.

When a child's own parent is absent, that child might fill in as a partner to their remaining parent and, in doing so, may trump their siblings. There are many ways we trespass and distort love. A child can never replace their own parents or become the fill-in spouse to a broken-hearted parent after a divorce. But children try to help. Though it is an innocent, well-meaning mistake, it is a distortion and a great burden to the child. It's all cozy until the parent remarries, and the child then feels dethroned. Or it is all well until the child grows up and tries to marry a peer and fears their parent feels put out. Loyalties and boundaries become confused, and Love is stunted.

To avoid trespassing, we must stay in our own station with deep reverence for the hardships that come—with faith—that God is enough for all of our needs. And we pray that we see Him there. He gives each person what they need for their situation.

Injuries, by nature, are disorienting. When we lose our bearings in a crisis, it is common to experience role-confusion, and, instead of representing our own lives, we represent/take on/trespass into someone else's life burden. By including God in the realm of the family visually, the disorder can be seen and then can shift. Guilty people can receive the support they need to move through their own guilt and not hide it. We will continue to explore this further in later chapters.

God is good to, with, and for the guilty. We can leave the guilt with the guilty in fields of grace.

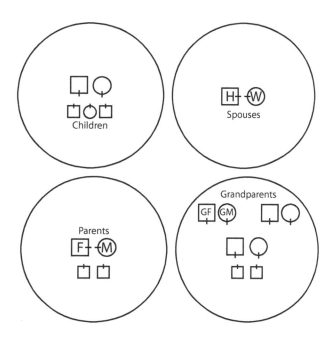

Diagram 4.7

Key: Each circle reflects a divine design: We begin as children, we become spouses, parents and grandparents.

Chapter Five: Biblical Patterns as Context

*"It is the glory of God to hide a thing
and the glory of a king to find it. "
(Proverbs 25:2)*

Wholeness through the ages

In Paul's letter to Rome, he explained that God had bound all men up in disobedience in order to show all men mercy. Joseph and his brother's rivalry story, as we read it backwards in the previous chapter, shows the bondage of our free will. We generally do not know what we are doing, nor who we are, particularly when we and the whole family are unconsciously identified with unresolved losses in the family that become a repetition saga. God's mercy would set us free, should we ever have more doubts about our own wills than we have about His. 'But wait!' a Bible student may reply, 'didn't God give Joseph prophetic dreams and destine him for all that He encountered in Egypt?' Joseph's reply to that was in Genesis 50:20, "As for you, you meant evil against me, but God meant it for good, to bring it about that many people should be kept alive, as they are today." ESV Paul understood similarly that God works all things together for good for those who are called according to his purposes. Romans 8:28. God can use all the evil and transform it when we invite His presence into all the inherited evils.

There is a rogue commitment in man's soul to disbelieve, that opens the door to ancestral flaws. In disbelief, we cut ourselves off from our best hope. When we resist the terms of our lives, and if we don't quite believe, our doubts justify our rebellion but we do not "have it our way." We only end up having it "history's way," thus the adage applies, the apple doesn't fall far from the tree.

Finding fault with the sacred text is never more easy than casting a hard glance at the flood. The enemy is ever-present to challenge the Word in us with suspicion and predictably provoke us to ask once again, "Did God really say that?" Our doubt projects an outright condemnation: "What kind of a God would flood the world?"

In times of suffering, the soul feels justified in taking over. The combination of a dead or disconnected internal spirit and the soul's temptation to dethrone God is enough to undermine the story that will do us the most good.

The days before the flood are "drowned" in large part, with little but the essential history saved. But a few years ago, two clever Bible teachers, Chuck Missler and Joseph Prince, both came to the exact same discovery. The first age of man's lineage between Adam and Noah has a surprising overarching plan for man in the ultimate treaty.

In the earliest epoch of Biblical history, hope was deeply embedded. These two teachers took the names found in the generational line between Adam and Noah, and translated them from English back into their Hebrew definitions. In doing so they found a sentence of prophecy.

Hebrew	English
Adam	Man
Seth	Appointed
Enosh	Mortal
Kenan	Sorrow
Mahalalel	The blessed God
Jared	Shall come down
Enoch	Teaching
Methuselah	His death shall bring
Lamech	The despairing
Noah	Rest, or comfort

Man appointed mortal sorrow; the Blessed God shall come down teaching; His death shall bring the despairing rest.

Be encouraged. God is sovereign over the ages. He has a plan unfolding in the worst of situations and we are safest when we entrust our toughest tangles to Him. Did God forget the pre-flood world, a world full of self-rule? No.

Twenty-five hundred years later, the Apostle Peter explained what he understood about that catastrophic event in human history. "For Christ died for sins once for all, the righteous for the unrighteous, to bring you to God. He was put to death in the body but made alive by the Spirit, through whom also he went and preached to the spirits in prison, who disobeyed long ago when God waited patiently in the days of Noah while the ark was being built" (1 Peter 3:18-20).

Pre-flood mankind was not forgotten. What happened is not entirely clear. But whatever mankind did, it was enough for God to bring things to a halt, demonstrating that what man needs is not just more time.

Time does not equal reformation; repentance does. God shortened man's days thereafter as a mercy. In our survivalist culture, we have politicized the right to end innocent life, but we judge the long-suffering God when He chooses to punish the guilty. We find ways to protect our rule and judge His.

Genesis gives us a bare bones look at family structures which build up or tear down societies. No one is good, but faith in *God's goodness* began to take root in Abraham's gnarley family. Now we will turn our attention again to the risen Christ as the promised 'blessed God who came down teaching, whose death brought the despairing rest.'

The Gospel writers give us systemic context for Jesus. Their lenses give us a few regal patterns to enjoy.

Patterns in Gospel Readings

The early Church Fathers who included the books in the canon of Scripture arranged them for us to start with Matthew's Gospel. This Jewish author introduced Jesus through his ancestral lineage. He demonstrated that the line of Jesus not only goes back to King David, but also Abraham. These clues make a statement. In Matthew's genealogy list, he bracketed the Lord's ancestry into epochs. Example:

"So all the generations from Abraham to David are fourteen generations, from David until the Babylonian exile are fourteen generations, and from the Babylonian exile until the Messiah are fourteen generations" (Matthew 1:17).

This writer makes us mindful of the key pivotal events in the Jewish history, thereby inferring that it was time for a new day, and the story he is reporting is of a man who ranks above Abraham and David.

Additionally, depending upon the translation a person studies, the lineage verses may read like a tedious line of 28 begats; Abraham begat Isaac, etc. But if we read it in a Messianic translation, the verses are more poignant. "Abraham fathered Isaac." 28 repetitions of the word fathered is a clear message that the story of Jesus is actually about a Fatherhood emerging in the purpose of Jesus. In Christ, man's representative, a paternal relationship is being redeemed between God and man.

Luke, the single Gentile author in the Bible, recorded Jesus's line all the way back to Adam, thereby including the interests of the entire human race, inferring that his Messiah King is for everyone. The God who formed Adam from dust in order to reveal Himself to man as Father, is demonstrated perfectly in the New Testament as the Father of Jesus, who was our representative, and God's.

The Gospel writers, after having contextualized Jesus as the promise Word of God descended from of old, gave us an earthly political context for contrast to His heavenly one. They present the earthly reigning king Herod as an evil man, unworthy of the title of monarch in Israel, who attempted to kill Jesus as a small boy in a sweeping slaughter of other children in the same region.

That was the shape Israel was in at the advent of the birth of Christ. It was a preview of what was to come and a statement of the end of their age which would come to a complete destruction forty years post resurrection. Herod is the perfect contrast of man and God, an example of the free will of man under no restraints. If we can imagine a world of Herod's making, we might wish for a flood ourselves. Give Herod a thousand years for a life span, and the upshot would be flood-worthy.

But there is Jesus, a boy of twelve, confounding the Temple elite, and growing in favor with God and man. This is a new kind of human being. How many twelve-year-old boys have ever been interested in discussing theology with their ministers for days on end? We hardly know this way of Being, and yet He is one of us to show us our heavenly design, who we are and what we lost.

Matthew detailed the baptism of Jesus and wrote that the Heavens opened and the Spirit of God came on Jesus as a dove and "the Voice" was heard, saying, "This is my beloved son, in whom I'm well pleased." This story is about the Father and Son dynamic. One up - one down is a luxury when you are the son of the King. There is only true authority under God. There is a particular dynamic, an order, between a Father and a Son, that makes everything Jesus did possible. Jesus said He only did what He saw His Father do. His doing was directly related to how He was stationed in the relationship.

Sonship is a place of being in a right station to one's paternal authority. This way of belonging was what was lost in Adam, but it was revealed in Jesus. This authority is personal; it is not a business exchange, nor is it political; it is the way Love moves in a family, and Jesus was the master of order and impeccable obedience also known as trust. It required both parties to represent what they were looking for with us. Obedience to God is the highest love.

> *"The proper good of a creature is to surrender itself to its creator —*
> *to enact intellectually, volitionally, and emotionally that relationship which*
> *is given in the mere fact of its being a creature. When it does so, it is good*
> *and happy. Lest we should think this a hardship, this kind of good begins*
> *on a level far above the creatures, for God Himself as Son, from all eternity*
> *renders back to God as Father by filial obedience the being which the Father*
> *by paternal love eternally generates in the Son. This is the pattern which*
> *man was made to imitate — which paradisal man did imitate — and*
> *wherever the will conferred by the creator is thus perfectly offered back in*
> *delighted and delighting obedience by the creature, there, most*
> *undoubtedly is heaven, and there the Holy Ghost proceeds."*
> *—C. S. Lewis, The Problem of Pain*

In a Father-Son relationship, the Father's blessing of favor flows freely to a son becoming hidden only if the son presents himself as a rival. The favor of this blessing is key as a normal way of being in order. It is a gift to know and be known by God in one's own place as His own. Child-ship is the only way the Father will recognize us because it is the only way He will be able to be seen as Father and not as a peer, nor as a condemning judge. The first order of love for man is receiving the blessing of God's benevolence. Fathers give blessings. Sons receive them. This was the original template for man that was disordered.

Paul explained the matter in Philippians 3:14: *"Jesus did not think equality with God was something to be grasped but made himself nothing; taking on the role of a servant, he humbled himself even to the point of death, even death on a cross."* This was the ultimate trust-fall. Adam fell. Jesus fell for Adam. God held us all up in Christ's resurrection. This action let us know Jesus trusted the faithfulness of God to raise us in Him. He was right to trust and commit His Spirit to God by faith.

Now as Matthew saw Jesus in a King's line and emphasized a line of the Fathers, Luke gave us the scope of Jesus as a King and a Priest, and he had a particular reader in mind: a Most Excellent Theophilus. Luke was a gentile writer whose audience was a Roman gentile dignitary. When Luke gives us lineage he goes all the way back to Adam, "who was the son of God." This included all men everywhere as sons. These good news books are about the Father-Son dynamic. Jesus' teaching on prayer, which taught the disciples to call God Father, was considered heresy. "Who has the audacity to call God their Father?," the religious leaders balked. Calling God Father implies that the speaker is identifying himself as a Son. This type of heresy leads to exclusion. We should so identify with such company.

Reading Luke's letter as if we are reading another's mail invites us to read the way the recipient would read it. From one Gentile to another, Luke needed Theophilus to have the entire story and understand Jesus as the Savior of the world including Rome. Luke's purpose was "that you may know the truth concerning the things of which you have been informed."

The first three chapters are details of Jesus' family tree intertwined with the nation's soul, embedded in the soul of humanity. He gives us those pertinent details of people, places and events to help the reader orient around the facts, not his opinion of the facts. All three layers enrich the weight of the document, making us take a breath knowing that Luke wrote such an important message to a friend!

Luke's Gospel assured the Roman reader that the kingship of Christ was not a threat but was a blessing to all people. This story about God is a story about God's longing for man to be put into right place with the Father. God's attention is also Luke's intention—reconciliation—to make sons of us all. Roman polytheism had no such good news. What god in Rome would die to make them know that they belonged? Rome was as brutal as their gods were.

Romans conquered territory through the vehicle of polytheism. Israel was no threat to Rome since they didn't proselytize as a people; their law kept them segregated which is not what it means to be "set apart" as mentioned earlier. To play god and to belong to God as a son differs. Rome garnered some favor with many Jews by building synagogues for them, which was how Rome made political progress without excessive bloodshed. That was palatable to the Jews scattered throughout the empire and, to some degree, within the land of Israel, but the Jews did not appreciate paying taxes in Israel to an external figurehead, Caesar. Nor did they appreciate the temples to Zeus set up in their territories beyond the Jordan. The religious tension was a certain irritation for Rome because the Jews did not like their plan to conquer.

This political figure Theophilus was given the details of the Jesus events. Luke included Caesar in the history in a clever way. He didn't hedge the issue for Roman allegiance since he quickly introduced him to a higher head than a mere man. He demonstrated that God Himself was the force behind that which moved Caesar to even call for the first census in the first year that Quirinius was governor of Syria. It was God's idea to move Caesar in order to accurately record His Son's time of birth in history.

This is how he started the account, with Caesar as a human, being moved by the one God. With that thought, how might that reader absorb the finale of the document when, at the crucifixion site, Pilate declared Jesus the king of the Jews, and then a Roman Centurion confessed the man was the "Son of God?" Polytheistic religion was going to need to bow.

This is good news like none other because the Jesus figure overcame death. This report would be an intense piece of information—uncomfortably intense: both troubling and exciting. We don't know the reaction to the letter. But we do know in later books that when Paul took the news out, it provoked an immediate and an intense response. There was nothing dismissive about the person and work of Jesus called the Christ. If we identify Him correctly, He has a claim on us to re-identify us correctly — as sons. This will create serious liberty in the souls of men. Until we know who God is, we can not identify ourselves. Identity is formed in relationships. And His should trump all lesser relationships.

But how also might a Jewish reader compare and contrast the fact that the advent records basically embarrass the religious elite? Zechariah, an elderly high priest and a good man—not perfect but good—is contrasted with Mary, a young Israeli virgin. Both had a visitation from the same angel but with entirely different reactions.

Zechariah was from a group of elites who shared the ranks of folks who had been hearing from angels for thousands of years, but had not heard from The Word in hundreds of years. A dusty letter of the law without Spirit was all they had. The angelic messenger was not out of the ordinary historically, but it had surely been a while since a message had been sent. Shockingly, Gabriel's message from heaven was dismissed by the priest. His goodness was not of the ilk that was really looking for God. But a virgin girl believed an even grander message. Religion was going to need to bow.

And yet both families received a child through a miracle. Thank God nothing He intends depends too heavily upon us. The priest's elderly and barren wife conceived a prophet, and the Jewish virgin girl conceived a Savior—for the sake of the world. These events would have been insurmountable for both audiences, had it not been for faith.

The records quickly move to the adult lives of these two babies. John, the son of a good but doubting priest, grew up. John did not go into the priesthood in the same way his father did. He transcended. He did not serve in the Temple. He was not dressed like his father, wearing a linen ephod covering his chest with jewels to represent the twelve tribes of Israel at the altar. He did not go into the Holy of Holies at the Temple as a representative intercessor for the nation of Israel.

Rather, he was a prophet who made a bold declaration that the Lamb of God—a heavenly lamb—had come. This was bringing earthly priestly duties to a close. He called for the nation to just repent and have baptism or mikvah in the river not the Temple. The gospel writers are all talking about another Kingdom that is breaking in on the earthly ones, both Rome and Israel were going to need to bow into reality.

This is an intense letter if we appreciate the race of the writer and the recipient. If we read it also from the perspective of a Jew, it is over the top. How might a gentile and a Jew hear the letter if read to them both at the same time? How do these groups interface? How might they see each other?

Ancient Israel—Persian-Greco-Roman Empire—Israel
Prophets (Quiet-exile forward) Angels-Zechariah-John-Jesus

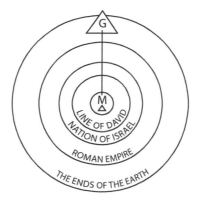

Diagram 5.1

The chart shows us what God was doing during the quiet epoch between the Jewish exile and Christ. He had a plan for all people. While God was drawing the Jews further out into dispersion throughout nations, He was also drawing Gentiles into the land of Promise albeit through occupation to have a front row seat to the ransom moment.

Throughout the quiet years, synagogues had been strategically set up, creating a fast track of evangelism throughout Rome before the birth of the Church. The news came first to the Jews, who then became the hubs for faith in Christ, the King of the Kingdom of God.

Luke, who wrote this record, also wrote the sequel, "The Book of the Acts of the Apostles." Acts chronicled the work of the evangelists throughout the Roman empire. The missionaries went abroad, synagogue by synagogue, house by house, and shared the miracle of Salvation which was designated for everyone. The God of Abraham, Isaac and Jacob, had been plotting for thousands of years to bring light to the nations declaring that there is only one God and one Father of us all. If you will not bow to be a son, you will be an orphan.

Seen in the light of the author-to-reader context, the tensions played out between the Christ and the Jews actually give credibility to the fact that this King had a Kingdom that was not of this world — not earthly but spiritual — it had greater claims on the nations. Be still my heart.

We've lost this note of impact. In Acts, Luke explained that the Holy Spirit fell on the disciples of Jesus during the Jewish Festival of Pentecost, and that the same Spirit also fell on Gentile believers soon thereafter. Father knows man's address, even if man does not know his own. Gentiles were bowing.

In Acts, Peter saw a vision of a sheet of animals descending to him with the command to eat food previously considered unclean by Jews. He couldn't let himself be like the gentiles and eat anything. So the message came three times and at the last, he received the knock on the door with a request for him to go with the gentiles with the gospel. The direct command to tell Cornelius, who was a high-ranking Roman — and to deliver the news inside the 'unclean' man's house — reinforced to Peter that His Father was not a God of favorites. God told Peter, "Do not call unclean what I have made clean."

Whatever this gift was, it was going to reconcile groups of people under one Father. That was the union the Jews could never have agreed to host prior to the resurrection. This salvation cleared ground for a friendship with all people via the Holy Spirit, who helped them see each other as God saw all men: loved with an ever-lasting Love. This was an extension of an olive branch; it was not an invitation to war against Caesar. But the unbelieving Jews would be the first persecutors of their own brothers — think again of Joseph — betrayed by his brothers in Genesis as a prefigured Jesus. We can rest assured, the great reconciliation is on the horizon. It's about that time on God's clock of 500 hundred year interventions.

Reconsider the introduction Luke gave for Jesus in light of this time line. *"In the fifteenth year of the reign of Tiberius Caesar, Pontius Pilate (a Gentile appointment) being governor of Judea, and Herod (half Jewish, half Edomite) being Tetrarch of Galilee, and his brother Phillip Tetrarch of the region of Ituraea and Trachonitis, and Lysanias tetrarch of Abilene, in the high-priesthood of Annas and Caiaphas, the Word of God came to John, the son of Zechariah, in the wilderness. He went into all the region about the Jordan preaching a baptism of repentance for the forgiveness of sins" (Luke 3:1).*

This doesn't read well for a 21st-century American reader, but it is a fiery introduction to a report. Luke quoted John, quoting the prophet Isaiah:

"The voice of one crying in the wilderness, prepare the way of the Lord; make his paths straight. Every valley shall be filled and every mountain and hill shall be brought low, and the crooked shall be made straight, and the rough ways shall be made smooth; and all flesh shall see the salvation of God" *(Luke 3:4-6).*

Theophilus could make no mistake. Jesus is of greater consequence than a political figure head in any nation. The recipient knows parts of the story, but he knows all of the names, and this is a detailed account sent for his assurance of God's grace to him personally. He is targeted as a Son. What the writer did for Theophilus he does for everyone who ever sees the document in its context. He contextualized Jesus as Christ in His time and also in ours by way of the eternity of the resurrection. It changes the way you view yourself as a mere human.

The Isaiah text quoted by John the Baptist could be paraphrased, 'Dearest: get your house in order so you can recognize the messiah when you see Him see you. He is coming to the house. Prepare to bow.'

From Macro to Gospel to Us

The Gospel writers provide dates, times, places, cloths, lineage, history context backward and forward, patterns, epochs age to age, as well as live dialogue with a Devil, angels, demons, and a long series of staggering miracles. The Scriptures are written so that we can trust the Creator of the macro as a personal redeemer of the micro family story.

Earth is the station of cosmic battle between chaos and order. From the micro of individuals trying to make loving connections with other people, to the macro of nations balancing power and establishing their place in the world, there is conflict. All the battles ask the same question that was proposed by the accuser in Eden, and again in the wilderness of Judea to Jesus, and to the audience of scriptures: Who is in charge of you? Who is your true King? Do you know who you are? If we bow, to whom do we bow and what does it mean to be a steward of Love? In simple terms, 'Who is your Father?'

Theophilus, along with all other leaders in the Roman world, knew the despotism in the heart of Herod the Great. Herod, horribly deceived, would not bow and died of venereal diseases shortly after the slaughter of innocent children when Christ was born. His sons thereafter received a divided Israel to rule in three parts. In Acts, Luke made mention that the Herod who mocked the Lord, before returning him to Pilate to be crucified, was suddenly eaten by worms for accepting worship shortly after the death of Jesus. Oy vey.

Israel's true God is the Father of the entire world. He came first to the Jews and then to the Gentiles. Both needed to understand that the kind of Lord to whom the Christians bowed was no small demigod; Jesus was the rightful owner of the souls of men: all men everywhere, and He offered the life path back to their own Father God by representing us as our ransom.

With all this in mind, we are ready to explore family life directly with order in mind. If a person sees the orders as they are presented in the sacred texts through patterns and generations and the life of the Lord, they see that they point to a greater Father. By putting our own houses in order, it is easier to transcend family patterns, as well as transcend the chaos of culture. Identifying as a Son is an entirely different way to be in the world of our own families. Our Father changes everything we know about Love and how He moves in our relations.

In the next several chapters, we will focus directly on common tangles in love. Symptoms belong to the system that produced them. By studying the way a system is organized, we can find solutions to problems its members. We aren't selves. We are souls and we are all connected. Now we will see how to go about getting our houses in order. Everyone can transcend.

Chapter Six: Unlikely Reconciliations, Sexual Orientation, Faith and Hope

"A bad man, happy, is a man without the least inkling
that his actions do not 'answer,' that [his actions] are not
in accord with the laws of the universe."
—C. S. Lewis

New Arrangements: Sexual Orientations

A couple had been married for many years when the husband told to his wife that he thought he was gay. They'd not been physically intimate in several years, and both of them were becoming increasingly hopeless about their marriage. He expressed having some same-sex attractions and, though he didn't permit himself to act upon them, he knew there was a growing distance in the marriage. When he made it clear that he wanted their marriage to work if there

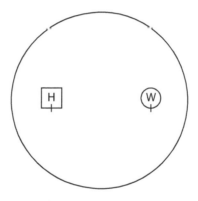

Diagram 6.1

was a way, she too was interested in repairing their love life—if there was a way. He had a clear wish. With her agreement, he began work in hope, and to work we went. We used pen and paper to diagram a model of their relationship.

In the sketch he drew, they were not particularly out of order, though there was significant distance. Prior to their marriage, they'd both had significant intimate opposite-sex partners, but there were no prior marriages, and there were reportedly no children. They reported no aggression, no neglect, nor any sexual abuse in either childhood. There was nothing particularly eventful in their history. So, I asked him to set

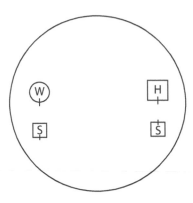

Diagram 6.2

up his family of origin. Sketching a similar distance between his parents, the only difference was he placed his mother (W- Wife in the above diagram) as the first of the two equals in their married relationship. He placed himself and his brother (S- Son) also at a similar distance from each other as their parents.

I wondered why he placed his mother first and asked him to describe their marriage. He said he didn't believe his father cared much for his mother, and their distance felt like an emotional burden for him to carry. Since he didn't like the family assignment, he stayed away. He found it difficult to be around them and said he had nothing in common with his brother, who seemed to get along fine with their father.

I wondered what events occurred with his folks and asked about their story. He could not relay any facts or events. In fact, he knew nothing about their meeting, dating, or decision to marry, nor could he report any significant life events in either of their families of origin. All he knew was that his dad had always seemed irritated with his mom, so he always felt sorry for her but also resented being the person expected to make it better for her—thus, he was estranged from the family, but it looked as if everyone was.

As it typically seems to go, once people start giving their attention to issues in their family souls, movement happens. Thus, an ironic occasion popped up in a timely manner that just so happened to call him back home. While he was there, he decided to ask his father how he met his mom. He reported this event.

His dad was deeply in love with a woman before he married this man's mother. He bought the woman a ring to propose marriage. When he proposed, she refused him on the grounds of infertility. Out of love, she wanted him to have a full life and a chance to marry a woman who could give him children. A year later, this man's father and mother were married.

He married a woman he did not love in the same way. But they married, successfully passed life on to two children, and lived unhappily ever after.

This story changed his mind entirely about his parents. He had compassion for them both. So we set up a new image, and I asked him to give his father's first love a place in their family soul. He immediately recognized a strong identification with her.

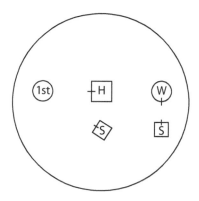

Diagram 6.3

I asked him to imagine her in his mind's eye, there in the office. He became moved in his heart and felt a strange joy at the idea of contact with her, and he soon recognized she actually held a place in their family. Giving her a place in his family soul, he began to see her sacrifice.

Her refusal and his father's surrender is what made room for his own mother and, specifically, for his own life to come to be. Looking at her on the level of the soul, he laughed and noticed how much he liked her and was drawn to her. His hidden identification was conscious now.

I asked him if he could recognize and honor her loss of his father, and his loss of her, and to honor her sacrifice. He did so easily with a warm bow. It was a person his whole family needed to honor and integrate as part of their wholeness.

It seems odd to honor someone besides a parent. But it is critical to acknowledge those people whose lives have impacted a family in such a way that the trajectory of a system is entirely changed.

The events are not always a sacrifice; sometimes, it is a great gift or a destructive event that was deeply impactful. We include them, either acknowledging the gift or their guilt, and in seeing their place, release those who might otherwise be compelled in some deep way to represent the forgotten or hidden.

Honoring one's parents helps children take their place as children and not burden-bearers. By seeing parents in context, the adult-children better understand their own place. For this man, seeing the first love changed the image of his parents. But more importantly, he was disentangled from representing her in her absence.

We all have certain terms in life with which we must reconcile with providence. I asked him to look at her in context of his parents. We re-sketched the diagram to include her. I offered the words to him to speak aloud.

"I live in part because you gave up your place to my mother. Thank you."

Next, I asked him to bow to his father and mother, giving respect and warmer regard for the limits of their relationship. Life passed on to him on these terms.

I said, "Tell you father, 'Now I see your hurt.' " He did so.

"And tell your own mother, 'You're the right mom for me.' " He did so.

He was immediately light-hearted and uplifted. He felt much freer to enjoy his father without responsibility for his mom's unmet needs. It made perfect sense to him, and a weight was lifted.

What did this have to do with his own marriage?

Soon after this session, the man quickly settled into a new freedom of life. His identification with the feminine soon disappeared. He felt a sudden and strong need to buy a motorcycle, which he did. He also left a home-decorating career. Within weeks, he reported that his attractions to the same sex were completely gone. That was a confirmation to me that he'd been carrying a burden of representing a missing woman in his family soul. He was disentangled, able to connect with his parents equally, as well as with his previously estranged brother.

He decided to go on some personal pilgrimages into various retreats to pray through his discoveries, solidifying them in more ways spiritually and with sacred ritual. He had a new freedom spiritually to worship and felt the miraculous around him. He was alive to his own presence in a new way.

During this entire process, from the start and for his wife's sake, since she was available but uncertain as to how things would move, or if things would move for her husband, I had recommended an in-house separation. My supposition was that living in different rooms as roommates would either lessen the shock of separating, if it came to that, or it could stimulate a latent appetite for each other to emerge again if hope was restored.

About a month after his clearing himself of a burden of representing, they both came in for a session during a time that happened to be his lunch break. He sat on the floor to use the coffee table as a dining table. While he ate, she talked and grieved over an incident in her own life. As she did, he unconsciously moved one inch at a time in her direction. By the time he was finished eating, he was on the sofa entirely wrapping her up in his arms while she cried.

Oddly, though, the next week he asked for an individual session and announced two things. "I don't feel any interest in same-sex attractions at all now. That feeling is totally gone. But— I don't think I love my wife."

Remembering the previous session, I reviewed in careful detail what I saw and heard, mentioning also that, "It took you about twenty minutes to get to her from how far away you were seated, but, unconsciously, inch by inch by inch, you figured out how to rearrange your seat in the room to close the gap. You made your way to her effortlessly, moving closer to her every few minutes. You weren't still until you wrapped her up in your arms."

He stared ahead into the distance of his own memory. And I sat watching him process his internal images. After seeing the memory and looking internally he literally yelled in my office, more so to himself than to me, "Oh my God! I am in love with my wife! I love her! I do love her! How did I not see that?!"

His brain assimilated her on new terms. He had seen his family soul and then seen himself, and now he could see her as she was with him. He connected with himself as a husband and with her as his own wife. Now, he saw them together as one. He was startled to discover himself as being entirely devoted to her. Then he started to laugh with joy. He continued with his shock and surprise.

He was free from a family entanglement. It is always a tragedy to be held captive to someone else's story, but it is also an opportunity to check to see if one is simply representing and receiving an opportunity to heal the past. Seeing the history as belonging to his father, he was able to honor it, and turn to his own life and be a devoted husband, which was new territory for his family soul. Now, more than ten years later, he is still in a happily-ever-after marriage.

I have to admit that when the couple came in, upon hearing their issue, I had to fight my own inclination to offer advice that would not have had one thing to do with their wish. Thankfully, we all stayed clear on the wish and followed the mystery.

Comments

Set-ups give us a window into the family soul. Whether we do them as a sketch, a figure set-up, or in live group-work, set-ups give us a chance to see the gaze of our soul. It's a good practice when someone has a snag that they cannot account for to stop and do a meditation on their whole family and just check to see where the soul has cast its gaze.

We are often not fully present to our own lives because we are preoccupied with something unfinished for someone in the whole. In our soul, we often look at the missing person. If we do not look, we will not see.

If we are identified with a missing person, we are not identified fully with the Lord in our own lives and His good terms for love. These loyalties can be better served in Christ by transcending them.

Homosexuality in a Church Organization

I attended a workshop training where husband and wife Jakob and Seiglinde Schneider—German facilitators who are experienced in models—were presenting in the United States.

A woman presented an organization issue related to the church. She was acquainted with the wife of a priest whose church had split over the issue of homosexuality. She was wondering if she could be of any assistance to the body of the organization in promoting reconciliation.

Although they had not formally asked for her to assist yet, she was interested in looking at the issue to see for herself what the elements were in the organization. Hearing her out, Jakob checked around the group to see if there was an openness to exploring that conflict. The group was available. Her wish reflected what she believed was their wish—to reconcile their local fellowship. She just wanted to take a look.

The facilitator chose participants to represent the following: the woman, her friend who was the wife of the priest, the priest, three people to represent those who left the church, and then he asked me to represent those who identified as homosexual, a.k.a. same-sex attraction. The set-up looked like the model below.

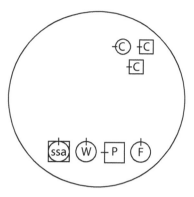

Diagram 6.4

The three who represented the church split (c) were in great pain. One pounded her fist on the wall in anguish saying, "God's law's will never change." The second of the three expressed deep grief saying, "I can't believe they let us go; I can't believe they don't care that we are gone; I can't believe they won't come for us," and the third sat down on the ground quietly in loss. The representatives for the priest, his wife, and the potential facilitator were all in a line, looking at the pain but being unable to respond.

As the same sex attraction representative, I was aware of the loss in the church split and was drawn more to those who left than to the leadership, but I too couldn't move. When Jakob asked what I was noticing, I reported the image that crossed my mind: "I see many small fish all over the floor: some are already dead, and others are flopping and struggling for water, but there is no water in this room at all."

The interviews of the others didn't allow for any movement. So the facilitator then added two more representatives: one to represent faith and one to represent politics.

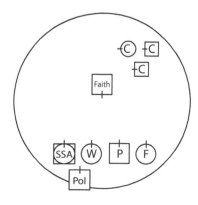

Diagram 6.5

Faith came in to stand at the center. He stood between those who left and faced those who remained. Politics stood centered behind homosexuality and the priest's wife. Jakob asked what effect the additions had.

I turned to look behind me and felt used. I wanted to go and bow to faith and perhaps even join those who were in anguish, but I felt stuck. I reported, "I am either going to bow to faith, or I will die like a fish outside of water." But I felt so stuck that I never moved, but I was aware that the leadership was stuck as well. And it seemed like the pressure was from Politics. When I turned to look at Politics, I felt used.

It became clearer that the issue was not as much about homosexuality but was rather more about the priest having faith in God and being able to follow faith instead of being owned by politics. The organization was driven by politics instead of faith, and the movements became stuck. It was an example of the leadership's need to transcend a cultural conscience.

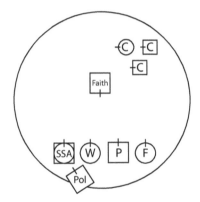

Diagram 6.6

Comments

We may wonder whether or not Jesus had much to say about this among many specific "issues" that the Bible identifies as sin. We know how he treated adulterers, robbers, sick people, and the proud.

We know when Jesus was greeted by a rich young ruler who called him "good teacher," that He asked why the man called Him good, saying, "There is none good but the Father." That is a leveling statement—no one is good but God. Period. Any goodness we have does not come from us, but from the Father. But we like to find ways to inherit eternal life. We like to justify ourselves instead of die to ourselves. We will come to that.

So, we might ask, did Jesus or did he not ever address homosexuality? He did, and He did it exactly as the model above demonstrated. Look at this passage and sketch it. He indicted an entire town, but not for homosexuality. He indited the entire town for the ultimate sin that opens the door to all other sins.

"And you, Capernaum, will you be lifted to heaven? No, you will go down to hell! If the miracles that had been worked in you had been worked in Sodom, it would still be there today. I can guarantee that judgment day will be better for Sodom than for you." At that time Jesus said, "I praise you, Father, Lord of heaven and earth, for hiding these things from wise and intelligent people and revealing them to little children. Yes, Father, this is what pleases you" (Matthew 11: 23 - 26).

Unbelief is the only issue in any issue. Capernaum had been given so many miracles, and still they would not believe. The Old Testament City completely given over to an insatiable and violent homosexual order was figured in the mind of Christ as a place of more hope than a city that refused faith in the presence of Christ.

The main issue is faith—a particular faith: Christ's faith in God. To that point, it is God's goodness that was evident in Christ, whose goodness Jesus honored as His Life. How Christ demonstrates faith in God as His Father is the favor God wants to grant His children.

If we set this particular text up visually—on paper, in group, or in our mind's eye—we see that his warning is sharp, and it is centered around faith. Unbelief is the issue; the fruit of unbelief is varied. To be lost in the fruitlessness and deadness in any form is to miss the issue of faith: in God's faith in Jesus, and in Jesus's faith in God. Their dynamics are the central issue of the universe.

The upshot of unbelief is the original and only issue in Eden. By dismissing God's Fatherhood, we lose touch with Life. Faith in Jesus redeems the image of man as a Son in union with the Father. In absence of this order, we opt to fill in his place with self rule.

Perhaps the preceding chapter would be better placed here, but I placed it as a foundation in understanding that faith in Christ is not a racial issue: it is not a Gentile, Roman, or Jewish conflict; it is not a denominational question, and it cannot be co-opted into a political issue.

Christ is simply supreme. He has no equal, no peer, no competition, no rival. He commands faith in the Father from the children of God. The disciples asked what they should do to do the works of God, and He said, "Believe in the one He sent." This is a union we are to grasp: the orders and the "way" of being with God. There are earthly terms of entanglement. These we see. The point of seeing them is to clear them, demonstrate the power of order, and then, in knowing that truth, we must contemplate the greater soul of Jesus who has bought us and brought us to the Father as His own. This is where we are all headed. Home.

Scripture is clear on issues of immorality, be it sex, drunkenness, greed, or rage. So, we all have one question, the same question, once again: do we believe God or not? It's the same question of Adam. And the same question of Jesus in the wilderness of temptation: Did God really say...?

God's opinion of us is Jesus. And just as the bronze snake was lifted up in the wilderness, where snake-bitten people could look upon it and the poison would be drawn out of them so that they would be healed—so, too, we have Jesus who also was lifted up on a cross and has drawn all our sin unto himself and separated us from it, so that we might be dead to sin and alive to His resurrected life inside us.

What we need most is faith in His face and no other. Look to the Lord, and be saved. Look to the Lord and let Love invade every part of our hearts, giving us assurance, hope, and peace, and wherever we need a way of escape, He gives us light enough to find our next steps.

Just bow.

Chapter Seven: From Parentage to Parenting

"Whatever you have done to the least
of these, you've done to me."
— Jesus

In this chapter, the reader will see several family arrangements where children were directly affected by the parents and grandparents. Keep in mind that every family is unique, which is why we must set it up in a model to see what that system is working on. But many families, like we saw in Joseph's backwards reading, are working out entanglements that speak to something long forgotten that needs to be remembered and reconciled. In the midst of all of our estrangements, there is the Lord ultimately working in and through the trouble to conform us to Love. A few reminders of the is-ness of heaven's reality are in order—once again.

Before we begin a word of caution is in order. The enemy of God loves to accuse us without mercy. The Old Testament story of Job, which precedes Moses and the patriarchs in time line, reminds us that there is an enemy in the world, bent on our destruction. Job lost everything. He lost his children, his livelihood, his friends became a voice of accusation, and he was estranged from his wife. I mention Job because losing children in death either physically or spiritually is a torment to parents like little else. Job's horror brings us face to face with the arch enemy of God. It was and is a cosmic battle that is behind all generational entanglement all the way back to Adam. Even when we try to do right by our kids, we know that God himself gave Adam paradise, but there was still an enemy. We must do our best as parents to take a burden off of our children, to clear the generational lines as much as we can to be faithful to God, but they have to work out their own faith like everyone else on the planet.

That said, we set things up in order to see things fairly. The following examples demonstrate where things could be reconciled. We don't set things up to make an accusation but to give us a way to relieve a burden where possible. God will show a way to persevere and intercede for children in the family.

Family Wholeness

The family is a whole body, and that is not to say that it ought to be, but that it truly is. When we fail to accept this as reality, and we attempt to dismiss people, we deny reality. In denying reality, we deny God in that we've role-played His part and acted as judge in having dismembered a part of the family body. This has great application to the body of Christ as well, which the family was designed to reflect.

The work of Rupert Sheldrake, a highly-credentialed biologist, highlights the connectivity of all things in the field to which they belong, explaining the cooperation of ants, birds, fish, and wolves as a natural phenomenon he calls morphic resonance.

This is a natural observation of what the Scriptures declare as Christ, the sum of all things. "All things were made by and for Him, and in Him, all things hold together," said the Apostle Paul. The observations of nature that Sheldrake presents are compelling and draw our attention to the spiritual nature moving behind and throughout the physical world and through that of the soul. This wonder inspires worship of the creator as we notice the calling card of Jesus.

All things are connected in Christ. Naturally, then, when there is a breakdown in relationships, we have lost alignment with our created order. Disorder is alien to the Trinity's wholeness. There is, therefore, no separation nor disunity between the members of the Godhead, in whose image we are made. This is our design as heirs. We are and should be in discord when we have disorder; it is a call to reconciliation.

When we imagine another person as inconsequential, or we dismiss their place or confuse it, someone else will often bear the burden of re-membering the forgotten and will become like the missing person as a representative with some of the similar conflicts. This is the kind of representing that members of a family do in an unconscious form and lose their attention to their own lives, as their soul hosts an unconscious gaze toward a hidden other.

Mis-arranged

If a woman started frying chicken for her family when she was seven years old because her father was hungover on the sofa, and her mother was at work, she was essentially reared in a way that is known as out of place. Competent enough to pull a step stool up to the stove and get ingredients together to fry chicken, her place was arranged structurally as a mini-provider. Later, as an adult, it was hard for her to take men seriously. The structure had to change for Love to have a chance.

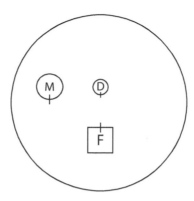

Diagram 7.1

In this diagram the inner picture of the arrangement visually demonstrates the disorders. The father is in the position of a child, the mother is in the father's place and nearing "the edge" perhaps of leaving, and the daughter is in the central place of the family. To appreciate the stress on a child who doesn't get to be a child, imagine her trying to piggy back her father. The burden, born long enough, is crippling.

Little Mirrors

A man asked me to see his daughter for substance abuse. We set up her family and reinstated her mother, to whom the father had forbidden their daughter's access after their divorce. While the daughter carried her mother in her soul, she became estranged from her father. Though she lived with him, they had no peace. The daughter's substance abuse subsided when she reconnected with her mother, though her father's alcoholism continued.

A woman asked me to see her daughter for her daughter's sexual acting out. Turned out, it was more helpful for the mother to address her husband's affair. Reconciling the spouses had a good effect on the girl.

A mother asked me to see her young son, who was troubled with bullies. I explained that I didn't do play therapy and tried to refer her to my colleague. Not to be put off, she said that she was given my name and preferred to see me, and again I explained how thoroughly competent my colleague was at play therapy. But when she said, "My son is asking to see a woman," I was stunned that a ten-year-old boy would specifically request counseling with a woman. I clarified, "Is your son actually the one requesting counseling for himself?"

"Yes, he is, and he is asking for a woman." Intrigued, I agreed.

We had a few chatty visits, and I gave the son some ideas about setting boundaries around himself to protect him from bullies, and then I requested time with the mother. When she came in, we set up her family of origin. She too had been bullied repeatedly but not at school. She had been bullied by a family member as a child. Originally from another country, she had since married an American and moved to the U.S., leaving her own home country. The son was born in the States.

We honored her family 'back home' in order to remember them with love, including her estranged bully sibling. I had her imagine speaking to her family in her mind's eye from her heart. She addressed the hurt in her mental Field of Grace and did a ritual bowing in her mind as a meditation of reconciliation. She made her peace with her sorrow of leaving her home country as well as leaving her sibling.

She called me later that same afternoon with a short report she left as a message. "My son came home this afternoon and told me he was on the playground today, and the bully came after him again, and this time he side-swiped the fellow's legs out from under him. He said his teacher was watching him, but he didn't get into any trouble. He said she just smiled at him and told him that the boy had had it coming, and she didn't think he would bother him again. This occurred at 11:30 a.m., which was halfway through the time of our appointment."

In each of the three examples above, the children were representing another family member who was present in the family soul. Many symptoms in one person are echoes of an unresolved issue in the family. In this way, symptoms belong to the system. The best thing a parent can do for a child is to unburden them. By asking the question, "has this issue ever been my own experience," we can connect with the larger wound.

An Elderly Child

When another mother was concerned about her adult son not fitting into his community, at first, it sounded like she didn't have all the facts straight from him, or maybe she was enabling. But when she said he had actually been kicked out of a religious organization for something that sounded benign, I suddenly noticed the strength of her accent as if it were suddenly being amplified. I wondered if the child was perhaps carrying a burden of her not fitting in well. So we began exploring how the mother had come to the United States.

As we talked, I could hear how much it cost her to immigrate. She had left her homeland for the love of her life. They raised a family together in the United States. When she came to me, her husband had recently died. Without him, the cost was increased. I asked her to think of a symbol of her country which we could include in our Field of Grace. She warmly described a statue. I had her imagine that she could bow to her homeland with reverence and speak to the soul of her country of origin directly. I helped her get started with words like, "I miss my homeland; I hope you will be friendly with me as I live abroad."

Once she got started, she spilled out the loss in her heart. "I hope I have never done anything while in this country to bring shame to you, and I still hold you in my heart." Then suddenly, bursting out a rapid-fire, staccato-like, weeping confession, she said, "And I want you to know that when I said my vows for citizenship, I crossed my fingers!"

In all these examples, "honoring" means that at the very least we include what is, or what is still there; the homeland abroad, the bully who represented the family at a distance, and even the affair. Honoring what is there allows us to put things into order. We have to acknowledge what "is." This is the whole system.

Grandparents Re-membered

At a workshop, a woman presented an issue of wishing to feel brave and free, particularly with men, with whom she often felt stupid. Knowing she had already worked through many core orders and knew this kind of work well herself, I asked her to choose two people from the group; one to represent her soul and another to represent feeling stupid. The woman and I both stayed seated, and I asked the representatives to set themselves up wherever it seemed they were in relationship to one another.

The station chosen by both representatives was in the lower part of the room, meaning, placement-wise in the circle, they stood in the child's sphere, which left a vast amount of empty space behind them. That empty space would soon be filled with those whose burdens were being born by this adult child's soul. The very way they set up made room for someone to be re-membered.

Interestingly, the person representing her Soul stood centered with arms wide in joy and wonder and declared that she was brave and free. So, the feeling of stupidity was with her, but it did not belong to her. The representative for Stupid was off center and on the left side, which is a male/father's side of the space. She stood facing the Soul. But Soul did not seem to connect to Stupid.

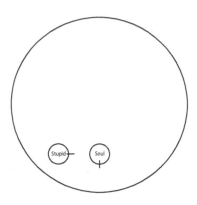

Diagram 7.2

The representative for Stupid, upon seeing the happiness in her Soul, said she didn't know where to go. She wanted to go with the Soul but couldn't connect there, so she sat down for a moment to think. 'Stupid' was a bit lost.

At that, the Soul started laughing very hard, and soon the laughter became contagious and filled the entire room, even to the point of tickling the representative for Stupid. To explain herself, the Soul said, "I'm just happy and free!"

The client watching this set up also started laughing hysterically.

The Soul laughed and said, "I'm about to wet my pants!"

I told her, "That's the representation; she's about to wet her pants all the time." The client laughed and squealed, "I am! I am about to wet my pants!"

Laughter rolled until Stupid finally began to move and found herself a comfortable place at the top right of the room. The Soul turned around and angled over to where Stupid had previously been. Stupid then smiled at her very sweetly and blew her a kiss.

As laughter began to settle, I began to work with the two representatives in their new stations, checking in with their experiences of seeing each other at this distance.

Shortly, something dawned on the client. She recognized now who Stupid actually represented. She identified the representative as her paternal grandmother and tenderly called her by a special pet name. She spoke of her tenderly and in the voice of a small child again. Everything became very still and quiet.

"What happened to your grandmother?" I asked.

She explained, "My father's mother was treated for mental illness all her life and was in and out of the hospital and had many rounds of shock treatment."

In that way, her grandmother had been excluded.

The healing words came to me almost immediately. I had the Soul representative tell the grandmother, "I have given my entire professional life to re-member-ing you by serving others in similar struggles."

The soul bowed deeply, and the beloved grandmother representative began to tear up at being recognized and honored in this way.

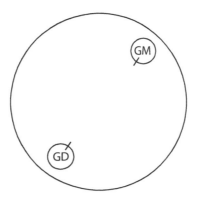

Diagram 7.3

Then the grandmother blew her another kiss. I had the soul representative step aside to let the real granddaughter, who was now free from the burden of her exile, take her place now as an innocent and loyal grandchild who had carried her assignment with great love and devotion.

As soon as she stepped into her soul's place, the representative for her grandmother blew her another kiss. The granddaughter wanted to go hug the grandmother. She walked toward her grandmother, and they embraced, reconciled.

In the group discussion that followed, the woman said men in her family had been very hard on women; in particular, in her father's family, they would often criticize women and call them idiots. She felt stupid, too. It stood to reason that her father perhaps had hardened feelings of loss from many interruptions in care and contact with his own mother. That anger about women belonged to him. The woman could better leave his criticisms with him and could honor both him and his mother, in addition to their hardships, with new respect. Her father's anger and loss belonged to him now, and other men were not to be feared. She was free.

Adoptions with Dicey Dynamics

A young woman was identified to me as a 'failed adoption' by her foster case worker. She'd been adopted by an American couple and brought to the United States from another country. The adoptive parents later placed her in a foster care home.

"What's your wish?" I asked.

She wasted no time. "I'd like to be able to get along with my adoptive father."

We set it up to have a look at her inner image of herself in her family.

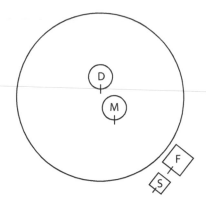

Diagram 7.4

Notice the size of the figures she chose as representatives. She, the daughter, is centered in the circle as an adult figure. Below her figure she placed the adoptive mother, and outside the circle she placed the adoptive father with their natural son who was small and younger than she.

I asked her who was in charge. She said she was. That matched her image of her placement. Her parents were beneath her, and the father and his son were outside the circle.

The main event in her life was her adoption. In our discussion about her relationships, I asked her what her theory was about why these folks adopted her, and she said, "I guess they couldn't have children at the time, and now they do." This also fit the display where she had placed herself in the provider position.

I asked her to choose figures to show me her birth parents.

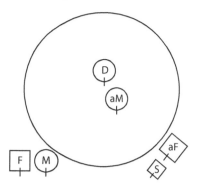

Diagram 7.5

She also placed them beneath her to the left and outside her circle. That also fit her image since these people were first, (thus to the left) and yet they were outside her world, beneath her, and were somehow in emotional debt to her, as if they owed her something.

That was an external display of how life appeared to her internally as an image. There was exclusion and parental debt with all parties; therefore, she was in charge. But in being stationed there, no one stood behind her for support. She had no backing. She was still an orphan at heart. And now that her father had a son of his own, he was no longer in her circle at all.

I noticed those two figures were rightly oriented in that the father was bigger than the son and above him, and they were close. This she also owned in the display. The two children in this family were absolutely, necessarily, and naturally treated differently.

To address first things first, for her soul, we needed to look at the loss of her own parents.

Children may or may not know the details of why they were separated from their parents, but some children who feel cast off experience the separation like a death, even a murder to their soul. They aren't dead, of course, but that relationship dynamic is deeply injured, and trust is challenging.

Added to that is the shock to a child's body. Einstein's theory called 'spooky action at a distance' supposed that if we separate two previously connected molecules and stimulate one, the other also vibrates. This relates also to Rupert Sheldrake's theory of morphic resonance, and it points toward a simple bow to the grace that Christ is our context: "In Him, we live and move and have our being." If we know this, we know that there is a fundamental connection.

Though the womb is gone, and so is that voice, what is still present are the soul and physical connections, both in the ether and in the hormones, and also the tensions surrounding the adult contemplations, whatever shade of emotion they may be.

In physical reality, we embody our parents' DNA. In the soul, the connection continues, and the state of the soul can be relayed in either direction until a Word, fittingly spoken, restructures the disordered connection from the heart like a prayer.

To put things into a better working order for this foster girl who needed to be in a less-burdened place, I said, "Close your eyes and imagine a wide-open Field of Grace, and tell me what you see when you get there."

"I'm looking at the ocean," she softly said.

Of course, her parents were an ocean away. "Call your birth parents and let them appear over the oceans of waters that separate you, and let them see you see them."

"... I can see them," she replied. In truth, I suppose in her soul that she was always looking for them.

"Tell your parents, 'You are my parents; I'm your daughter.'"

"You are my parents. I'm your daughter," she repeated the words calmly, taking deep breaths spontaneously.

"What do you notice about them?" I asked.

"He looks sad now."

There was her truth in the whole matter: his grief and sadness revealed her value. It would be appropriate for a father to feel grief and to express pain upon seeing a daughter who is impossibly out of his reach to touch physically. Upon her seeing him in loss, a burden lifted off of her. One cannot be lost unless one belonged.

"So, tell your parents," I said, " 'Whatever separated us made room for an ocean to come in between us. But this is not the only life; there is one to come. I'll meet you there.' "

She took a deep breath, and repeated the words slowly and warmly. When she opened her eyes, she had peace on her face and a gentle smile. She acknowledged that she was the child of two people. These were her parents. In her soul, she needed to see them. And it needed to be okay to see them. And it was important to see them seeing her see them. It reconciles them in the depths. '

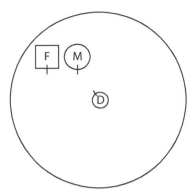

Diagram 7.6

To put things into working order for her whole family soul, we then rearranged everyone. We gave her birth parents a place in her circle above her to honor the loss and to recognize that they were. This allowed her to give them responsibility and reality in her story. At the same time we replaced her adult sized model figure on the board with a child-size one. This left her birth parents' responsibility effectively 'over her head.'

Next we addressed the relationships she had with her adoptive parents. I asked her again to tell me why she thought she was adopted, and she repeated that they couldn't have children. "So, does that mean you became responsible for making them something they couldn't be at that time?"

"Yes."

"I guess that's why you felt bigger than them, since you had the assignment to make them something God hadn't made them into yet."

"Yes."

"Do you think it's true that you meet their needs?"

"No. But that's why they needed me. And then they had a baby after me."

"Yes. Where does that leave you?"

"I don't know."

We frankly discussed the fact that infertility is an adult burden that is not solved by adoption. It's their burden and pain and loss. It is doubly burdensome when an adopted child, already bereaved down deep, grows up feeling like a disappointment, since adoption never solves the infertility.

I asked her to close her eyes and go to a Field of Grace again and call her second family: her adoptive parents. She saw her adoptive parents on the sea shore near her. I offered her these words to speak to her image for clarity.

"Dad, your son is the right son for you. Mom, I could not make you a mother. I was just a baby."

She said the words comfortably with breath. And we continued.

"'Thank you for helping me live and for caring for me. I'm taking what I need from foster care now, and what I cannot get from them, I will get from God, others, and myself. Thank you for helping where you could. I'll do something good with my life."

She could breathe with those words as well. While she was speaking, I arranged the figures to reflect the arrangement of their life together.

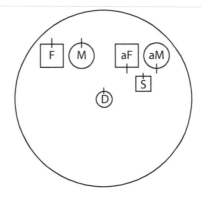

Diagram 7.7

I turned her birth parents away from her to consider that they may have been prohibited by something in their own back field. She looked like she had peace.

Discussion

Many of these reality words were clarified for me and others by a family-systems philosopher/former priest, Bert Hellinger, who once said in a workshop that adopted children are like guests in the adoptive family's home. That was a startling image for me when I heard him say it. But it seems true for some children. In those cases it is a relief to have it put into words.

Each family dynamic is different. The adults' motivations have everything to do with the dynamics of relationship and the way in which the children can take love from them. Adopting parents have a better relationship when they are clear that they are there to give for the sake of the child.

Let us say that an adopting family got off on the wrong dynamic. If an adopted child is a guest in the home, but the parents become clear that they are the givers, and if they also come to see the stewardship of a child of God is in their keeping as a heritage of grace, perhaps a shift can happen. The child can come to trust that they are deeply welcomed and are a pleasure. If the children are welcome to stay as long as they like, perhaps they will begin to trust and agree.

The orphan in the world is a rich child of God, and they can be won, but only as a treasure of God and should be stewarded as His own. Their terms are their terms. They, like everyone else, learn God's way in those specific terms. If seen on those terms, and if welcomed, then they have a choice to stay with dignity, not a sense of failure or—God forbid—as a provider to the adults. God has terms to shepherd and care for the children lost to their mothers. They were His children first, and His children last. He is the Father in between. Adoptive parents must represent Him.

Every adoption is unique. It's imperative to know how the child views himself or herself in relation to the parents and the their adoptive parents. And it is important that the adoptive parents are aware of their own view of the whole family. The birth parents are hidden, but present. When all the views line up with the Father's view, Love has a chance.

Some households are blended with biological children. Every image is unique. Some biological children are injured when they hear their parents say they love them all the same, as if children are replaceable. It is good to have children show us how they see these events when the stress is present.

The same thing happens in blended families with step children. Sometimes, it is the grandparents who see the is-ness, or facts, better than the immediate family, and they do not force themselves to be what they are not. If they favor their own, it is because it is true.

Worse, when a child of a divorce is legally adopted by a stepparent, they are forced to take another man's name. It creates a burden as we saw earlier with Johnny's wish, but it also creates an identity question. How does the child look at his own father's parents? The wider we open the frame, the more we see. By having his name changed, the male child, has now been separated in identity from a long line of men. It is not necessary.

And what if, someone may ask, a child is the product of rape? It is impossible to see this child as a mistake. A child is a heritage of the Lord; the fruit of the womb is a reward. A child is only and always a product of Our Father who decided to grant life and sovereignly determined for good to come of a painful event.

God is the life-giver. In this way, the guilt of a rape stays with the man who raped a woman—and yet—he became a father. This is fact, life, terms, and goodness. The victim/perpetrator relationship belongs to the adults. The child belongs to God, as do the parents. His mercy is seen in the baby.

An Image for a Child and His Adopted Mother

There are many delightful, open-hearted, and generous adoptions that reflect the benevolence of a heavenly family. I like to imagine those adoptions artfully. I want to introduce another image in another Field of Grace to support the generous souls who recognize that they are stewards of a child of God. It is presented as a simple vignette for reflection:

This field was wet with a recent rain; the air was clearer, and the nearby creek was muddy as it hurried on toward a greater river and on towards the ocean. The grass sparkled bright green, and the tree branches sprayed mist in the breeze. The heavy clouds having let down their storm of thunder and lightning, bellied on along to soften neighboring grounds on their path. The sun was shining again, no longer directly overhead but in no hurry to set. Everything was fresh.

A small child and his favorite angel walked out together, barefooted, and lay down on a thick blanket as was their habit, sometimes to nap, sometimes just to be still. They both giggled when the rainwater dripped onto their cheeks. Soon, their breaths matched as they became quiet under a wide, shady tree. The birds began to stretch their wings overhead. The wildflowers were no worse for wear after the storm. The two lying down became present to all the sounds in nature.

The young child spoke the way a child can when they are comforted, without any inclination to censor around a tender spot.

"Mommy," he whispered to his earthly angel, "I wish I'd grown in your tummy."

She smiled and brushed his hair with her fingers without verbal reply.

The boy was still, quietly listening to the birds overhead call out to the birds nearby in conversation.

The angel's thoughts moved toward his birth parents, not knowing who or where they were. "You know," she said, "when I think about it, I think it's too bad for your birth parents and your grandparents, too. I am so happy we are a family, but I know my happiness came because of a lot of sadness over your separation from them. She must ache sometimes."

"Mommy, I'm glad I'm here with you."

"So glad," said she, "I am so glad you are with me now. It's lucky for me that I get to be second. I didn't get you in my tummy, but I got you in my pouch!"

"We're like kangaroos," he snickered. "I'm a little 'Roo, and you're a big 'Roo, and God is our Super 'Roo."

"Super 'Roo," his angel repeated, smiling.

"Dear Super 'Roo," the boy began to pray, "thanks for putting me in my mommy's tummy, and then in my second mommy's pouch, and for putting the whole world in your pouch."

The Psalmist was clear when he observed that "When your father and mother forsake you, I the Lord will take you up" (Psalm 27:10). Guardian Angels and Shepherds alike all care for the princes and princesses of God. Magi are simply those who recognize the face of Christ when they see him and bring their treasures to give and bless. May God bless those who've seen to the needs of the orphans. And for those who've started a relationship off in the wrong order, may God help each find a new place to give.

Life and Death in Mothers and Children: an Abortion Dynamic

One of the most remarkable pieces of family work I'd ever seen was as a participant. I was asked to represent the eldest of two teen daughters for a mother who could not connect with her girls as she wished. The facilitator asked about special events in her life with her girls, and nothing was noted, and so he asked about her relationship with her own mother. There was a very poor connection. She was the youngest of eight children, but she and her mother both almost died in childbirth, and their bonding was fragile. The facilitator helped her set up the story live.

In working with the representatives, it was apparent that the representative for the client's mother was slow to "come to," as she connected with the difficulties of the client's birth experience. Once the 'mother' was clearer, she tried to shake the representative of the 'daughter' into full presence. The facilitator instructed the representing mother to tell the representing daughter, "We are alive; we both made it—we are alive. We are here; it's okay now." After saying it several times, the representative for the daughter was able to respond in full connection. A traumatic birth experience was identified and revisited for resolution. Then the real woman stepped into her part and made the solid connection to her mother via proxy. At that point, the facilitator had her turn to her two daughters, but the connection in that direction was still flat. It didn't have an impact yet.

However, in the circle of observers, there was a woman who had been making a rhythmic drumming sound on the floor much like a heartbeat. The facilitator had the mother turn to face her own daughters and in seeing the blankness he asked if there were any other children who were lost. Reluctantly, she said she'd had an abortion.

He began to search the room for a person to represent that child but then instinctively he stopped to check again. "Just one?" he asked.

"No," she answered. "There were two."

Again, he turned to look, but stopped to ask again, "Just two?"

"No," she said. "There were three."

"Three?"

"No. I had four abortions."

When the mother said she had four abortions, the facilitator looked at the woman drumming the sound of a heart beat on the floor, pointed to her and to the next three people in the row with her and said, "There are your four children."

Immediately, the drummer threw her arms out wide towards the mother and smiled so big and so wide but stayed put on the edge of her seat until she saw a sign from the mother that she would receive her. The mother, seeing the love, began to weep and then released her arms to open. The facilitator motioned for them to come. And they rushed her. Swallowing her up in affection, they embraced her tightly as she began to wail out her sorrow.

The sound of her anguish was unlike any sound I have ever heard. It felt like the sound was coming up from the center of the earth channeling up through the floor and her body releasing in a roar. The representatives for the dead children embraced her tightly as she bore up under the full movement of her pain and their loss. The surge of grief seared through her chest and throat. It was loud, and it was raw, but she was held in Love. When she could get her breath more easily, the facilitator said, "Tell your children, 'I thought I would die.' "

She repeated the words that connected her with them and with her own life and her mother, and she wept again more softly.

Eventually, the wave subsided, she looked at each face representing her children, and then she could face the representatives of her live children. As a representative of the eldest of the two living, my heart was softened and opened toward the mother and the whole of us. The representative for the younger sibling and I moved to join the group connection. She was the mother of six children. She had found a place for them all.

That piece of work was one of the most compassionate movements I have ever witnessed. The grace and elegance of reconciliation was visible in the woman for the rest of the training week. Her gait changed as if she was lighter. Her face was radiant with peace.

A Kingdom Perspective

When a woman becomes pregnant, she becomes a mother. The man who conceived the child with the mother is now a father. Maternity and paternity begin at conception. The two parents are now a mother and a father of a child. They are the parents. This is the truth. The child does not become a child at delivery; the child is a family member from the start.

From the moment of conception, the child is taking resources for life development and support from the mother. Thus, the woman is already mothering. Until the child is delivered, the father and others are responsible to participate directly with the care and support of survival for the mother and child. To fail, is to forfeit one's place.

From a Kingdom perspective, God has given life on whatever terms that are. The terms vary, of course, but conception creates parents. God creates families in many situations.

In undergraduate school, I interned in a child protective agency where I observed children's group work. In the group, I met a very young woman of twelve or thirteen. She sat at a table with children all younger than her, whose lives had also been disrupted within their families due to sexual abuse. The children were all doing art work. She, however, sat at the table holding her baby doll. She was being treated for 'sexual abuse.'

She knew what her stepfather had done was not right, and that was the reason she wasn't living with her mother now. She knew that she had had a baby inside her from her stepfather. But she did not comprehend what the abortion involved. No one was looking at that squarely with her. The decision to discard the child in utero had been made by the little girl's mother.

As evidenced by her behavior, she was still looking for her baby. Most women still do, albeit in unconscious ways. It is good to help mothers find their children in a Field of Grace. It is good to help children find their mothers. In a Field of Grace, it is good to turn children over to Our Father. Mothers do not normally end the lives of their children. They do so at a high cost in the soul.

We can escort the bereaved to the broken. I ask women to close their eyes and go to a Field of Grace, and tell me what it looks like when they get there. Then they move out into their own internal Thin Space. There, they call for their children.

And they come.

The mothers often cry, and they also report that the children smile. They take hold of each other, every time. Then they call the child's father and show them their children.

The same thing is important for stillborns, miscarriages, and early-childhood death. We go find them together. That's what mothers do. They look for their lost children. And we find them in Thin Space.

Is it real?

Consider this.

A small boy died, and I had the privilege of escorting his mother to her own Thin Space Field of Grace. Immediately, she moved her arms up in the air, saying, "I see him! He is so big, and he's right here," pointing her hands towards herself. "He's huge." Their terms had changed but not their love. It was a new start. We will examine this again in chapter 9.

We typically memorialize a departed loved one with a service and burial of some kind, perhaps a marker in a cemetery, or an event of spreading ashes or keeping them in an urn. A ritual to anchor a thought of a continued "place" where perpetual light shines upon our departed loved ones, is an honor to the departed and our relationship to them. This is often missing for the parents and children who die in utero, be it miscarriage or abortion, where grief is compounded. It is important to own the relationship nevertheless, knowing the loss is temporary.

How a mother marks her loss is as unique as the child she received. By facing their presence in a Field of Grace, she may, with the Lord's presence abiding, sense the soul of the child and, from that sense, choose to honor their soul by going on her own treasure hunt for that special something to honor them. She can place that item in her surroundings at home or in a sacred place.

Everyone belongs, and finding some token of their continued existence in the Kingdom by giving them a name, and a token of having lived for a small time perhaps with an angel for the garden, or a bird for the mantel, is a way to be mindful of the whole and that motherhood continues and the child still belongs. Everyone belongs. We can't change the terms; the death cannot be undone by us. It has to be seen, and owned.

But in the words of King David, when he and Bathsheba lost their baby, "I will go to him, but he will not return to me," (2 Samuel 12:23). There is the hope.

To honor the whole can take a burden off of other children who, like in the earlier story, have a sense of unnamed loss. When I meet women who are overburdened with the needs of a long list of others, I wonder if they are driven by an unsatiated motherhood, and I wonder where they are gazing in their soul. It is good to give all things and all people a place and, with order, find rest.

No one can find peace in the dark where there is no sight, no acknowledgment, nor any connection. And yet, God dwells in deepest darkness. He waits for us, in the dark, keeping company with all those who are still waiting in the dark to be re-membered.

Chapter Eight: Stations for Couples to Consider

Marriage is built in hope. But there has to come a
disillusionment of false hopes. This can be a positive if you will
come down from that high hope to the fall and decide to understand each
other and build a household of faith and be committed to live by God's
Word. Open your heart to the work that has to be done.
— Bill Billingsley, Pastor
(Sheridan Hills Baptist Church Sermon notes on marriage June 1988)

Marriage Template: Christ and the Church

Ladies, if you are looking for Mr. Right, and gentlemen, if you would like to qualify as Mr. Right, understand that Mr. Right stands to her right. If Mr. Right would like to be left, he may stand to her left.

We have some natural instincts about men and women that our culture confuses with politics and economics. Though traditional roles have some functional positions that support the marriage relationship, the notion that there is such a thing as Mr. Right has more to do with the Lamb of God than with chemistry, luck, marriage assessment inventories, or traditional roles. In this chapter, we will discuss the overview of a philosophy of a covenant, and we will differentiate it from role-confusion and contracts.

The root of marriage is a union, and it constricts independence. The merging of two becoming one in marriage represents the Holy Union between Christ and His Church. If we can see the dynamics between Christ and the Church, we have a foundation and template for marriage.

In this regard, Mr. Right is the first, and his grace-based beloved has been made equal by reconciliation and is second. When she follows his lead, there is a lovely dance. This lead-and-follow dynamic is the design. To the degree that a husband and wife are in sync with the design and Designer, the Spirit draws us into Love.

In this way, marriage is a spiritual union, first and foremost. But in our carnal and tangled state, we tend to live life in general, body or soul first, not spirit. We reproduce tangles, not Love. Life has so many hurdles, though, that it gives us ample opportunity to figure out that we need to live spirit first in order for Love to make sense in us.

In the beginning, Adam and Eve didn't form a partnership. There was Adam, and out of Adam came Eve, from Adam's own being. Marriage was a reunion of their physical beings.

Now, if we pause here to consider the Lord and the Church, it is a breathtaking reality—it is startling. The Church is born of Christ's sacrifice and resurrection. His wounded side opened him to the birth of the Bride. In this gift, He has made us reconciled.

Heaven's Marriage is the destiny of the Church as the reconciled, reunified humanity that He came to restore to Himself. In the eyes of God, the redeemed of God are an inseparable part of Christ's own body. When I see this as the 'sameness in body' as Adam and Eve had, it leaves me speechless.

Marriage is of that kind of dynamic: the two shall become one—again.

Visualize it. If the Bride's right hand is held inside His, and if the Lord is at the right hand of God, the church is seated in the Father's lap. What a grace. Marriage, like children, belongs to the Lord, and the Lord determines and directs what makes for fruitful love. To Him, we yield in Love.

We will not follow the crowd of culture without dark consequence, nor will we yield to the Lord without good consequence. The situation below gives an example of things being out of place.

What's Not Fine

A young man scheduled an appointment for himself and his wife. When I greeted them, she let me know how unhappy she was to be there. If you imagine opening an oven door and feeling the heat threaten to burn your face, that is the kind of heat that filled the office.

Seeing that she had no wish to be there, I balked a bit and asked why she came. She made a vague mocking reference to some paperwork he needed filled out for his priest, which flew right over my head, but since she had to come, she figured she might as well let me know what had happened from her point of view. In a flash, she gave me a succinct history of their dynamics.

This was her account:

"We dated for a while and fell in love, and that was fine. He asked me to marry him, and I wanted to, and that was fine. We had different jobs, and I happened to make more money than he did, but we both liked our jobs, which is what is important in work, and so that was fine. I had a better apartment, of course, because I could afford more, but he wanted to feel like the man and wanted me to move into his place, so I did, and that was fine. He lived on a sketchy side of town; it's not all that safe, but as long as we are together, even that was fine. But now, whenever anything goes bump in the middle of the night, he wants me to go find out what it is! AND THAT'S NOT FINE!"

The reader is invited to mentally draw their own diagram as to what such an arrangement might look like in their own mind's eye. Where were they positioned in relation to each other? In these cases, size matters as well as placement. Whatever the arrangement was between the two, it was an untenable arrangement.

Apparently sacrificing himself for his wife to protect her from an intruder was not within his bounds of marriage. In whatever way he looked at her and at himself in relation to her, it was not on terms of a husband-to-wife order of orientation. The husband did not offer a different interpretation of events. Sadly, he was not actually there for counseling; he was there for a signature.

Apparently, if he could demonstrate that he went to counseling, and the marriage still failed, he could apply for an annulment. There was no wish for them; it was just for him, and that wish was to be free from guilt. Thus, she was doubly insulted.

Whatever his need for safety was, it could not be found in his wife, and whether or not his priest would lead him to grasp security was a question I left with him, along with his paperwork.

Marriage Stations

What does it mean, then, for a man to stand to the right? What does it say to us in earthly language mirroring heaven?

By design, it is normal and instinctive for a man to sacrifice first for the relationship. It tends to build faith in a woman, which calls for a response of mutual surrender. Sacrifice is a part of honor and trust.

There are many normal sacrifices that husbands make for their wives. The lover is tested by the costs, and his preparedness to offer himself to her is the way he demonstrates that he means it and that she can trust him. Love compels a man to initiate, defend, protect, provide, and sustain the union. That is first,

There is always a healthy cost to building a union. The cost is not a barter, nor is it a purchase; it is a gift. He should feel good to be spent on love, and, in spending, he finds his gift received. He initiates, and he leads.

The reader may think that this idea of positions and stations is wildly out-of-date and that it resurrects traditional values that many have discarded. But if we recall that the template is Christ—not popular culture—then we might notice that traditional values only serve love when they reflect the Designer. The stations actually exist in terms of what warms responsiveness.

By contrast, consider a seemingly innocent glitch on a woman's part. Is it questionable on some level for a woman to "make it easy" for him to propose marriage by suggesting they use a family heirloom from her grandmother as an engagement ring? In that scenario, who is proposing? Who is initiating? More importantly, if the initiation is from her family, who do they become together in identity? Do they become her grandparents' grandchildren?

As nice as it may feel to be so approved of, it is weakening for the man, and he becomes the debtor. How does that set up?

There is such a call to leave and cleave, noted in Genesis with Adam and Eve, in which two parties are to leave their origins and become one together. If a man is proposed to, he follows her family. It creates more doubt than security for him. It is no sacrifice for the grandparents and no sacrifice for the suitor. She doesn't have to count on him, and perhaps she won't.

In that set up, can the Bride of Christ be the initiator of Salvation?

No. The Gospel tells the better story. Christ is not counting on the Church; the Church is counting on God in Christ.

The sacrifice is the gift of self as a man invests in cutting his own path to the station of manhood and husbandry. Love is sacrifice with another in mind, and there is honor in that. Christ is able. Men are enabled by the Lord. Couples give themselves to one another at a certain cost. "He" goes first.

But some couples get off to a rough start. So, it matters how both parties see their image. If it is out of order, and she is in the first position as the head, it matters who moved where at the time when the arrangement became untenable.

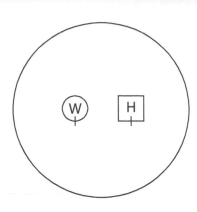

Diagram 8.1

Whatever it means for a couple to switch sides should be explored by both parties:

It means one thing if she trumps him; it means something else if he abdicates his place.

Similarly, if they both agree to the dis-order, it means one thing if the couple is newly wed, and it means something else if they are elderly when roles naturally must change, given that women often live longer and stay stronger than men.

So, first, if she trumps his station of leading, she has left her station open by vacating it, making him vulnerable to whoever may like to have a seat.

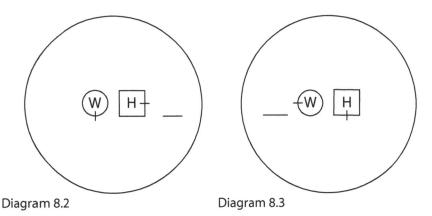

Diagram 8.2   Diagram 8.3

Alternatively, if he has abdicated, he has set her up as well. This is not a justification for her acting out on emptiness in the relationship; it is a way to see the dilemmas involved in boundaries and responsibilities.

There are hosts of other ways to be out-of-bounds with each other: by standing above as a parental authority, which is completely oppressive for the one-down position, or a debilitating dependency of some kind that situates them in a one-down placement.

Seasons come along on occasion where one partner loses some amount of independence due to an illness or crisis. For a time, it is a blessing to have someone who can hold the lion's share of support. Everyone gets the flu, and a partner can easily give the extra care in sickness. But for the long term crisis of illness or job-loss, one party who does the heavy-lifting is a difficult tax on the marriage, and a couple needs to find ways to draw on more support.

Love's varied loves

Let's review the distinctions in Love's stations in a family once again.

Parental love toward children is the benevolence of both people sacrificing for the child. As children take, they trust. Benevolence is necessarily a one-way offering since children do not reciprocate; they inherit, and they internalize security, and grow up to become givers to the next generation. This is the Father-to-Child dynamic that Christ insisted we enjoy in humbling ourselves as children before a good Father whom we can trust.

Next, as children grow up, as siblings and with friends, they learn fairness and sharing, and they internalize the love of justice and mutuality. This fidelity makes the world a safe place to engage in with confidence and children can invest in relationships beyond the family. Quid pro quo makes good business sense for fair exchanges of goods and services. It is a natural community form of love.

In benevolence and fairness, we grow into a readiness to learn to sacrifice and start a family. So, how we love in marriage is not parent-to-child benevolence. It is Sacrificial-like-Christ, and it is Surrender-like-the-Bride. Each party makes very specific sacrifices that allow a couple to become the foundation of a family. To that end, let's talk about covenants.

Holy Matrimony and Glitches

Covenant is the context that makes sacrifices sacred. Men and women are built for different sacrifices. These are more than traditional roles because we aren't role-playing; we are representing a sacrifice as unto the Lord.

If couples engage in a performance-based relationship of exchange, like a business model, the justice becomes corrupt because we can't earn love.

Sometimes, a man, as the primary bread-winner, might turn towards his spouse as if he is her boss instead of his soul mate.

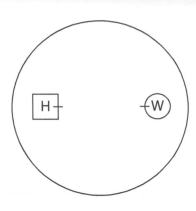

Diagram 8.4

In this diagram, the husband is in the lead, but they are apart. The relationship is not intimate; it is at a distance and the couple is at odds. If his love is trapped in a business agreement, then for her to earn his love, she has to work, and that is called prostitution. If the worker part of him comes home and doesn't change clothes, so to speak, and he expects her to make his day up for him, she might begin to feel like a concubine instead of a part of him. This forms a demand, which is aggression.

Quid pro quo does not make for happily ever after; it makes for good business. Marriage is not a business agreement; it is a covenant. It is not a deal a man makes with a woman; it is a covenant a man makes with God and expresses to his wife.

Mutual Sacrifices

For Love to have a chance, two people must be willing to forsake all others as future options. If a life of fidelity is too hard of a sacrifice, then there is a tangle, and the gaze of the soul is elsewhere.

Affairs happen for any number of reasons: sometimes vengeance, sometimes family patterns. Conflicts should be "set up" to see the root. Rarely is it love, since the nature of married love is the covenant.

There are other examples of "forsaking all others" that make for sacrifice. I've mentioned already the "leave and cleave"—leaving one's parents to start a new family. But imagine for a moment this distortion:

Perhaps a child's father died when the child was young, and his uncle innocently conferred upon him the headship of the house: "You're the man of the house now, so take care of your mother." A son whose devotion is his mother may feel guilty about marriage. This sacrifice is difficult. But it is also the price of admission into adulthood and matrimony. Forsaking all others includes families of origin as primary allegiances. To refuse to make the switch is to make rivals of wives and mothers.

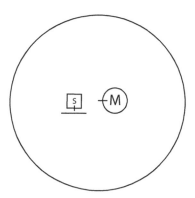

Diagram 8.5

In this diagram the son has been assigned the place of his father and has become his mother's emotional partner.

A son is not the right husband for his mother. Nor is a daughter the right wife for her father. An innocent word spoken by a well-meaning uncle planted the seed of a burden. But it happens. The words need to be re-spoken by an adult child. "With my parent, I'm just a kid, and with my spouse, I'm an adult. I will trust that you, my parent, can find appropriate support."

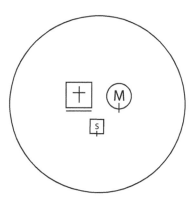

Diagram 8.6

Simple but powerful words can change the arrangement. In the above diagram, the deceased father still has a place in the family that belongs to him, not the son.

At-one-ment

So, we come to understand that we are not just surrendering other dating options; we are leaving the loyalty of childhood to become someone else—a sense of being at one, or having at-one-ment—with another. Atonement is an odd thing to refer to through marriage. But in a real sense, the idea of God presenting Eve to Adam is a re-unification of sorts, as the Church is with the Lord.

God knows that, given the many struggles in life, there are ample opportunities in marriage to renounce independence for harmony. There is a deeper union happening in the mutual sacrifice, and the biggest sacrifice is our selfishness.

Moses instructed men (Deut. 24:5) to stay home, not go to war or have any other duty for a year but to find out how to make their wives happy. In forsaking all others, we will transfer the childhood dependence from parents to God, and leaving childhood, we will establish ourselves as adults, becoming free to take up the responsibilities of spousing.

In doing this, a man becomes a little bit more like the God who made him, capable of sacrificing for the wellbeing of a woman and their children. The general call is to die to singleness, to childishness, and to independence, and to come into the intimacy of living for the good of another. Thus, we have the cross.

Sacrifice in this form is a surrendering of a possession—one's life—as an offering to God, and to a divine/supernatural figure—one's spouse. This raises the bar of marriage. Romans 12:1-2 comes to mind as it mentions having the identity of being a living sacrifice. This is not the traditional role-play; this is a covenant.

The "Holy" in the matrimony is the personal intent to live a Romans 12:1 life. We present ourselves daily to God as a living sacrifice. Our fidelity is unto the Lord first. We surrender both ourselves and our union to its rightful owners: Christ and His Bride. When put in these terms, intimacy is a fruit of the shared spiritual identification with the Lord.

Wives are in a covenant, following Christ in their husbands. Many women yearn for a man to have a spiritual depth that reveals Christ within him. The fundamental intimacy they seek first is soul/spirit. Sexuality comes second. A wife's trust in her husband is never more important than when she bears children, trusting that he is sufficient for the lion's share of the load of provisions.

Childbearing is her great sacrifice, and she needs it to be seen for what it is. No one can bear life except women. These burdens are exclusive. In our current culture, the gift of life is sometimes shamed and not always honored. It is a sacrifice to pass on life, and a woman bears the burden at the risk of her own life. It is a serious and a glorious sacrifice.

Thus, the root of the division of labor in the home is a given. This is not a political statement; it is a biological and a spiritual reality. A woman cannot easily both provide and reproduce. If she does both, she over-functions and becomes the false husband or worse. A man clearly cannot bear children. A woman will never make a good husband for her man nor a good father for their children.

Now, picture the mandate for us to abide in Christ to bear fruit. Abiding is what is happening as a woman bears the fruit of life. It is not always easy, given the morning sickness, the weight gain, the loss of sleep, and all the many changes, but she is abiding. When the labor and the delivery of both the child and the mother begin, it is a painful labor with an effort but an abiding effort since the uterus is going to do the work. The risk of death to the mother and the child is why we say they are both delivered. A stroll through an older cemetery gives a clear report of how often women did not survive prior to modern interventions.

It is not easy; it is a dangerous sacrifice, but it is by "abiding" that a miracle of life is knit together by God in the hidden parts of a woman's body. This is an incredible wonder. If she endures the trauma, then comes the nursing and nurturing. This is a holy sacrifice.

If he will do his part and she will agree to hers, they give it all they have, and God makes them able to do that and more. If a woman must sacrifice her role as provider for a trust, then holy wholeness has a chance. God will come through; that is what Love does, and this is His story.

Role-play vs. Representing

To better understand the limitations of role-playing, even 'traditional' role playing, now we consider the so called "committed" relationship that is neither legal nor spiritual in foundation. No matter how common the arrangement is today, there are a few issues afloat that may sabotage the arrangement if the foundation does not become corrected into covenant.

Living together, "committed" but unmarried, is like playing house. Unmarried, the couple is still trying to make up their mind, meaning, that they are not all in yet, but they are not 'out' either. This is not a sacrifice; it is either a taking, like a child, or a sharing, like a friend. Someone does not want someone else to slip away. For whatever reason, there is a hold-up on one end at least.

What can we see about this? One may be still shopping, while the other is still hoping. In effect, they are trying each other out, perhaps mutually getting their needs met. Neediness is dependency, and a partner is never the right parent. There is a place for tryouts, of course, but it is called dating, which is categorically different than mating.

Probation periods are also a part of other kinds of relationship vetting in business or in a community. It may even have a place in marriage when there has been a betrayal of love and a need to rebuild trust is present. But as a foundation, it is cracked.

Tryouts of any kind incur a natural stress of indecision after the initial high has diminished, and two parties are pushed to make a discovery of truth about the caliber and fit of the relationship. To date with questions is real; to delay decision is fraud. And to live together is a form of infidelity to the covenant relationship itself—meaning to Christ. Partaking of another's body and soul while outside of covenant and inside indecision is taking comfort without regard for meaning it.

That type of relationship is actually uncommitted. It could use a model set-up to see who the two have each other confused with. Fear of commitment is often related to childhood when a child could not reach out to the parents and connect securely. So, now, a would-be partner reaches out, but then draws back, uncertain.

By living together without covenant, there is an illegitimacy or an imbalance that undermines the nature of sacrifice, which would otherwise bring security. Taking instead of sacrificing presents a dependency need, which is better-suited as a task for God to satisfy. He meant it when He came here to give entirely to save humanity. It was no gamble, no joke, no question; He was and is all in. He is marriage in the core dynamic. Just as it is not a good idea to take communion if one is not a believer, it is not good to take intimacy without devotion.

Imagine it this way, once again. Adam was the first, and Eve was initially Adam's own body. She was taken out of and reconciled with Adam becoming one with him again. Jesus is our Adam, and we are His Eve, taken out of his bleeding side and reconciled to our original life. This is a sacred surprise.

Imagine if the decision to 'commit' was made under the duress of outsiders, or a job move was on the horizon, or pressure from the inside in a pregnancy made a couple 'parents' before they were partners. Then, we have the notion of obligation, not an intentional gift. How will that be for the child? The child is at risk of inheriting a burden of providing security as 'the reason' the parents stayed, instead of covenant being the reason. It is a pity when a young man or woman feels trapped by their own usury and compromise. It's also a pity for a child to have to slog through the idea of being the reason their parents are "stuck" with each other. The child needs to know that he is, nevertheless, a good gift.

If marriage requires anything of two people, it requires them to be sincere, to mean it, and that is why we need vows and witnesses and intentional celibacy beforehand; it protects the sacrifice of devotion in a sure foundation. This is why we want a covenant over a commitment.

The 20th and 21st-century sexual freedom is not a new expression of capricious role-playing. As we've seen in ancient history, it was the first thing God addressed in a covenant with Abraham. His sexual organ was marked by his relationship with God.

Circumcision had no power to change the appetites of sexuality. It was a signal to make a covenant of the heart with God, and it was a statement that the hard heart would be softened by an experience with the living God.

Role-playing marriage out of selfish appetites, with little regard or respect for the dignity of the risk of a sacred conception and the demands it would place on a woman's body, is blindness; it is not representative of Christ, who always means it.

Hope in the Spirit of Loving Sacrifice

Given that the marriage relationship is a picture of, and the property of, Christ and the Church, we have two things as resources. One is the great hope that He is present and able to do what is needed when we apply to Him. If Christ is the context, Love has a strong chance of blossoming when the couple depends upon the Lord's Spirit.

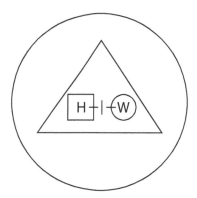

Diagram 8.7

Secondly—curiously, perhaps—we have an example of Christ's own rocky honeymoon in the book of Acts for our encouragement. As Christ became at-one with the Bride, and the Church was born, the new at-one-ment had a few exciting conflicts. We might not think of Acts as a marriage testimony, but it sets up like it is just that. It's nice to know it was rough getting started as a new union for Jesus and his Church.

In Acts and in the letters that followed in the nascent 'abiding' Bride, the disciples were filled with the Spirit, and they did the exact same works of Jesus. Jesus meant it in them. He made His Love real to them, in and through them. Miracles abounded.

But there are a few stories that seem a little edgy if you see just the surface and dismiss the context of the marriage. They tell us a lot about the passion of the Spirit that is moving us toward completion. This Spirit of Christ means it.

The new fellowship was fiercely guarded by that hovering dove, who was not opposed to showing his claws if needed to defend the Bride. The first example of ferocity is similar to leave and cleave, which is to say 'mean it or leave.' When Ananias and Sapphira lied to the Spirit—seemingly about money (Acts 5:1-11), the Lord would not have a couple deceive the fellowship of believers with pretense.

The couple wanted to seem to be as invested as Barnabas, who had given all his possessions to the Church. Instead of being honest that they did not yet have the whole heart he had, they pretended that they had sacrificed everything. That lie cost them their lives.

It was the role-play that killed them. It would have been better had they said, 'This is what we want to give at this point.' They were still on 'dating terms' and weren't ready to go all the way.

Again, it is not a good idea to take communion in Church if one is not a believer. Faith is not a role-play fellowship. Peter was clear when he said that they didn't lie to him; they lied to the Spirit. When that couple lied and died, others took joining the faith community seriously.

Acts 5: Lying Betrays Love

There are two other stories related to a few people who had no faith in Jesus yet, and they thought posing would suffice. The situations occurred for both Peter and Paul separately.

Simon, called "the Sorcerer", upon witnessing miracles moving through Peter, assumed the apostle was a trickster like himself. Misunderstanding the person of the Holy Spirit, Simon offered to purchase the Spirit's power, not respecting that the miracles were of God's abiding presence and covenant. Peter was so stunned at the idea of prostituting the Spirit that he rebuked Simon and warned him that he was at risk of hell (Acts 8:9-24). The Holy Spirit is not a trickster and is not for sale. Pure grace is not for sale, it is a gift, not a barter.

Likewise, Paul was also challenged by another magician, who was posing as a Jewish prophet but was actually hostile toward the work of grace. Paul's movement of the Spirit was to strike him blind—for a time (Acts 13: 4-12). Paul had greatly benefited by his own episode in the dark, and it was only 'for a time.' In our group study of this part of Acts, the person representing the blinded magician said, "I am listening now."

Perhaps it doesn't sound very gracious of the Spirit; I've not written the many miracles the Spirit did in the fellowship of believers. But think of how fiercely protective a husband is of his bride or a young mother is of her newborn. We can hypocritically criticize the protection of God's holy jealousy and the defense He expresses for His beloved young fellowship. But rest assured that God means to love and protect the fellowship of His people.

Today, it is hard to know who means it and who doesn't in the leadership of the Church. In the early days, persecution culled out all the frauds.

Lest we forget, Christ and His followers are not strangers to suffering. We will discuss suffering at length shortly. Certainly, Peter and Paul suffered for the message they embodied. They meant it, and their endurance in persecution demonstrated their trust. Their love gave the gospel a chance to find us. They became a Church family and brought the light of life to the nations.

Persecution doesn't belong in marriage, but there are practical sacrifices in the earthly and heavenly covenants of marriage.

Sacrifice is glamorous in the days of a wooing through dating, proposal, the engagement period, wedding, honeymoon, and setting up house together. The love drug, as we often call it, is inspiring but is unsustainable.

As love matures, sacrifices are not so glamorous, but they become—when seen over a lifetime—glorious as they conform us to Christ and one another. Love is always bigger than we are, and we are made to grow into the destiny of Love, but we can't look at the process of maturing love through the narrow lens of a peephole at the beginning of a relationship. It takes years to work Love into the depths of togetherness.

Every day, couples cope with work, service, community, and children, and make thousands of sacrifices in both the small incidentals and the large, near-death experiences. Cumulatively speaking, married love is about supporting the lives that have transformed a romantic couple into a parenting couple with a family.

I saw an art piece at a local store recently that held a quote by Mother Teresa: "If you want to do something for God, go home and love your family." When Love survives struggles, it expands heaven's reach into the earthly realm. Making spiritual covenants on the terms of the Kingdom makes it possible to escape the earthly terms of me, my lonely self, and I.

For a season, the way parents give to their children is also one of the ways they give to one another because it takes two people to get the needs of their dependent children met. Family Love makes us grow up. Children make parents less able to be conveniently selfish since their demands are life-and-death serious.

When the children are little, folding a bunch of odd socks together after the little ones are asleep can be a form of foreplay simply because it is a shared task that can be quietly reflective. When the children are older, the kindest thing a husband can do for his wife is to go on a search-and-rescue mission for the wandering soul of their child whose launch pad had a bad fuse.

Love finds a way; it's what He does. You can't kill this kind of love. But you do have to learn it slowly over time because, although oneness is the outcome, we are slow learners.

If sin is strong enough to destroy immortality, it is sharp enough to end a union early. Sin is not our identity, but it is a real disease. It must not be the master.

Imagine the scene

It is 6:00 p.m., and dinner is hurriedly prepared and on the table. The wife/mom is on her way out, in a hurry for an important business meeting when, suddenly, an opportunity for what we know as Thin Space presents itself on the kitchen sliding glass door in the form of her child's small hand prints.

Now is the time for a truly critical decision to be made.

It's suddenly all about that sliding glass door. She stands and looks at the door, which opens to a beautiful vista, but all she can really see are the small, greasy hand prints on the glass… and if she honors the rising sense of awareness and pure presence, she will admit that she cannot bear to wipe the hand prints off with Windex because this is the last baby and the last of the small prints.

A realtor is coming, and the glass should be cleaned. But she suddenly recalls the day that a little crafted clay hand print, brought home from preschool was broken.

This current moment shows her how these days are passing too quickly. How do we save hand prints like these?

Do we sacrifice the hand prints for a clear window?

A question hangs in the balance between one kind of beauty and another.

Slow motion sets in for this wife and mother to experience a longer moment of reality testing; maybe she likes the mess because of how it was made and what it means. This mess is where heaven and earth meet, and so is the house: mess that it is. A little bit of dirt is precious and a lot of it is all the more precious. Didn't God make us all out of dirt? Isn't dirt holy because when holy breath is in it, dirt comes to life?

If we look at the prints—if we SEE our children inside them— we can see the breath of their spirits even on a warm, sunny day. That's what that hand print is on the glass: it is the printed evidence of a living spirit! God is still in the room and in another perfect baby—as usual.

What would happen if baby Jesus left a greasy print on the window or the wall? It would become a tourist attraction! We'd rope the section off and keep people back from it at least fifteen feet, and we would charge admission to see the blessed work of art. It would be documented in reports, and filmed along with all the supporting elements in the vicinity leading up to the sacred hand print. In addition, whatever the babe had eaten that left the grease on his hands would soon become a feature dish in a new restaurant chain called 'Sanctuary Chicken Nuggets.'

What is on the glass? The hand print of a little image-bearer, complete with signs of life. Maybe his mother will decide not to wash that glass — especially when it has become a portal to awareness. Maybe she should cancel her meeting, go change her clothes, or make time for her husband, anything to keep her from cleaning the glass, at least for today, the day it became a holy relic. That's how Love sees the glass.

These moments exist to slow us down to see what is right here, right now, like that hummingbird that is preaching on the porch with the sound of floating flight. If the spouse or parent sees and cancels the evening plans with the realtor, changes clothes, and settles in for a night of the holy oil of chicken grease, even the crumbs on the floor below the table are fine, as the dog nibbling them will suffice for vacuuming.

Mess will take care of itself if we can slow down, not panic, and settle in because, when Love suffers long, it becomes kind. True Love Himself does the heavy lifting on the wings of a winded man or woman whose simple prayer is an all-encompassing single word, "Lord." That's all. He was there all along. The parent can breathe right past that hurdle.

The Long Love

Marriage and family are a blessed terror show because of all things that leave a person speechless: both the near-misses and the horrible hits. Someone mowed down a rabbit in a bed of flowers, or ran over the dog, the fish are floating again, Grandpa's funeral was sad, layoffs are scary, and this is all the norm, and must be survived in love.

Tough things happen.

Then, along come days of the unspeakable: infertility, miscarriage, the incomprehensible death or a severe and threatening illness in a loved one. You fill in the blank of tragedy, and Love Himself marches right into that dark abyss and finds a way to keep you breathing through the inconsolable. God dwells in deepest darkness.

Even when God is measured as an F for failed, and we forsake our faith and put Him in the dog house, for a season, we find that His Love stays, and suffering exposes our utter dependency on a God we do not understand or even always know how to trust for the moment. But He weeps with us in the dark. Those are dreary, non-negotiable, non-functioning eternal days, and during those times it seems like a couple has nothing left.

When the pain is insurmountable, and someone is likely able to find a hidden way to follow the departed (in death,) Love sees. Sometimes, God permits the second departure, and sometimes He does not. This calls for more of something that no one has until that Eternal Someone rises up and comes into the room of the empty heart and, in a felt and palpable way, exhales again, and a family keeps breathing when some might prefer not.

This is all serious and sacrificial living. Just living is a sacrifice. But what's important is how we come to keep on "meaning it" together.

This is why we need to know how Love sees this life on these covenant terms; how Love finds a way. Maturing on this side of the veil is going to take a lifetime of growing up into Love.

Love deliberately chisels people over and over and over because He has covenanted Himself to make us turn out just like we already are in Christ in the heavenly realm, where things are already whole. In Him, we are already flawless, but God has to make that promise come to exist in us on earth as it is in heaven. Love will make it real.

Marriage and family life will literally sanctify the hell right out of you. Love is designed to help you lose your fallen mind. Marriage is not the task of a mere human; it is the quest of a God for the sake of the gods.

Love has made up His mind about us, and He means to help us make up our minds about Him and each other over and over and over again. This is not a role-play. This is God. This is about faith in the Gospel.

The gods in the Bride of Christ

In Paul's letters to the churches, he had a pattern of communication. He addressed his readers by telling them who they were as Saints. He knew who his reader was, even when they didn't comprehend Christ in themselves fully. Paul saw them finished.

After much affection, he would then reinforce his claims about his readers with instructions about Christ in them and about their inheritance of resources; this was doctrine.

Following that support came his application, which was directed toward the family. He began with the wife. He basically said that the Christian house must come into order. He brought Jesus to the house.

Question: If Man was first, why address the woman first?

Answer: The wife has the power to follow Christ now.

Paul plants wives securely in their stations as holders of inspiration and reinstates them with weight and dignity.

When our study group set up this Colossians 3:18 text, the initial set up was disorder.

The representatives included below are: Husband, Wife, Love, Christ and Inheritance. The husband was above the wife, who is shown standing in front of Christ, who is supported by Inheritance.

The representative for Love specifically chose the role with an interest in knowing what love would experience. She stood directly behind the husband but reported feeling no Love at all and was disappointed, wondering why she felt nothing at all.

The wife reported being able to see the husband, but he was too far away and above her to feel interest. When she looked at Christ, she felt her need to bow. In her submission to Christ, she let go of her disconnect from her husband. Watching her bow, though, was touching to the husband. Soon, he was moved to cross over and face her on the other side of Christ. He then humbled himself and felt a strong need to ask her for forgiveness.

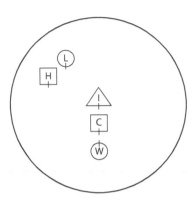

Diagram 8.8

In his original position, he towered over her as her ruler at a distance. Soon, he felt a deep sorrow looking at her, and then he went to the ground in a bow to her and asked for her forgiveness.

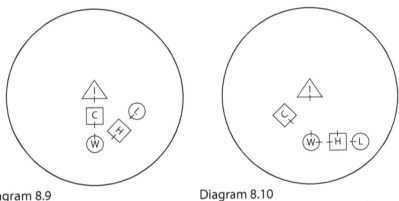

Diagram 8.9   Diagram 8.10

The representative for the wife was entirely overcome by the movement of the husband. In that moment, she integrated a piece of her own healing as a woman. Then, the representative for Love followed the husband in support of his reconciliation to their union and reported feeling a great flow and tenderness of Love.

At that, Christ moved aside to reveal their joint 'inheritance' in God, and the Inheritance blessed them and gave them their peace and wholeness as joint-heirs to the gift of the covenant.

In terms of placement, as the couple faces God (Inheritance,) they are in the right place with one another. Notice that the couple is looking up toward God together. The husband is still to the right of the wife. In his original position, he towered over her as her ruler at a distance initially and this was similar to one we saw earlier at a workshop mentioned in Chapter Four.

In the study week that followed in Colossians, Paul addressed the relationship dynamics between masters and slaves. The masters in the text were eager to find level ground with their bond-servants as fellow heirs of Christ. The wives, the children, and the slaves were each called to submit by faith in someone greater than the person to whom they were yielding, which was where they found their power to effect change in the whole. Though these stations are vulnerable positions in the family, in Christ they have a special influence on the Spirit when the person sets their hope in Christ. Then they have a strong hidden influence. Even slaves inspire their masters. These are living words. Paul, who penned them, was beheaded for his faith in the power of surrender. (Colossians 3:18-4:1)

He meant it.

A New Vision for Wives

Jesus said He was going to leave in order that the Spirit of Truth would come and that the disciples must wait on her to arrive. Her?

"But when she is come, the Spirit of truth, she will take you by the hand and guide you into the path of all truth. She will not draw attention to herself but will communicate and unveil everything she hears and discerns from a heavenly perspective about the things that are about to happen within you" (John 16:13, The Mirror Bible).

Revelation is gender-neutral, but I chose the above translation because Jesus described the Spirit as the Friend of Comfort. The Spirit was called a helpmate in other translations, but in this rendering was called the Great Companion to Jesus's friends. This was the same designation given to Eve in the beginning of our mortal time; Eve was called helpmate. This was an honor she lost. This was a station restored to the families of God. Paul restored this station first. This is the station of redeemed influence for wives, former daughters of Eve.

Eve was originally the mother of all living. Now, the Spirit is the helpmate energy that reproduces the life of Christ in the Church. The friend, the Holy Spirit is the constant energy and inspiration in our relationships drawing us all into order. In our Colossians study set up, the wife surrendered first. Embracing her vulnerability before the Lord, her surrender had an effect on the whole group.

Practically speaking, when a woman is stationed as wife, to her husband's left, she is positioned in order and does not trespass. In order, she is able to receive revelations, guidance, wisdom, and discernment to help—but not control. Her bow to Christ inspires the Spirit to move her husband. This is what we saw both in the study and in the earlier workshop. The Christian woman has a blessed chance to redeem what was lost in the deception of Eve. She's empowered to hear and to see when she is standing in the right place before God, in submission. This is completely contrary to the cultural narrative which insists that we force the naturally weaker more vulnerable positions in family and society into the first place of power. When we allow for that kind of distortion, we trespass against Love. Jesus, Paul and all the disciples discovered the mystery of submission. And in his letters to the churches, Paul reinstates this gift to women.

Women have a feminine template designed for spiritual discernment. It is not given to usurp a man's lead, but instead it is given to resist his carnality, affirm his faith, and assist in what God is calling him and his wife to do. God calls them walk out together in the Kingdom. She dovetails, and follows the Holy Spirit. Surely, Pilate wished he had listened to his wife when she received wisdom in a dream. It was specifically given to her to give to Pilate, for him to avoid the turmoil concerning the condemnation of Jesus. And recall that Pilate was a Roman governor presiding over an unjust judgment. God offered him a way of escape through her wisdom. This hearkened the beginning of the shift that was on the way.

Jesus fully reinstated women in service to the Kingdom through surrender and sensitivity. Beginning with the incarnation, He hallowed the womb. At his home visit in the house of Lazarus, He put Mary and Martha in a new working order and liberated Mary's devotion to learning firsthand from Him. And she positioned herself at his feet.

In the resurrection, He honored the testimony of women first. The disenfranchised of the culture heard his voice first. A wife absolutely must submit to the movements of Christ inside her heart in relationship to her husband in order to bless her household and come into the agreement that Eve forfeited. She is often in the role of prophetess to her husband, as the prophets were to the Kings.

The sorry demise of Israel happened in part when their men intermarried with pagan women. Jezebel and King Ahab are the most prominent examples of this in the Old Testament. The wife's station of surrender is host to the Lord's influence who moves in her in the way her family needs when she is in her right placement. A man does not need to be led by her nor to come into rivalry with her, but he does need to be inspired by her. By her seeing Christ in him when he can't see Christ for himself, she is helping in his salvation. It is a beautiful thing to know that when a culture beats a man to the dirt, his wife continues to see his worth.

She must protect her witness in the home. To do that, she needs to have her own internal soul image in order. Battles will come, and when they do, she must fight like the Holy Ghost. The flesh and the spirit are at war.

But when she fights with her man, she should keep in mind that she is doing battle with a god. May God help her mean it and mean it for the good, because wife-ing is a spiritual task. She bears life physically and guards lives spiritually in submission.

Husbands and Fathers as gods

A man was created first as a son of God. He is the first to initiate, the first to sacrifice, the first to serve, the first to trust, the first to engage, the first to restore, the first to follow the Lord, the first to lead accordingly, and the first to provide and protect. He hides behind no woman; he walks with her as part of himself.

As a prince of God, a man is a co-heir with Christ and is in a league of Royal Priests of the Most High, seated together in Christ on a throne which has the regal name of Mercy, the highest attribute of God.

Contrary to the earthly thrones of dominance through sex or money, in the Highest Kingdom, Mercy rules. A man is first in this order, loving the attributes of kindness, compassion, and, most of all, covenant.

God leads men for the sake of all those counting on him. He is not a functionary, holding down a fort, but is a living stone erected in the Living Temple of God whose cornerstone is Jesus. Causing grief for his wife is akin to grieving the Holy Spirit.

Extinguishing the Spirit in her disheartens the children, who will then resist his leadership to justify their own temptations to living a bankrupt self-life. If a man loses his children's faith in his love for their mother, he will discredit the Lord to them. This is a failure to represent Christ.

A woman resides in a fragile physical frame. The husband can neither ask her nor expect her to work like a man. She bears up like a saint in childbirth. And this sacrifice should not be denigrated nor forgotten. She no more earns her keep than the children earn theirs. Everything he provides and brings to her, she passes on for their benefit. A husband who discovers his wife to be pregnant, and asks her to have an abortion, is in reality, asking her for a divorce.

Leading by developing a spiritually intimate life is the quickest way to create like-mindedness. Couples who come from different faith expressions in their upbringing might give some serious consideration to exploring a place of worship that is new to them both. But they need a place for both of them to go deep and wide.

Having a fellowship of believers to build community with in family life is an indispensable part of marriage. These are the friends that will support a marriage equally, without undermining the union, particularly when there has been a breakdown.

Family-of-origin members can often interfere when there is trouble, and naturally take sides. But couples leaning into other couples provide a rich help during tough growing seasons. The Family of God helps us grow our families in faith.

A merciful man is a tender man. This is the circumcision of the heart.

Chapter Nine: Making a Space for Reconciling Grief

I heard of Edward Burrough's decease. Being sensible, how great a grief and exercise it would be to Friends to part with him, I wrote the following lines for the staying and settling of their minds:

Friends:
Be still and quiet in your own conditions
and settled in the Seed of God that doth not change:
that in that ye may feel dear Edward Burrough among you in the Seed,
in which and by which he begat you to God, with whom he is;
and that in the Seed ye may all see and feel him,
in which is the unity with him in the life:
and so enjoy him the life that doth not change,
which is invisible.

— George Fox
An Autobiography

Relating to the Whole: Past and Present with the Future in Mind.

People have interesting facial expressions when they speak. The large majority of all of our communication is non-verbal. I used to know a man who always looked at the ground when he spoke to folks. He seemed to be in two places at once. A smile, a genuine "hello," and then it was like talking to someone who was unable to force his eyes up off the ground.

He would keep the listener engaged, though, with raised eyebrows and his head tilted in their direction, but from there, only occasionally would eyes meet. He was jovial, interested, and lucid in the conversations, but the gaze was constantly sweeping the floor. I always wondered who his soul was looking for. He was a vet. Some vets are deeply burdened. It's not easy to be hired to kill. Soldiers wear it in the soul long after their service. The cost of protecting a nation is higher for some than it is for others.

Finding a place for reconciliation with the dead, whoever they are and however they died, is a part of the inheritance of the Saints. It matters not the flag under which one kills; after a time, the soul doesn't see the flag—the soul sees the soul of the other who happened to be born and hired under another flag.

Making peace with the dead is possible. I encourage vets to imagine a Field of Grace, and to go to look, and notice where their gaze falls, and make peace with the dead by turning them over to the Lord, to whom the battle always belonged.

In live model set-ups, when people are staring at the ground, generally they are preoccupied with the dead, and then, supporting facts confirm the expressions of the representatives.

When people get stuck in unfinished business with the dead, or if death comes in terms that are impossible to accept, a person's presence can become distracted. It is a task of faith to part with a significant soul with grace and to find the new terms on which to relate. Where there is guilt or a tangle, this task becomes more tedious, and the work becomes all the more important to finish. Grief needs to be clear and clean.

The following stories will demonstrate different dynamics that people found themselves in with their deceased loved ones and how they made new peaceful arrangements.

The Widow

A woman phoned me, reluctant to schedule an appointment. She said she thought folks were expecting too much from her since her husband had only been dead a short time. She went on to explain that she'd been hospitalized for physical issues and treated for anxiety, but she felt she was forced to agree with her doctor to make an appointment with me.

She was clearly in a tangle, which was making it hard for her to move forward. Soon after she made the appointment, she canceled it, stating that her physical symptoms were sending her back to her doctor. Interestingly, though, she asked to reschedule.

We spoke briefly, and I could hear how challenged she was, and she asked if I would pray for her. I'm always ready to pray, and given the physical struggle she was having in her body, I asked her a straightforward question.

"Do you want to stay?"

"I don't know what you mean by that."

"Do you want to stay here in this life, or would you prefer to follow your husband?"

To be clear, I wasn't asking her if she was suicidal; she wasn't having a mental break; she was having a physical separation reaction. I was asking her to notice her wish before I joined in with her doctor and relatives in their wishes and prayers for her wellness.

When she paused a beat to think, I felt perhaps this could be all she needed; just five minutes on the phone to get her to notice her own desire, and the direction of her attention.

"Oh," she said after a moment of thought. "Are you asking me if I want to die?"

"Or," I replied, "if you want to stay?" I included both—excluding neither.

"Oh—," with another thoughtful beat. "—well—I don't want to die." She had answered with a non-wish and then owned it fully with, "I do want to live!" More earnestly now, she clarified for herself, "Oh! I want to stay with my children, and I have grandchildren too. No, I want to live!"

At that, I felt at liberty to pray, and we did, and then we hung up. I didn't know if she'd need to come in or not after that short chat.

She went to her doctor and he insisted again that she make an appointment with me, and she called me again in two days, saying, "Actually, for some reason, I'm really feeling better already. But I will go ahead and come on in."

She arrived—with a family member—and we got right to work.

"Close your eyes and picture a wide open Field of Grace, whatever that looks like for you. Tell me what you see when you get there."

She said, "I see a big field of flowers: purple and yellow. It's like I'm waiting on children to pop up."

There was the clue: children. I wanted to chase that rabbit but determined that the field would direct, and we would come back to that hint later, if need be.

"Call your husband, and tell me when you can see him."

"I see him. He looks peaceful, but he's not too happy with me and wonders why I'm being so sad." I told her to tell him why she was so sad.

She said, "I've never ever been alone. We've been together 35 years. And I don't want to be without you."

I said, "Tell him these are hard terms."

She did, and then she cried a while. "Now, ask Jesus to the field."

She motioned with her hands…waves of movement coming towards her. "He's all over. He's a comfort. He's big."

"Yes," I agreed, "and, with Him, you are small." I said. "Get smaller still and go to the ground; just bow, stretch out palms up. See if you can agree with his bigness and comfort."

She rested her hands in her lap and turned them upwards with open palms. "Tell him too, that these are hard terms."

"These are hard terms, Lord," she repeated.

She rested a while in that space. Her breathing deepened over the next few minutes. Then I said, "Tell him you will take up your life on these terms and ask Him to fill in your life with what's next." She did, and she continued deep, easy breaths.

Afterwards, we spent time talking about her faith in God, and I supported scripturally the ways God is the God of the living, including her husband, by referencing Jesus meeting up with Moses and Elijah on the Mount of Transfiguration and introducing them to his earthly friends Peter, James, and John.

The disciples had a little glitch in the experience and were considering worshiping the three as equals until the Father's voice instructed them to understand Jesus was His Son, and they were to listen to Him. All of that is important for doctrine, of course, but the point is that people aren't dead if they are glorified! That was helpful to her.

Then she discussed some of the things that people say to her that are not a comfort, and I suggested that she might ask God to help her find room for their words if they were meant for her or to help her discard them if they were coming from people who were just trying to push her into another way of being in order to relieve their own discomfort and loss.

With time still allowing then, I asked about her children. She had two that were alive, and she and her husband had had two miscarriages. I repeated to her the choice of words she'd used in describing her field of grace being "a field of flowers ... It's like I'm waiting on children to pop up."

"Close your eyes, and call them," I said.

"They are hiding," she said.

"Find your children."

"They are shy, but I hear them laughing. They are hiding behind someone's legs."

I smiled inwardly, knowing that these were her miscarried children, now reunited with their father.

After she reclaimed her lost babies, we discussed her naming them and shopping for something to represent them in her home. She agreed to carry both of them, along with her husband, in her heart.

She left buoyant.

People generally tell us where they are. If we will listen, we can bear witness by seeing issues with them in our mind's eye. These visioning tools are training wheels that help us see what we are saying in the depths of our hearts, beneath the surface of life tensions. They help us check in with our inner world and study the tensions as tender places and help us come into agreement with God's terms working in us.

Years ago, prior to my using these family models and set ups so often, a young widow spent a few sessions with me, and in God's grace, we 'saw it' together at the same moment.

She'd buried her late husband of nearly a decade in the year prior and was being pursued by a kind man about whom she felt flat and stuck. The friendship was increasingly feeling imbalanced with the weight of her not being free to reciprocate his friendship or interest. This was creating guilt in her. He was nice, but she didn't feel anything for him, though she wanted to be able to move forward in her life and feel something eventually for someone, even if it were not him.

Although I had had family systems training in grad school, I didn't immediately look at her in this framework but through the general stages of grief, which yielded no movement. Then, during one session, off the cuff, I happened to ask a wider family context question, "Do you ever see your former in-laws?"

"Oh, yes; every week," she answered.

"Every week?" I repeated a bit surprised.

"Yes."

"You see your in-laws every single week?" I repeated perplexed.

"Yes."

"How? Why? What is the occasion? Do you go to their house, or have them over? What? Why do you see them, and where?"

"We see each other every Tuesday at 4:00. It's kind of a standing appointment now. We meet at the cemetery, at my husband's grave site. We've been meeting weekly ever since he died."

I noticed she referred to him as her 'husband,' and not by his name.

"Why do you guys do this? Do they expect you to come? Is this a ritual you guys do for him, or for you, or for them?"

"No, we didn't really plan it; it just kinda happened. I went back to his grave site a week after the funeral. I went on Tuesday at 4:00 because that was when his funeral was. So I chose the same day and time, and they happened to be there too. And then I went again the next week, and they did too, and then we just kept meeting up, and it became a habit like that."

This had been going on for almost a year at this point. After a pause, during which I tried to put it together in my head, I summarized out loud to her while she stared at the floor.

"So, your husband died almost a year ago. And you guys all buried your husband, their son, but you did not bury your husband's wife because she didn't die. But the dead man's wife keeps coming back weekly to wife her dead husband—at the cemetery."

We were quiet together for a few beats. Then, very slowly—her gaze gradually lifted up from the floor until her eyes met mine. At that moment, the woman let go of her life as his wife. It was a sacred privilege watching her soul step back from his grave. Her face showed that she had life in her again. She noticed that she didn't die when he did.

We sat in stillness together, quiet in the peace. Here we were; both of us were sitting together, breathing, and feeling breath.

It's hard to describe the feeling of the holy: whether it is a feeling in the body, or a sense of integration in the soul, or perhaps a sense of presence in the spirit, that which holds us together inside and out—whatever it is, it is a Thin Space encounter.

If it is presence—whose presence it was for her entirely, I can't say—maybe God's or her husband's, or her own, or all of the above and more. When I see her in my memory, I also see light pouring in through the afternoon window shade in my westward-facing office window. I can still feel the awe of that holy moment of life made whole.

How profoundly loyal she'd remained, utterly faithful as a wife whose role in life as his wife was also finally now released. Her peace was palpable.

"Welcome back," I said.

I saw her only once more. She married her kind friend within six months. I would say she bowed to life on new terms and agreed to love again.

A Timely Following

When I was a little girl, there was an elderly couple who lived at the end of my block. I enjoyed seeing the way the husband kept up his trees by trimming them into perfect circular mushroom shapes.

I saw his wife only once a year when he invited us into their home as small, threatening little trick-or-treaters so that his wife could greet us from her wheelchair, appreciate our sing-song threat, and then happily surrender her treats.

The day came when whatever it was that ailed her finished its job, and she died. Her husband, who seemed to be in perfect health, died three weeks later. Young as I was at the time, I remember thinking to myself how nicely that worked out. In their case, unlike others, his death had my full agreement as a reconciliation. I could not begrudge the mushroom shaped trees losing their form, knowing that the old couple was together again, and likely young again, becoming their truer selves.

That death was easy. It was also down the street and didn't involve my own next of kin.

The Illness

Sometimes, a live model can assist us in coming into agreement with harder partings. Sometimes, the death to face is one's own. Though the Scriptures instruct us that everyone has an appointed time for death, it doesn't mean that we are able to consent easily when the threshold is visible.

At a workshop, my husband once represented an illness for a man who had cancer. The illness was set up facing away until the man agreed to look at the cancer. The disease turned, and when the sick man faced the illness, it didn't seem scary or threatening. Nor did the illness change or morph into an alternative representative with human qualities like a lost loved one that the man perhaps wanted to follow.

They simply stood facing each other in a neutral way until the man made his peace with his next step in life and finally took a deep breath and said, "I'm not afraid now."

With that, he came into peace and agreement with his own door into what was next.

A Small Child

A young mother's family brought her to see me immediately after the sudden death of her toddler. Her own family was determined to keep her in the land of the living and escorted her with insistence that she come in. The only thing that made sense to me for her immediate relief was to help the young woman see that she could connect.

"Close your eyes." I said. "Imagine a large wide open Field of Grace, and tell me what you see when you get there."

Soon, she described the beauty she saw in her mind's eye. I asked her to allow herself to be there, then I said, "Call him."

She spoke her son's name in whispered tones and immediately upon saying his name, she gasped, and the tears began to flow.

"Oh! He's here!" She took a deep breath and said it again, "He is here. I see him." Her eyes still closed, she moved her hands upward in the air to demonstrate. "He's huge, He's not gone at all. He's right here in my face.

I can feel him." Her breathing changed from the deep gasp to a deeper movement into peace. Mercy attended, and she could find him.

Weeks later she came back in to do some basic work around adjusting to these seemingly impossible terms with her child. She said that although she'd not seen him again the way she did the first day she was in my office, she knew he most certainly still existed and that she could sense him.

In Christ, we live and move and have our being. In Him are all the treasures hidden.

Arranging Matters with the Dead

I attended a workshop in Kentucky many years ago when the German family systemic facilitator, Bert Hellinger, was presenting. Though I'd studied family systems, family sculpting, family psycho-dramas, and mapping in graduate school in the 1980s, it would be years before the European slant crossed the pond. It was in his training that I agreed to facilitate my first live set-up. I was still on the fence about his slant on the systemic method, and, as the Lord would have it, the issue we first-timer facilitators would explore was for those who needed to acknowledge a dead person.

After we grouped up, a woman said she wanted to go first. She asked a woman opposite her in the circle to represent someone she needed to see. When they stood up opposite each other, the participant refused to look at the representative for the dead. Since she refused to look at her, I dismissed the representative, and left the wonder of it with the woman. What I learned from that was the sense of starting and stopping a piece of work in facilitating. It is okay to look if you need to, and it is also okay not to look at that reality if you are not yet fully willing to do so.

Next, another woman said, "I'd like to see my father."

She chose a man to represent him, and they both stood up opposite each other. He took two steps forward into the circle, and she also approached and fully faced him. Moments after centering himself as a representative for her father, his eyes went to the floor, and he literally never looked at the woman again. He began to stretch his jaw, and repositioned himself in his stance and stared at the ground.

They shared no more eye contact at all.

Meanwhile, the woman who had previously represented the dead, slumped over in her chair as if asleep demonstrating that she had a place in this story. Noticing a simple movement of unction, I got up, gently tapped her on her shoulder, and directed her to go and do this on the floor in front of where his eyes were landing. She did so immediately.

When she laid down on the floor in front of his gaze, her hair covered her face entirely. Soon, the representative for the father also laid himself down on the ground next to the other dead person. The woman's dead father focused intently on the sleeper, and he began trying to move her hair out of her face to get her to look at him. But she remained utterly still and unresponsive. Eventually he also came to a rest of stillness but not until he'd snuggled up close to her, and then, he too became peaceful. After staring at the scene for a while, the woman who wanted to see her father stopped the process and said, "Thank you," with a surprising tone of joy.

"Thank you so much; that was perfect. It was just exactly what I needed to see. Thank you so much. Thank you for representing; you can de-role now."

The two representatives stood, bowed to her to de-role, and returned to their seats. She sat down next to me with a new warmth and sense of hope and then explained to the group what she had just seen.

She introduced herself to us and told us where she was from in the United States and offered to us a small slice of her rich heritage as a Jewish woman. Her father, who she said had had the exact kind of jaw action the representative demonstrated, was the only survivor from his family of origin, all of whom had died in Europe in the Holocaust. After the war, he'd immigrated to the United States and married this woman's mother, an American Jewish woman, and they had several children together.

She said her father had seemed distracted her whole life, and she could never seem to get his attention. It bothered her. She had always wanted him to look at her just once and see her. She'd hoped to see him see her in the live model—but once again— as usual—as consistently as ever, this didn't happen.

But the miraculous thing that came to her as she watched the representatives was that she recalled something he'd always said to her when he was alive. Now he made perfect sense to her. He used to say, "I just wish I could have said goodbye or could have seen them just one more time." She said, "That picture was just exactly what I needed to see. He is with his family and is at peace. I can leave it alone now. I now see what he was always looking at. Now I understand."

So she was satisfied. She understood him better; she saw what his soul was always occupied with, and she could let him go. They both shared the same wish.

Summary Thoughts

At the beginning of this chapter, there is a quote by Quaker George Fox, giving encouragement for us to find our departed loved ones in the Seed of Christ.

To end this section, I'd like to share a comforting narrative by George MacDonald, taken from his book of sermons, Miracles of Our Lord. A portion of this sermon offers a reflection on one of the miracles of Jesus when he raised a widow's deceased son. The way he discusses how the two of them might reconsider death thereafter is not only beautiful, but really reasonable.

MacDonald's writing style is wordy but worth our patient attention. This is a lovely reflection on a resurrection miracle that invites us to think about the feelings of the departed as well as our own.

Friends crowded around a loss—the center of the gathering that which was not—the sole presence the hopeless sign of a vanished treasure—an open gulf, as it were, down which love and tears and sad memories went plunging in a soundless cataract: the weeping mother—the dead man borne in the midst. They were going to the house of death, but Life was between them and it—was walking to meet them, although they knew it not. A face of tender pity looks down on the mother. She heeds him not. He goes up to the bier, and lays his hand on it. The bearers recognize authority, and stand. A word, and the dead sits up. A moment more, and he is in the arms of his mother. O mother! mother!

Wast thou more favored than other mothers? Or was it that, for the sake of all mothers as well as thyself, thou wast made the type of the universal mother with the dead son—the raising of him but a foretaste of the one universal bliss of mothers with dead sons? That thou wert an exception would have ill met thy need, for thy motherhood could not be justified in thyself alone. It could not have its rights save on grounds universal. Thy motherhood was common to all thy sisters. To have helped thee by exceptional favor would not have been to acknowledge thy motherhood. That must go mourning still, even with thy restored son in its bosom, for its claims are universal or they are not. Thou wast indeed a chosen one, but that thou mightest show to all the last fate of the mourning mother; for in God's dealing there are no exceptions. His law are universal as he is infinite. Jesus wrought no new thing—only the works of the Father. What matters it that the dead come not back to us, if we go to them?! What matters it? said I! It is tenfold better. Dear as home is, he who loves it best must know that what he calls home is not home, is but a shadow of home, is but the open porch of home, where all the winds of the world rave by turns, and the glowing fire of the true home casts lovely gleams from within.

Certainly this mother did not his lose her son again. Doubtless next she died first, knowing then at last that she had only to wait. The dead must have their sorrow too, but then they find it is well with them, they can sit and wait by the mouth of the coming stream better than those can wait who see the going stream bear their loves down to the ocean of the unknown. The dead sit by the river-mouths of Time: the living mourn upon its higher banks.

But for the joy of the mother, we cannot conceive it. No mother ever who has lost her son, and hopes one blessed eternal day to find him again, can conceive her gladness. Had it been all a dream? A dream surely in this sense that the final, which alone, in the full sense, is God's will, must ever cast the look of a dream over all that has gone before. When we last awake, we shall know that we dreamed. Even every honest judgment, feeling, hope, desire, will show itself a dream—with this difference from some dreams, that the waking is the more lovely, that nothing is lost, but everything gained, in the full blaze of restored completeness. How triumphant would this mother die, when her turn came!

And how calmly would the restored son go about the duties of the world...

Introduction to Part Two

All this energy issues from Christ: God raised him from death and set him on a throne in deep heaven, in charge of running the universe, everything from galaxies to governments, no name and no power exempt from his rule. And not just for the time being, but forever. He is in charge of it all, has the final word on everything. At the center of all this, Christ rules the church. The church, you see, is not peripheral to the world; the world is peripheral to the church. The church is Christ's body, in which he speaks and acts, by which he fills everything with his presence.
—Paul to the Ephesians (from the Message)

Without the heavenly order in the spirit, earthly orders in the soul have the strength of a house of cards. "Unless the Lord builds the house the laborers labor in vain."Psalm 127:1 What holds Love in place is our Father. He keeps us standing oriented even if others are running wild around us. Everything in the preceding chapters are a leveling tool, clearing the way for a higher view of ultimate placement in the spirit. The next three chapters may seem like they should be in a different book. But the fruit of the Spirit is a gift to the soul. Without spiritual orientation we are unable to maintain change.

In the next chapter I'll take a symbol and use it as a key for the whole book of John. We can take any symbol and use it as a lens and see where it takes the reader. It is offered as a simple way to use patterns as excavation tools in scripture.

The chapter that follows is a novella. There are no graphs, the history is there but the story line is fictional. I use it here because I've retold the story "in the round," so to speak. The point is cosmic in scope and presents a very real and serious consideration for what it means to bow in the most impossible situation when everything inside a person normally demands resistance. Even in trauma we learn to bow to God's terms for love.

The last chapter is a synthesized look at souls in Biblical systems who came into agreement with the terms of heaven. Together these last chapters bring us into a whole view of "thy will be done on earth as it is in heaven." We may ask, how is it in heaven? And how might we see with any confidence? How should we visualize the spiritual terrain? John, Jesus, Mary, Jacob and David show us what it is to bow in the Spirit. The Epilogue is a true story that demonstrates the simplicity of the bow.

Chapter Ten: John's Wish: Key Code of Covenant Waters

Thus far in this book we've explored how to see family order and anchor systems in scripture in a visual and an embodied way. We have touched on the common relationship themes having not yet addressed victim-perpetrator connections. How do we heal those traumas with order? How do we make whole what is irreparably damaged? All true change comes from grace. With God all things are possible. The subject of trauma is coming in chapter 11, and to stomach it we need a biblical foundation that leads to a field of grace that supplies us with what we need for repentance and a powerful love. We need a bigger spirit and that grows from a bigger and bigger definition of love, big as the sea. Where do we find that? Scripture holds the wisdom of God for all things.

How do we plumb the depths when we are not in a group fellowship? We have to read in such a way as to see. All the tools we've used in this book are seeing tools. In this chapter we will look at another way to glean an understanding of orders from the fields of grace in the holy texts. We will take one word and use it as a key to help us understand the entire testimony. The process is similar to a word study, except that it will look at the way the word creates an image. We are, after all, image bearers and we need to bear the images that heal us.

A word is in order about approaching the texts with confidence. Some readers live in the Word daily, others are afraid to go there. I sat in my undergrad dorm room when a gal entered and saw me reading and underling in my Bible and very nearly ran screaming out of my room for fear of lightning striking me in her presence. Her tradition did not encourage her to study at all let alone make a mark with a pen in the Bible. Some people are far more comfortable being told what the Bible says and allowing it to be fenced off from them. But it is a fallacy that one needs to be a theologian with seminary background to be able to go fishing in the texts. For the majority of human history, the scriptures were only read in synagogues or churches for good reasons—vocational priests were hired to study, many people were illiterate, and there were not many copies of the bible, most of which were not in the language of the people. Sadly, if you didn't speak Latin, what you heard read by priests didn't help you.

In the last five hundred years thanks to the protestant reformation and the printing press, everyone has access to scriptures in their own language. Sincere vocational priests and pastors are clearly gifts of discipleship, but as part of the priesthood of believers, we have reasons to study for ourselves, both in groups and in private. And if we find something that seems odd, research is easy for us through technology. Everyone needs to venture to trust the Holy Spirit to lead them into truth—as promised. The Bible is spiritually discerned, so when we ask for guidance, we can expect to receive it.

It is imperative that Believers become intentional about the entire counsel of God if we intend to transcend the fallen conscience in Adam's race. To have the mind of Christ and be lead by the Spirit, we must know the Word. Faith comes by hearing the Word and together with fellowship the Lord Himself transfers our allegiance to the Spirit's teaching. Hiding His logic in our hearts becomes for us a shield for our faith, much needed for transcending a perverse world. We cannot bind our conscience to the Word if we remain ignorant of the scriptures.

In the Old Testament, the prophets used themes which Jesus later owned as symbols of Himself. Jesus as 'the way' is a reference to Jeremiah's prophecy of the Lord. Jesus being "the Shepherd" is a reference to Ezekiel's experience. Isaiah called him the Light but all of them referenced the Word of the Lord coming to them.

A doctor might see Jesus leading him in his field as the Great Physician; a farmer may emphasis Jesus as the Lord of the Harvest; a musician might experience the Lord as the Song, and a writer finds Him as the main subject. John's gospel testimony uses many of these same symbols but the water symbol is another lens that offers us a glimpse into what happens when a couple of fishermen are finally caught in a net by the great fisherman, who owns the water and all that live in it.

The symbol shows up in nearly every chapter. If we give water our attention, if we give it a living voice, and give it a place in the story, we give it a platform for hearing and seeing the message. Water begins to show us reconciliation with God, and also with one another, which is the great point of being made whole. John shows us Jesus in the water. He also shows us his best friends and what he thinks of them, and how he came to see them better through the lens of the water. Before we dive in, there are several other symbols in his introductory chapter that I'd like to point out to the reader for future study on their own.

The Apostle John was originally a disciple of the Prophet John the Baptizer, the cousin of Jesus. In the synoptic Gospels—Matthew, Mark, and Luke—the writers contextualize Jesus in his family and in his culture and nation. John went a step further to contextualize Jesus as context Himself—the entire human story exists within the cosmos of God. He opens his testimony by calling Jesus the Logos, the Logic or Word of God. Calling Jesus the Word, is a powerful statement to a Gentile reader because they sought after logos and believed in a living logic behind all material things. But for a Jew, the "Word of God" typically came to a prophet; this was about that in the flesh. The notion that "I Am" is here is a startle for a start.

"To go back to the very beginning is to find the Word already present there, face to face with God. The Word is I Am; God's eloquence echoes and concludes in Him. The Word equals God" (John 1:1, The Mirror Bible).

John briefly discussed the baptizer, the cousin of the Lord, as his first spiritual teacher who turned him over to their master, Jesus. John the baptizer called Jesus the Lamb of God, who takes away the sin of the world. The baptizing prophet John demonstrated faithful and necessary transfer of John to become a disciple of the Lord. There was no rivalry in ministry. John maintained the message of repentance throughout his Gospel, speaking of it as a kind of water in most every chapter. He understood the movement of water.

John also declared Jesus to be the Light of the world. A Jewish reader might understand this light to be a reference to the Shekinah glory of God in the Old Covenant. As Light, Jesus was superior to the Baptizer, as well as Moses and Abraham.

He also introduced Jesus to his readers visually by way of the placement Jesus had with God. God was Father, and Jesus was His son. Jesus is the Son of God. They together invite us into our place with them in this way.

This message was as outrageous for the Jew as it was for the Greek. If misunderstood—this could seem like heresy for a Jew and could be seditious for a Gentile. John's earliest audience would know immediately that the text they were hearing was hazardous material; surely, it would explain the motive behind the most famous crucifixion.

In any case, then or now, if this narrative was true, it required a new seating arrangement in all of humanity. This was deity material. In a land where Caesar was called Lord, the writing could have been viewed as propaganda—at least until it was thoroughly read.

The Apostle John was neither shy nor careful in his opening chapter because this was not a political statement; this was cosmic good news. He introduced his reader to God in the flesh, not Moses and not Zeus, not

Caesar but God incarnate had come to invite us home to His Love, by way of the cross, his benevolent sacrifice. John understood thirst for home and waters of repentance.

There was a reason Jesus called him one of the sons of thunder. Indeed, John was the disciple who knew Jesus loved him. He was secured. And as we will see at the end, John was also the disciple who knew Jesus loved everyone. In this Love that moves like water, we are free to connect to God and one another in a new way: by the Spirit through repentance of our blindness.

John took the placements of the individual's soul, the nation's soul, and their historical leaders, as well as the Greeks, and he revealed them all as subordinate to Jesus when he saw Jesus's placement as the son of God.

"The law came through Moses, but grace and truth came through Jesus; no one has ever seen God except the son who is seated in the Father's lap" (John 1:17, The Delitzsch Hebrew Gospels).

That is the image supreme in fields of grace, a son who is seated in the Father's lap. This is where love comes from. The Father is the seat of love.

"He came to that which was his own, but his own did not receive him, yet to all who received him, to those who believed in his name, he gave the right to become children of God" (John 1: 11-12, NIV). This seats man, by faith, also in the Father's lap.

John believed Jesus was God; he also believed Jesus was making humans into children of God. If Jews were waiting on the Messiah to arrive and confirm their boast in their race, this man had a different wish. John nullified the rights of lineage in that statement. This is a gift of inheritance and a sharing in the love of a Kingdom family: a homecoming where we leave the chaos of self rule and cling to the Father. Jews were not the only recipients of the invitation. This was for everyone, including the oppressors occupying Israel.

It was not a new faith, but the root of the faith God gave to Abraham when He promised Abraham would be the father of many nations. That promise was coming to fruition. His plan was always to close the gaps between God and man, and man and man. The wall of the flesh of Adam's race was torn down in Jesus.

Jesus Himself was entirely a watershed event. The message given wasn't inviting people to a Kingdom of Israel, but to a Kingdom of the God of His own children. This may have stunned a Gentile audience—becoming a child of God was a matter of faith: not race and not mythical philosophy.

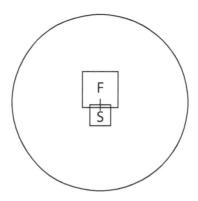

Diagram 10.1

The diagram pictures the dynamic of a Son being seated in the Father's lap and shows the proximity of intimacy, and dependency as a model for all humanity. With God we are all small.

The first, the next, the middle, and the very last thing John invites his reader to do is to see the water symbol as a way to repent our way into a new way of being in the world as a child of an eternal Father. In his testimony, the gods were comforted as children again and called to become their true selves.

John may have been a fisherman, and may have been tutored by the greatest prophet who ever lived, but he was discipled by the Mind of the universe. This is the wish of Christ for us all — to be discipled by the Spirit. Notice in the following highlights of each chapter, how often Jesus goes home with people and gives them the water they've been thirsting for all their lives. The book is not long and if the reader is familiar with it, the water theme will be a delightful surprise. By focusing on a theme, the ministry of reconciliation in relationships both to God and to others, is clearer.

All the symbols mentioned above can be used as a filter for further study in the book. What follows now, is how I've summarized through the lens of water. The patterns demonstrate one more way to dive in.

Married With Water

After his shocking introduction John tells us about Jesus's first public miracle. In chapter 2, Jesus re-ordered places with his mother at a wedding, when he turned water into wine. Of all the images he could have chosen to present first, this is the one that represented the whole situation: when vessels for purification were filled with water, the water was transformed into wine inside the vessels.

Weddings weren't short afternoon events; they lasted for days, sometimes even a week of feasting. Apparently, in wine presentations, the best was given early, not late. When the wine ran out at this wedding, Jesus's mother took notice and mentioned it to her son.

Whether she reported in a spirit of compassion for a need, or doubtfully with a loose tongue, or as a confidant or a prompt for his assistance to them or to her, we cannot know. Not knowing her exact station with the celebrants, we do not know her reasoning, which requires a careful handling of his reply.

What she did, in any case, was mediate. He asked a question: a common pattern in his teaching style. "What does that have to do with you or me?"

If we drew a picture from the question, we'd see the question was about an arrangement. If we imagine the question as a literal one for her to answer we notice the question is about relationship. Where are we in the matter, Mother? What's our place? Do we have the right to take action? What gives us the right? Who are we to act? Are we to act as the providers for them, and, if so, do you think they know it yet? Have we been asked? Do we have to be asked? Are you asking on their behalf? Is this their wish? The relationship has to be in order for something corrective to happen.

If this is Jesus's first public miracle, and if He can only do what His Father does, He must act in regard to the relationship orders, or within His divine rights to act as a Son to His Father ever mindful that God is the doer of the deed. He always operates in order—to then establish order.

There is an entire thesis on prayer in this question. Briefly, recall that God in Genesis had become hidden or veiled to man when man hid behind a tree. By human disorder, man couldn't see God from where he was standing hiding behind a tree. God was there of course, seeking and available, but man had to be called out of hiding.

Man has been historically blinding himself by hiding God from himself and placing a tree between them. God must be revealed again, reinstated, person by person, with a bow of recognition that comes of waters. If we make a request, and if we want to make room for Him to act as He would act, we must agree to the terms John shows us behind another tree which he comes to later.

Jesus gave extensive teachings on "asking" and affirmed that God knows what we need before we ask. Asking gives a place for an answer to come when it reseats the asker as a dependent rather than the authority.

Jesus didn't move or act without a humble jurisdiction under His Father and in His service. His mother petitioned for the couple, their family, and the village to have new wine. So another question is present: What did this need/miracle have to do with Jesus and his mother? We might even ask, what would the upshot be for them and their relationship?

From here forward, she would be sharing Him publicly and releasing Him to wherever ministry took him. Public ministry would change things.

A wedding was a beautiful place for God to act first. In this water-to-wine miracle Jesus rescued a young couple from the humiliation of lack. Spiritually speaking, he set them in order through the gift of the sign of filling the vessels of repentance. This gift would protect the young couple from the enmity in a new marriage. In this miracle, Jesus brought them Eden's grace of repentance and covered them.

Remember that the skin covers. If we superimpose the bridegroom and bride's names as Adam and Eve, the wine is not only gone already, but the vessels of purification are bone dry. This was not just the state of affairs for the couple, but for the nation. A new wine was called for so that no enmity would come between these two representative lovers so long as the servants did what Jesus told them to do.

So Mary, taking His question as an answer, took a re-ordering action. She made new arrangements by putting the servants under His command. By instructing them to obey Jesus, she put the servants in an order through which Jesus would legally act. He doesn't usurp the power Adam surrendered to the enemy. He waited for a legal space to act.

Mary had held the promised seed of Eve and had agreed to incarnate Christ. He now, as He did in Eden in the first crisis, acted to woo mankind into wedding themselves unto God willingly.

What was his first move here?

He addressed the first thing: repentance, which, as John demonstrates over and over, is not how we might all define repentance. There were in their vicinity water jars which were normally used for purification. They were empty. Emptiness in purity represented the spiritual emptiness of mankind's entire wedding story with God.

Jesus addressed the servants with that most needed wedding gift and called for the purification jars to be filled with water; all six of them together held 25 gallons. This wasn't just for the couple; this water was for everyone. He then told the servant to draw out some water and give it to the head waiter who, upon tasting it, immediately went to the groom to ask how it was that he had saved the best wine for last.

At that, Jesus won the hearts of His disciples; they believed when He turned water into wine. It's no accident that this was the setting for the beginning of His unveiling, and the cross and the empty tomb were his finale for reunion.

Marriage was attacked in the Garden of Eden. It was a first order of business in His public ministry to set up a station for restoration in a union between husband and wife through purification. Repentance would lead to wine, which is the joy of being in union with God. Marriage, as we've already discussed, belongs to Jesus, who is the Bridegroom. No marriage can survive without a common habit of reconciliation; we are the vessels of purification.

In a couples' workshop once, we embodied this story at the beginning of our work, and then again at the end of the workshop to recap the entire work by pulling the representatives from the earlier set-up back in for a summary piece. The participants stood as representatives, facing each other to reflect this passage.

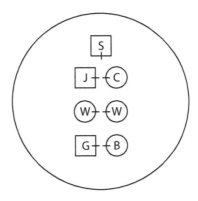

Diagram 10.2

Representatives for the groom and bride faced each other.
Representatives for the wine and water faced each other as well.
Jesus and the Church faced each other, and the "Spirit of Expectation"
stood over them all, like a cloud, a covering of water.

As the seven stood in such a pattern, I asked the bride, the water, and the church to bow to their partners. The response that the receiving representatives had in reaction to their partner's bowing was immediate.

The groom was taken aback and touching his own heart said he felt very humbled. The wine reported a felt physical stirring of empowerment in their core. The representative for Christ was moved with compassion. And the 'Spirit of Expectation' with long extended arms arching high over the couples was full of love and a desire to pass life on. It's a wonder and a mystery how bowing to order inspires life and love.

More Water Please

In John, chapter 3, Jesus explained to Nicodemus—a highly-educated teacher in Israel who came to him at night to talk—that until one was born of Water and the Spirit, one wouldn't be able to enter the Kingdom of God. That would be hard for a Jewish teacher to hear if he thought he was already secure in the Kingdom of God.

According to the text, Nicodemus was unclear about what water meant. He was also unclear about the Spirit and could not grasp the concept of being born again at his age. But one's identity, when it is located in the ego of the soul hangs in the balance until identity is relocated in the spiritual realm and is made subject to God as a child of the Father. We hang our sense of self on many things, people and places in earth, bowing to many things, giving our power to idols that can not produce life in us.

In chapter 4, John answered all of Nicodemus's questions by giving the answers to the reader through an opposite kind of character, one who, unlike Nicodemus, had no respect in Israel. Jesus settled himself at noon at Jacob's Well, which was a water source with an ancient history in Israel.

A woman arrived at midday—another way of hiding, since most women drew water early—and here, beside the well, she found God waiting for her. He has a way of coming for us behind the proverbial tree. Nicodemus came at night, this nameless woman came at midday.

However, Jesus asked her for some water. He still asks us for water. If he can ever get some from us, we shall both drink and become drunk in the Spirit of Love together. But rather than giving Jesus water, she pushed back with a racial slur to challenge His right to speak to her by assuming Jesus was more like the religious Nicodemus perhaps than God.

Jesus explained that if she knew who He was, she'd ask him for water. And if she would ask, He'd give her water like a river flowing out of her, and she'd never be thirsty again. She wondered how He could do that without a bucket. She had no idea that she *was* the bucket, like an empty jar for purification, waiting to be filled His living water.

So, He gave her a demonstration by telling her to go get her husband. She said she didn't have a husband.

Agreeing, He assisted her fragmented confession and told her how many husbands she'd had—five—and that the man she was living with now was not her husband. He drew her sin up from the deep well of her emptiness and drank her into his compassion.

She was so vulnerable and thirsty, that no one understood her but Jesus. He was her watershed event. He knew her better than anyone can know anyone, even in marriage. He saw her soul.

Let's not imagine that He revealed his knowledge of her like a condemnation; that was not the truth. The truth was that she was God's princess, a lost daughter, and no one saw her rightly until Jesus did, and this had consequently been a hard life.

She was vulnerable. The angst of the shift in her life was coming to the surface; She was going to have to release and bow to true love.

To be seen and come out of hiding, to be present as one was, was part one — the water. Ministering to help her see who God was as her deeper home was part two, the wine. This was the food the disciples did not know about when they questioned the engagement of Jesus with her. He gave her the good news that worship was in Spirit and in Truth… not in Jerusalem. Worship was everywhere. At the moment, it was at the well.

The truth is this. We are in need, and God is in Love with us and wells up in us when we go inside with Him. This woman's empty vessel was filling with presence.

Now, this was cause for fellowship, the koinonia, or community union that people are looking for is the Love of the Spirit of God. She immediately and shamelessly introduced him to her entire town, and all received him and asked him to stay. They had all had a long drink of water.

Water In The Temple

In Chapter 5, Jesus acted out at the Temple's water source, at the pool of Siloam. John tells us that the sick would often sit and wait for an angel to stir the water, and the first one into the moving waters would be healed.

A crippled man had been waiting for such a chance for 38 years. Being crippled, though, he could never get in first. What a sad situation it is to compete for healing.

Jesus, the commander of heavenly hosts himself, came to the pool and upon seeing the man who had been waiting nearly forty years, healed the man—on the Sabbath—during a Holy Week. His timing was impeccable.

The healing command issued was to, "Take up your bed and walk." The man's obedience drew out the elite self-appointed police, of course. Were they more appalled that a healed man carried his bed, or that the fellow was healed on the wrong day of the week? They demanded that he identify the criminal healer. But the healed fellow didn't know who Jesus was. This kind of healing begs a few questions regarding illness and the soul. Can we be healed by someone we do not know? Can we get sick in relation to someone we do know?

Jesus came back to the man later with another protective instruction. He told the man to be careful not to continue sinning, or something worse may happen to him. This is interesting.

I've heard people balk at the idea that sin wreaks havoc on our bodies. Nothing is more reasonable. If we are image-bearers and as such are also temples of the Holy Spirit individually, there is incompatibility and conflict with sin and our spirit. The conflict manifests often enough in the body. Jesus offered him a word of protection from further illness. We don't know the man's heart, but we know the company he kept wasn't helpful to his soul. I wonder if Jesus was protecting the man from taking up an offense with the religious elite.

Water Outside

In John, chapter 6, Jesus went out to the Sea of Galilee, the largest body of water in the gospel narratives. At these lake shores, Jesus fed thousands with very little fish from a lunch sacrificed or offered up to Jesus by a believing boy.

Jesus would have to out-give the gift, of course, to keep the child's dear little soul in order. Can you imagine what the child thought when he saw his offering expand into a miracle to feed the thousands? Would he ever consider holding anything back from God after that? I hope his parents were there too, because he'd surely have gotten in trouble for "lying" if they weren't. Imagine going home with a fish tale like that, and not being believed.

The upshot of the crowd being fed though, was not an increase in faith in God. The crowd wanted to install Jesus as their political king. Certainly, they had reason to long for his rule. But his kingdom was more than taxes, wars, and the prosperity of fish. He was the Greater King David, and He wasn't just seeking Israel's prosperity; He sought Rome's and the prosperity of rest of the world's thirst for water and true substance.

His enemy was not the Roman Empire. His enemy was the Liar, the Devil, who sows seeds of discord and division, and who installs fame and ego and self-rule as king. His enemy is the dis-order that yields death.

After feeding and teaching them, Jesus slipped off to a mountain to pray, sending his disciples away on a boat—into the water. The sea became a torrent of wind and water that threatened to swallow them. Jesus took that occasion to walk to them on the water.

Jesus owns the water. It is his solid foundation in approaching us. It's his channel of quenching thirst for reconciliation, the disciples were floating on it and also being whipped by winds threatening to empty their vessel, capsizing them into the water. Once they received Jesus into the boat, they were immediately on the farther shore, in joy no doubt. The crowds were mystified that He and his disciples were found on the far side of the lake. But their interest in Jesus was still shortsighted.

"Rabbi, when did you get here?" asked the curious.

Jesus replied, "I tell you the truth: you want to be with me because I fed you, not because you understood the miraculous signs. But don't be so concerned about perishable things like food. Spend your energy seeking the eternal life that the Son of Man can give you. For God the Father has given me the seal of his approval."

They replied, "We want to perform God's works too. What should we do?"

Jesus told them, "This is the only work God wants from you: Believe in the one He has sent" (New Living Translation).

What a fish is to water, man is to repentance. We need to be swimming in it. That story is coming.

The Festival of Water

In Chapters 7 and 8 in John's narrative, we come to the highest festival in Jewish life. Among the several annual festivals celebrated in Judaism, some major holidays called for a pilgrimage to Jerusalem.

In the spring was Passover, the celebration of deliverance from slavery, and also Pentecost, which marked the beginning of the harvest of barley and continued throughout the wheat harvest: a 50-day cycle, the "first fruits" of Pentecost.

In the fall were two more festivals, the Day of At-one-ment or repentance, followed by The Feast of Tabernacles, which was the highest celebration trumpeting the season of reconciliation with God. It was the most joyful time in their calendar year. Think of the marriage supper of the Lamb in eternity when we are home with God!

On the last day of the eight-day feast, the priests typically took golden pitchers to the pool of Siloam and filled them with water to bring into the Temple in high ceremonial fashion. As they made their way toward the altar, they were escorted by loud choirs singing and dancing, and musicians accompanying the priest to the altar, where they would pour both water from the pool and also wine together as one stream onto the altar.

This is like the wedding at Cana. Study that sacred image in your mind's eye, and hold it there forever. We will shortly see it again.

Visually, this scene is Christ's strongest prophetic sign: four-story massive towers of menorah posts lit up the Temple in the city of Jerusalem so it could be seen for miles.

At the highest point of the highest festival, at the moment when the priests poured the water and wine over the alter of sacrifice, Jesus began to shout out to the masses the same exact thing He said privately to the Samaritan woman at Jacob's Well. "Come unto me all you who are thirsty, and I will cause rivers of living waters to flow from you."

What does this mean? What is He doing here?

If we can begin to appreciate the gravity of the festival and all that is represented to the nation, we can respect the weight of the situation. This is Jesus; He and his father own the Temple and all the ceremonies. These are and always have been representations of Him, and this sign is about to be demonstrated fully.

If the man who made this claim was not God, and if he was not really The Word made flesh, then this is the most audacious thing a mere mortal could ever do—profaning God's name as his own—and doing it at the most sacred ceremony of reconciliation!

But what would an eye-witness think about his deeds? His acts of kindness and generosity, his ability to handle water in a storm, and the blessed way He handled sinners and the sick? Moses was enabled to part the waters of the Red Sea, and Joshua parted the Jordan, but this man walks on water and now makes a claim about water itself. Does He think he is one with the water too? Could Adam have done this?

If we accept this story, and his identity, then we have to ask what He meant by the pouring out and the mixing of water and wine together over an altar.

This is the exact image representing what would soon become reality at the cross. After He declared, "It is finished!", He committed his spirit to God and exhaled his last breath. Here is the son of man, the son of Adam exhaling the race of Adam's last breath, and then "the Roman speared his side, and blood and water poured "(John 19:34). Water and wine come into transformational agreement. Man's repentance is a movement of the Spirit and draws us to meet Jesus in his sacrifice and see the devotion of sacrificial giving—not retaliating in the name of God. He becomes wine to us because his blood is the pouring out of his life for ours, as seen from the heart of God, who is behind the tree.

He owns the Temple of humanity. Could anyone at the festival begin to imagine that He would soon split the veil itself? This water business is about his wine business. This revelation would provoke man's judgment of Jesus, and once that was behind us all, this would soon transform our destiny "into a happily ever after."

This is the wish Jesus had and was declaring at the Feast of Trumpets as the great wish of God. The Lamb of God was setting himself up to take away the sin of the world. This was an extravagant act of generosity, hope and delight, a revelation surprise, an unveiling, a wonder of love, and the climax of the festival that would happen only once in the lifetime of a nation tucked royally inside a cosmos.

"Come to me! You are a vessel! I'm inside you! I'm at home in you! Come sink down into me!" This is God's wish to reconcile humanity to his mercy.

But this was not seen yet by those who called themselves temple rulers. They started plotting to kill him. The sinful nature in man does not want to be governed by God, but wants to govern God instead. This is not a Jewish sin; it's an Adam sin. We reject the breath that gives us life and wonder why we are suffocating.

The blessed story is still coming together. What a long winter our Jewish brothers have endured waiting until the number of the Gentiles is complete. And what will the world be like when we all see together? But I digress.

A Taste of Water

In Chapter 9, the water key opened a door to both political and spiritual recalibration of conscience. Would one ever even imagine their own conscience needed to be reconstructed? We never suspect our rules are skewed, let alone entertain that our conscience is corrupt. We are much more comfortable believing that we are right.

Earlier, we discussed the role of conscience. Here, John detailed the cost of allegiance to a misinformed conscience when Jesus met up with a man blind from birth, and in healing him, addressed the blind community in which he lived.

Jesus covered the man's eyes with mud from his own watery spit and sent him, muddy-eyed, to the same pool of Siloam where the crippled man was made whole, and also where water was drawn at the Feast of Trumpets. There, he too was to wash off the mud of Adam's blindness and receive sight in the temple among the blind leaders. Jesus was extending himself to give sight to all with his own clear view of life.

Personally, I like my doctors to be healers, not bankers; and I like my ministers to be filled with the Holy Spirit and actually know the Jesus for whom they speak. But this is not always the case, and when it's not, if you go beyond the current level of development of conscience among the local authority, you might be punished with eviction or worse. The conscience works that way in a group. A group conscience will not easily accept that a group member can exceed the level of the group.

This man's eyes were healed, and he was punished for it with excommunication. This happens when people get well. It doesn't feel like protection, but it is.

In this water, could it have been any clearer?

Jesus is in charge of the temple of humanity; the elite are not. The leaders had mud in their eyes. No one suspected it yet, but Jesus is the Temple of Humanity that the temple in Jerusalem represented. Holy Water is here now, but it's a problem when those chosen for sharing the water contaminate it with their own blind refusal to bow and repent daily.

Tension at the temple continually builds around Jesus's water.

If the conscience is corrupt, the person is blind. A blind person cannot discern the difference between good and evil; only God can. So, the blind may feel fine doing evil things and then feel guilt and tension when getting things straight.

This man's family, for example, didn't want to speak for their son when pressed. Everyone is naturally afraid of being excluded until finding God as their true Father. We don't grow in the mind of the tribe; we grow in the mind of Christ.

Conscience gives us the sense of conviction within our community. It's a gift to humanity that allows us to form safe structures, and this is needed to survive. It gives us a felt sense of being under a rule or an authority, and in that way, it gives us a reading on "what it takes to belong, fit in, and avoid excommunication."

Everyone has a community that they've received from their family and their political or religious group. These communities guide our behaviors with a fear of separation and the anxiety that comes with crossing the boundary. Conscience is soothed by being secure in one's group. By maintaining one's place in the group through performance-based acceptance, a person feels good about doing their part and performing as the group expects.

In belonging, the conscience is quiet. The German Nazis had a strong group conscience, but it was not the mind of Christ. This is the nature of all humanity. God has mercy on us when He delivers us from the limits of the group and allows our highest allegiance to be to the Kingdom of Heaven. This is what transcendence is all about: seeing God and conforming to

His definition of belonging.

So, here, this newly-seeing man is not only given his sight; he is also given his spiritual eyes and can discern the nature of the group to which he and his family had always belonged, but were now excluded from.

In this deliverance (through exclusion), he was transferred to a new group and would now belong to the Kingdom of God. He received not only sight, but a new heart, which is a new conscience, where the laws are written by mercy—not to be confused with an innocent heart, which sees nothing wrong. There is no greater evil than that of a false innocence which never supposes its error or need for repentance and languishes in a condition of blindness as a slave to self or system as God.

When Jesus healed people on the Sabbath, it caused a stir within the consciences of the elite ruling body. Once the blind man saw, he saw things in a new manner; in short order, he learned that he stood in violation of the temple group conscience, which Jesus was eager to expose as a conscience bound to control. Theirs was a blind conscience. Would we rather be blind and secure in evil, or would we be healed and endure a cost for transcendence into great company?

This miracle was quite a demonstration of God's vision for man's freedom. In politics, religion, culture and family, we are only free to serve as puppets. We are not free to transcend.

Waterless But for Tears

In the next chapter of John, Jesus offered water as tears from his own eyes. Jesus wept. Then He raised Lazarus from the dead.

One might ask how much a tear of Jesus weighs in value. Tears have weight in heaven. God saves our tears in a bottle (Psalm 56:8). Wouldn't we love to see the compassion of Christ in his tears as he weeps with us when we are suffering what looks like an impossible situation?

Mary and Martha, the sisters of Lazarus, and many others saw Jesus weep publicly. He is above all things compassionate and will enter into our every sorrow. If we will go there, He will be there with us, for He weeps with those who weep and is near the broken hearted. If we will not go there, He will still go there and wait for us to find Him there, where he is waiting to turn our water into his wine.

Following her brother's resurrection, Mary, the sister of Lazarus—the one who ceased obeying her sister in order to sit at Jesus's feet and learn from him—now after her brother's revival once again placed herself beneath Him, bowing, to anoint Jesus's feet with oil. Now she wept, naturally.

She understood exactly what immense suffering was going to come of His compassion and generosity. He had by then explained Himself repeatedly. And she got it. She heard Him. She saw Him. And she believed Him. Thus, she anointed Him for burial. She understood Him.

The growing tension among the elite at the temple was untenable. From the perception of mockery at the temple, the impossible miracle of opening blind eyes, healing lame men on the Sabbath, and now the raising of the dead, climaxed in the true but anxiety loaded words of the rulers who lamented that, "the whole world has gone after Him" (John 12:19).

Within days, people were shouting "Hosanna" in the streets as Passover was approaching, and Jesus had not slowed in service momentum. He'd begun to purge the temple grounds with fire in His belly. He turned over tables in the temple and set doves and other animals free that were slated for sacrifice. His behavior demonstrated a reference to the ancient prophet Samuel who declared to the first king of Israel how God loved obedience more than sacrifice, and how rebellion was the sin of witchcraft.

The time had come when sacrificial animals were no longer representative of the Lamb of God. The temple originally intended to be a house of prayer for the nations was being gutted, and the structure itself within less than one generation would become a trash heap. Soon enough, not a symbol of God's presence would remain there once the false-innocent power over men was stripped and the true Lamb was on display on an altar hill outside the city.

All that would happen to this temple would also happen to The Temple—the body of Jesus. But on Resurrection Day, The House of Prayer for all nations would rise again. Jesus had finally come to the house of humanity, and He meant it. If the dead heard His voice, we can be sure, the depths of earth and the farthest reaches of the cosmos heard the voice of The Lord Most High. And there was no room to negotiate the universal throne.

Since Jesus raised a dead man who lived so close to Jerusalem, there was simply no living with Jesus. He was bigger than life. Mary, sister to Lazarus, seemed to be the only person who visibly understood who Jesus was and what He was going to do. She humbly bowed at His feet and treated His feet with dignity and worship before they suffered crucifixion for the world. There she wept in her bow and rightly so. Nothing rivaled her allegiance to her faith in Him, not money, not family, not nationality, everything was His. However even some of the disciples rebuked her for squandering such an expensive amount of oil on Jesus's feet. "Leave her alone; she has anointed me for burial" (John 12:7).

She saw Him for who He was before He was crucified. Her bow was earnest. She meant it. She could not serve God and money. Now the water was found in her tears.

Covenant of Water

Now we have come to a clear and powerful water picture that unfortunately seems dismissed by the present-day Western church. In dismissing this water, we've lost part of the power in the Gospel. And in doing so we've dismissed the heart of Jesus's eternal plan to make one new mankind. If we don't retrieve this, we will not be able to represent the Lord as ambassadors of mercy. This is a key we've set aside and have since forgotten what lock it fits.

We have one covenant that was celebrated by Jesus in two parts: we've remembered and practiced only one. We must re-member-ship the other and begin in earnest to represent this water.

A man once asked Jesus what the greatest command was, and Jesus answered in two parts: one was to love God, and the other was to love one's neighbor, and then He had to explain what that meant with a parable that basically indicted religion that refuses mercy. Reconciliation with God always includes people. Heaven is full of people.

For a proper weight as a further introduction to this water story, let's consider the content with mathematics. The fraction of space John spends writing about the upper room teachings, the last teaching before the passion of Christ's sacrifice, is a full third of his book. Recall that four-fifths of the book of Genesis is about four generations of one family system. That John spent one-third of his book on one night in this one room is a significant focal point for his understanding of the Gospel message.

John gave us many details about the last supper. He gave us Jesus's frame of mind in his teachings, his consolations, his redeeming prayers, and he introduced them to their Friend the Holy Spirit. It is full and rich, and when we think of an image of the 'last supper' we might automatically mentally reference the image painted by Leonardo da Vinci. But that is not that image John described. If the reader will check it again, the reader will confirm that John did not once mention the new covenant sign as the bread or wine. It's not there in his upper room account, but something else is. The sign of the new covenant according to John is found in the water.

All three of the synoptic gospels, Matthew, Mark, and Luke, gave us the feast of bread and wine, and the Church has locked on to that practice.

While John does express Jesus's covenant teachings of being fruitful in the vine, and how it is that we are called to abide so that we will bear fruit, his version of the New Covenant symbol of communion is not about bread and wine. It's about water.

As mentioned earlier, for John, the New Covenant ritual is practiced through the service of washing one another's feet. And initially it was offensive, and highly offensive to Peter, and perhaps it still is to us as well. I don't think it even ranks with the Roman Catholics branch of faith as a sacrament, though the Eucharist does. And I don't think main-line denominations practice it more than once a year, and I don't believe it is an ordinance for the Baptists. Largely it is safe to say we don't yet see the message nor the value of humbly bowing to cleanse each other. We could say it has fallen out of practice for obvious reasons of travel and fully shod feet. I don't think Jesus chose a symbol that would be so easily lost to culture. Rather, Jesus told the reluctant Peter that they would all understand it later. And Peter, as we will come to see by John's ultimate testimony at the end, does come to an understanding.

John celebrated the new covenant, as the oldest command, which was to love one another the way Jesus loved. Jesus then demonstrated what we will come to call the Father's blessing. What is the seal of the love in the new koinonia community? It is being together in service of water. This is the sign that we love God by keeping His command to love one another by gently tending to the feet.

We celebrate love by washing each other's feet. We help each other repent and come into sonship; we do it humbly, to draw mercy. Mercy filled the empty vessels with water that transformed into wine. Mercy is how Nicodemus is born again, and how a thirsty woman at a well repents and surrenders to love. Mercy sees a need and bows to care for each other in need. There is no condemnation; of course Jesus could see the filth of Peter's upcoming betrayal, as well as the scattering of the rest of his friends, but in mercy, Jesus just bowed and washed their runaway feet first.

John wrote:
Jesus disrobed.
He wrapped a towel around himself and poured water in a basin.
He knelt down on the floor.
He washed the disciples' feet.

It's a new order between men, but it is an old order between God and man. The disciples had never seen this arrangement before God. Jesus was seated in his Father's lap, and both He and God washed their feet.

He came to Simon Peter, whose name meant "rock"— the first of the disciples to identify Jesus as God and to confess He was the Christ out loud. This same Peter resisted the humility of Jesus until the Lord told him, "If I don't wash you, you have no part with me." And Peter asked Jesus to wash all of him. Jesus said he was already clean and only needed his feet washed. Jesus accepted that they didn't know what He was doing then and, afterwards, explained:

"You call me Teacher and Master, and rightly you say, for I am. So, if I am your Master and Teacher and have washed your feet, you also ought to wash each other's feet. I have given you an example that you should do for each other what I have done for you. Amen, amen. I tell you, a servant isn't greater than his master, and the one who is sent isn't greater than the one who sent him. If you know these things, you are blessed if you do them" (John 13:16).

Are we obedient to this kind of bow? Is this how we love each other? Do we water each other humbly? It is a serious meditation. Whose life would you love to support in a set up to disentangle them through prayer?

"If you know these things, you are blessed if you do them."

Later in the scriptures, Paul taught the Galatians to restore a sinning brother or sister gently (Galatians 6:1). We cannot be any more gentle than to draw close to the person in a bow and kiss or wash their dirty feet. Consider again how extravagantly Mary ministered to the Lord's feet. How far does one extend themselves in an intimate act of mercy?

In a personal workshop setting, we often see the gentleness of having a representative stand and mediate in a painful story of broken relationship so that we can find the hope of mercy and reconciliation. We are called to stand in the gap and represent for each other, to stand with the victim as well as the perpetrators. We might tend to the pain of a person kneeling at an altar for prayer, or reach out to the seeming god-forsaken on a park bench and allow mercy to unfold into thin space where the water flows, cleanses, and reveals a human person again as beloved. Water is a practice of mercy and restoration.

Rivers of Water Poured

In chapters 18-19, John portrayed how Our Great Representative became sin for us. The trial of the cosmos demonstrated the displacement of the heads of state as they put on a grand display of false authority. Between Pilate's fear and powerlessness as he wrestled to weakly confront the contradictions, and the revelation of bankruptcy in the temple, John described the bone dry emptiness of man's vain attempt to vessel life. In

Matthew's Gospel, Pilate washed his hands of the guilt of Christ's death. John didn't include that water practice as a sufficient declaration of hope. Everyone has a need that can't be solved by personal denial of responsibility.

"Gall" is the only drink mentioned is in chapter (19:29-30), where the executioners gave Jesus something that was neither water nor wine as a sorry comfort aid. It is a bitter contrast to what Jesus gave at the wedding of Cana. But he drank our gall.

There was a jar filled with vinegar in which someone dipped a sponge attached to a branch of hyssop and lifted it to his mouth. When Jesus had taken the vinegar, he said, "It is finished!" He then bowed his head and surrendered His spirit.

And that was how Jesus saved the world. What a great exchange. He paid the bill in full. Forgiveness is full and free. Consequently it is a small thing to wash one another's feet.

And finally, in verses 19:33-34 we read about the fulfillment of the Feast of Tabernacles to which Jesus referred earlier:

"But when they came to Jesus and saw that he was already dead, they did not break his legs. But one of the soldiers pierced his side with a spear, and at once there came out blood and water. He who saw it has borne witness—his testimony is true and he knows that he is telling the truth—that you also may believe. For these things took place that the Scripture might be fulfilled: Not one of his bones will be broken. And again another Scripture says, They will look on him whom they have pierced."

On the Terms of the Weeping Water

Chapter 20:9-18 states: *It was as if they could not fully grasp that this was indeed what was predicted in scripture, that Jesus was destined to rise up out of death. The disciples went away to face their own thoughts. But Maria remained facing the tomb, weeping. Then she stooped down and gazed into the tomb. She saw two angels dressed in dazzling white, seated, one at the head and the other at the feet where Jesus's body had been lying.*

They asked her, "Woman why are you weeping? She said to them, "They took my Lord away, and I do not know where they have put him." As she said this, she looked around and saw Jesus standing but did not immediately recognize him.

Jesus said to her, "Woman, why are you weeping? Who are you looking for?" She thought he was a gardener and said, "Sir, if you have taken him away, please tell me where you put him so that I may fetch him!"

Jesus said to her, "Mariam!"

She turned in her step and exclaimed "Raboni!" which is Hebrew for, "My teacher!"

Verse 17 is wild and stark delight. "You'll have to let go of me so that I may continue on to the Father God, and tell my brothers that I am ascending to my Father and your Father; to my God and your God!" (The Mirror Bible).

She could not easily let go. That part is not hard to comprehend. Everyone wants to hang on every now and then, maybe savor this startling recalibrating moment. But, not to digress much, it is a little humorous. Just when you think God has taken an eternally long time to move a mountain of death, once He did it, He was up and running with a hurried tone... "Stop weeping, we've got things to do. Everyone needs to know we have the same Father. Now go tell it on that Mountain!" I love that tone.

Water Finale

And now for the extra amazing grace of Chapter 21. As if the life, death, burial and resurrection was not the central theme of the Gospel and more than we would ever need, John takes us one step more into unspeakable riches of water. This is how John wraps up this record. And on the surface, it seems he is telling a story about Peter. And in part that is true but as a vehicle. We have to get beneath the surface with him because this is where we learn what John thinks about his fishing partner, his friend, Simon, his heart brother, who, like himself, was a basic nobody from a practically no-where fishing village. Again, John wrote from a pool of stories and gave us this as the last one in this record.

Let's recall first that according to John, Peter was first brought to the Messiah by his brother Andrew. Together with James and John, they were two sets of fishing brothers. Peter was later revealed and seen by Jesus as the Rock upon which He would build His Kingdom. Jesus sees us as we are in God. But apart from that confession of faith, Peter, neither understanding his call nor his Christ, made a series of mistakes, and upon tempting Jesus to discard the death destiny plan was then called Satan by Jesus. Matthew and Mark record that incident but John did not use his pen for that remembrance. It is an interesting sidebar if in fact "Mark" wrote for Peter and Mark's Gospel is the foundational record for the synoptic writings, that Peter did not discard that mistake. John told us Peter didn't want his feet washed, that Peter resisted Jesus's arrest by cutting a man's ear off, and that Peter denied Jesus during his trial. It would be a perfect time for John to step into that place of leadership and accuse his friend of forfeit since John alone had staying grace at the foot of the cross and was now "the Lord's mother's new son." But that is not what John does. In fact, he does something opposite. He follows Peter. So who is Peter to John after it's all said and done? How does this disciple see his Kingdom brother? How does he describe his friend to us the reader? Very well as we will soon see, and without one hint of disrespect.

Peter and John were from Caesarea Philippi, the tribal lands of Zebullun and Naphtali, tribes of Jacob by his concubines, certainly not of Judah. And though John was given a staying grace, this man had suffered his betrayal during the three days the Lord was in the grave. But upon resurrection Sunday, the first day of a new week, he and John both got a new faith life. Although Peter was slower on the uptake, John began to see Peter as who Jesus saw him to be—which is the definition of a friend. Together they ran to the tomb, John outran Peter and looked inside the tomb but waited, allowing Peter to go in first.

Why did he wait? As they left the site, John declared he believed.

Recall that Mary had been there too and encountered Jesus, who then commanded her to go tell his brothers He was alive.

Brothers?

Yes, and Mark's gospel specifically adds these words: tell his brothers and Peter. The writers let us know the state Peter was in. He was in need of water. Jesus had to retrieve and restore Peter to his forfeited confession.

"Go tell his disciples and Peter" (Mark 16:7). Was Peter thinking he had lost his place as a disciple?

Here, in the last chapter of John, watch how John's beaming respect deepens with tenderness and affection for his friend as we learn to see Peter the way John saw Peter. The following excerpt is from The Delitzsch Hebrew Gospels in John chapter 20.

Petros left along with the other disciple, and they went to the tomb. Both of them ran together, but the other disciple ran faster, passed Petros, and came to the tomb first. He peered inside and saw the burial garments lying there, but he did not enter. Shim'on Petros came after him. He entered the tomb and saw the burial garments lying there. The scarf that had been on His head was not lying beside the burial garments; instead, it was folded up by itself in a separate place. The other disciple who came to the tomb first also entered. He saw and believed. For they did not yet understand what was written, that He would surely rise from among the dead. The disciples returned and went home.

They are a dear pair. They hurried to the tomb at the same time; they both ran, but though John was faster, he yielded, and Peter went in first, then he followed, and believed; he added to this, saying "they" didn't yet understand what was written. John ran faster, but he did not overstep his friend Peter.

John celebrated for us the details of Mary's story at the tomb, the woman who anointed Jesus's feet with oil. This too was a shift in how their relationship dynamics changed in their reverence and revelation. John would not have otherwise included a woman's testimony with his own.

He also told us that Jesus met them in the upper room again and filled them with His Spirit, as promised both by Jesus and in accordance to the scriptures. The upper room is a beautiful way of noting transcendence. We are in a higher place with each other and God. It is where filling happens with Spirit—in an upper room—it's where feet are washed.

John told the reader briefly about Thomas in chapter 20:24. Since Thomas was absent when Jesus first came to them, Thomas wouldn't believe the disciples' story. But apparently they were able to persuade him to hang in there with them. Eight days later, Jesus appeared to them, entering through a locked door and invited Thomas to touch his scars and believe. It's a gift to let readers know how present Jesus always is by the Spirit, which was His promise. Christ can enter into our awareness and draw back our veil, opening Thin Space at any point in our time line.

So apparently with John, no failure is permanent so long as there is breath and water; water and the Spirit as Jesus told Nicodemus. Now, John comes full circle, back to another large body of water, not a river Jordan with the Baptizer, but this time at sea with Peter the fisherman who transcends into the Rock.

So much happened at this sea. Boats were filled with fish, people were fed, storms were calmed, Jesus walked on it like he owned it, and, after the resurrection, Peter went back to the water and told his friends that he was going to go fishing again. Half of the disciples followed him. There were seven of them.

What was Peter thinking at this point? Was he reinstated yet? Was he useful to God? If Peter couldn't follow, surely he couldn't lead. All he could do was go back to what he knew. He could go fishing. If the Lord was back and was going to do something in Israel, perhaps He didn't need anyone like Peter after all.

Judas had taken his own life in despair, having been fully warned, he betrayed him anyway. Peter was alive, but might just slip on out into yesterday because, apparently, that is exactly where he still was — gone fishing. Now the seven of them fished all night and caught nothing… just like old times.

But in the morning, after the dark was over—Jesus.

What might we call that?

An arrival?

No. Jesus, alive again, had already demonstrated that He could enter locked doors and had had a conversation with Thomas that indicated that He can hear you when you think He's not there, as if He is there, even when you aren't seeing Him.

Does He show up on the shore?

Not if He is always everywhere. He just shows off on the shore beside the sea that He owns, and He gives Peter a do-over in front of the six.

The sweetest words of Jesus, "Children," He asked in verse 5, "do you have any fish?" Children and fish... Children: this is a word John later turned into poetry in his next writing in 1 John. Children? Who must be talking in the voice of Christ now? With God we are always small.

Jesus had previously referred to them as brothers and friends. Now he called them children. The Father was present, and full-on revealing Himself as fully present to them and coming nearer to His children.

"No," they answered Him.

"Cast the net on the right side of the boat, and you will find some."

He gave a simple familiar instruction to reassure them of his presence with them, as if nothing with God had changed in His affection. As an aside, there is always a right side of the boat. We are about to see Peter get married to Mr. Right. On the right side is where the leader guides.

"So they cast a net, and now they were not able to haul it in because of the quantity of fish. That disciple whom Jesus loved (John) said to Peter, "It is the Lord!" When Simon Peter heard that it was the Lord, he put on his outer garment, for he was stripped for work, and John writes that Peter THREW HIMSELF INTO THE SEA." Emphasis mine. Peter went full body into the *water*. On the left would be the only place left for Peter to jump.

Oh for a swim in these sacred waters. Peter threw himself into the sea. What an image of immersion. John had been baptized by the prophet in the beginning. Peter had wanted Jesus to wash him all over in the upper room. Now after his betrayal God gave him a new chance to mean it. He threw his whole self into all of the water. Dear Peter meant it with all his desperate heart.

Jesus, who had borrowed Peter's boat to preach and then sent Peter fishing as a 'thanks' and overwhelmed him with fish, gave Peter a similar sign. After a night of futility, Jesus met him there again in the same way. In a different Gospel Peter had been so humbled and convicted the first time he asked Jesus to depart from him because he was a sinful man, Luke 5. But not this time. He is all in.

Imagine taking a deep gasp of air and diving in like a fish hurrying to the risen Lord's shoreline. Peter had wanted his whole self washed, and now he got it.

These are the blessed waters of the deep that the Holy Spirit hovered over in the beginning of creation in Genesis 1:1. These are the deep waters of "starting over" in the days of Noah, that the Spirit flew over as a dove looking for a place to land. These are the waters of baptism that gave another dove a place to land on Jesus, the Son in whom God was well pleased. And now Peter gets his wish to be completely submerged.

Exactly what happened in the moments between Peter's arrival on the shore and the return of the other six disciples with the great catch of fish, we don't know. But we can assume Jesus and Peter had some private time together. Neither Peter nor John report on that tender conversation. Some things are still private, just between one heart and another. Peter was a child of the Father of Jesus, now and forever and I'm sure the Lord helped him understand the new family order.

Once they were all gathered together on shore, Jesus started giving his dear runaway orphans some words to help them come into koinonia fellowship with one another. He established Peter in his destiny. Simon, son of Jonah, became fully identified with the Rock of God. It's almost like a coronation as a servant leader.

Jesus already had breakfast ready, and He fed them. What he did for the thousands he did again for His crew. Then Jesus asked Simon Peter— son of John (Jonah)—if he loved Him more than these (John 21:15). Defining to what the 'these' referred is one way to widen the awareness of the heart. It's a perfect question for anyone, fisherman or otherwise; do you love me more than the fish? Do you love me more than you love these other disciples? Do you love me more than you think they love me? There had been that moment in Peter when he said he loved Jesus enough to die with him… "Others may leave, but not me!"

"Yes, Lord. You know that I love you."

Jesus said, "Feed my lambs."

"Simon, son of Jonah, do you love me?" He asked again and left off "more than these."

"Yes, Lord. You know that I love you."

"Take care of my sheep."

First lambs, now sheep; first feed, now take care. He is inching Simon onto new ground. Is feeding and caring for others the definition of loving Jesus?

"Simon, son of Jonah, do you love me?"

Peter was grieved because He asked him for a third time. But hadn't he denied the Master three times—at least? It's a very kind act of mercy to let him declare his love as many times as he denied it.

Water flows. Water heals. Water satisfies thirst, it cleanses, it brightens, and it clears things up. The Lord is spiritually washing Peter's feet again, now, not to mediate him to God or even himself but to mediate him to merciful treatment of his beloved.

"Lord, you know everything."

Ah, and here he leans into that very fact. The Lord was the one who told Peter he would betray Him. He had known the truth then, Peter knew the Lord knew the truth now. Beautiful. Is that not the very thing Jesus needed to establish in the heart of Peter before he gave him the promise he was about to reveal, a very special promise.

Of course God knows all things, and He knew for sure and for certain how it would be the next time it came right down to it and Peter was tempted to deny God. John 21:18-19, ESV: *"Truly, truly, I say to you, when you were young, you used to dress yourself and walk wherever you wanted, but when you are old, you will stretch out your hands, and another will dress you and carry you where you do not want to go."* This He said to show by what kind of death he was to glorify God. And after saying this, He said to him, 'Follow me.' "

I am certain it was a promise, not a warning, and not a test to get ready for. It was a promise. A promise targets a fear and a stronghold, a 'what if I blow it again?' concern. What was previously, and was likely still, his worst fear would one day become his own great privilege to 'mean it.' Jesus knew all things, and he knew Peter would suffer later in life, and he would do so faithfully and die for Jesus. When that time came, Peter would have rock-solid, fearless faith.

Church history tells us it happened, and that Peter was faithful. And he asked to be hung upside-down in honor and humility for Jesus. His faith had to grow and it did. We can see his faith grow through the accounts in the Acts of the Apostles.

Just as Eve was given a promise that her seed would crush the serpent's head, God gave Peter a living Word, that he would face another test and would mount in strength and not deny his Christ. This was personal good news. Jesus promised Peter he would not fail to "represent" in his own death. He would die full of faith. And he did.

John finished his account with Peter's new concern for what would happen to John. John loved Peter. Peter loved John. There were no Cain and Abel rivalries in the Kingdom, here the brotherhood was solid. Koinonia is the rule of love. "If I want him to live until I return, what is that to you? Follow me." John was in God's care, just as Peter was, and just as we all are. We have one Father, one Savior, one Baptism, one Spirit, one Church! Forty days after the resurrection the Spirit fell in mass in Jerusalem and Peter was filled with the Spirit's impartation of the gift of preaching and in one day three thousand confessed faith in Christ in Jerusalem, at the Temple, under the eye of those who had called for the Lord's execution, and the Church was born.

Persecution was not far behind. The gracious martyrs in the early church paved the way for us to hear and believe what they saw was true. They were all in and they demonstrated that they feared nothing and no one. They simply followed the Lord Jesus. Fear of man is a dis-order from which they were free. So what did happen to John after all?

He was also persecuted for his faith and was finally put in jail on an island called Patmos. On an island he was completely surrounded by water. There he encountered the presence of the transcendent Jesus, more grand than on the mountain with Peter and James. What he wrote became the last book of the Bible, Revelation, and it was an encouragement to seven churches who were suffering torment and persecution for the faith. Again, with math for weight, it is important to notice that five out of the seven churches were unfaithful and they had left their first love Jesus and were tempted to lose heart, faith and purpose. But John was given images to know how to encourage them with a fitting Word and restore them to love and worship and a sustaining hope that the end of hard times was imminent and the hope of an eternal future in a new world was certain.

James, John's brother, was killed by those who killed Jesus; Paul, who was converted from Judaism by a direct encounter with the risen Lord, was also persecuted and was beheaded. We are Christians today because they all bowed and drank living water. After they bowed, they stood upright, strong, full of faith, and marched the Gospel all over the known world. They give us a the true meaning for the word rock stars.

It all started around the water. "In the beginning, God created the heavens and the earth. Now the earth was chaos and waste, darkness was on the surface of the deep, and the Ruach Elohim [Holy Spirit] was hovering upon the surface of the water. Then God said, 'Let there be light!.' " (Genesis 1:1-3)

Let us continue around the water.

Be baptized in the waters of repentance.
We must be born of water and the Spirit.
Just bow. And then get up in power.

Chapter 11: Mary's Wish

*"If God is love, He is, by definition, something more than mere kindness.
And it appears, from all the records, that though He has often rebuked us
and condemned us, He has never regarded us with contempt.
He has paid us the intolerable compliment of loving us,
in the deepest, most tragic, most inexorable sense."*
– C.S. Lewis, The Problem of Pain

A Word About Suffering

The list of ways humans can hurt each other is long. Protection against suffering is one of the reasons why we tribe up, and, it is also why we divide up. On the playground, one boy takes up for another. In politics and religion, it is the same. Suffering often demands a protector, and with it, a prosecutor. In private stories, even in times when "it didn't happen to us," we still identify deeply with the injured party. We do not so much identify with the "sinner" or offender, or the guilty unless there is a favor that defends them regardless. This is an issue of exclusion and inclusion on many a faulty line.

In truth, suffering is felt across the landscape of the entire whole. But the pain of injury creates gaps too large for us to bridge unless we have a faith as big as Jesus. Without faith in God's own commitment to forgive, suffering creates a relational divide, and with it, an idea of an "us" against a "them." When the suffering crosses the boundaries of the unspeakable, the loss is catastrophic and can last many generations, effectively hiding the beginnings. Closing the gap that is beyond repair seems impossible. And humanely speaking, an honest person may concede that it is.

Suffering injustice threatens to make us lose quite a bit. We may lose the sense of our self that we once knew. It threatens to suspend faith in our community, our place in it, and the purpose of relationships. But at its worst, the faith-crippling kind of personal suffering makes us accuse God or deny the idea of God altogether. The 'How could God let this happen?' question seems like the most reasonable question. The temptation to deny God or His goodness is natural when the gods have mis-represented Him. Nevertheless, all of it, according to Calvary, is very personal to God; this is the true crux of the ultimate matter—His suffering.

When it comes to the arena of suffering, God might seem a liability instead of an asset depending upon one's wish. Given He does support justice but will not leave us the burden of vengeance, we must seek to understand Him here. Here, His wish matters to the well being of our soul. Praising God is easy when we are hosting gratitude for delightful events. But when we are suffering, humans ask, "My God, my God, why have you forsaken me?"

And if we are the cause of suffering—if we are the betrayer—the perpetrator—or the coward—or we simply did not have the right information and came to the whole thing sideways—we come to another kind of crossroads and experience guilt, accusation and condemnation. These demand punishment, and we find ways to suffer with or without the assistance of a judgment.

That said, actually, I'm not going to discuss the long varieties of particular kinds of suffering. We would love a book just on trauma. What we have in this chapter speaks directly to the point of orders between victims, perpetrators and witnesses.

In the general market place, books abound addressing personal trauma from the point of view of the victim, not the whole. What I am going to speak to here in this chapter is the entire whole of trauma. There are people on many sides of a trauma. How does the whole come together in a trauma that completely divides?

Seeing the whole terrain—which is nearly impossible to do in blinding pain—is key to healing. So we have to enlarge the picture because in any traumatic injury there are not just two parties; there are as many parties as there are witnesses, and all have reactions. From those reactions, different ideas emerge regarding needs for safety, justice, vengeance, escape, and other crisis management strategies. We have to widen the lens to include many other layers of entanglements in witnesses so as to appreciate, not only the enormous weight of a trauma as it reverberates across a relational landscape, but also discover the only solution. And we do have one—oh we do have one and it applies to us all.

So let me offer first an example of simple hurts and simple healings for contrast before we go to the crushing story.

Simple Healing:

When or if an injury is only between two people, and is a simple injury, guidance often finds them and enables them to address their pain privately and mend the relationship. This happens often. People can face things in a Field of Grace, or on bended knee at an altar, or in a moment of clarity at a picnic bench beside a lake, or in a subway, or at a check-out counter buying a box of ice cream. Enlightenment can rise up spontaneously from an insight into a beautiful book or movie, or in over hearing a comment a stranger makes to someone. Bing! Light shows up and something makes sense and the heart opens up again where pain had closed it, and the thaw melts the hardness off and away and a peace rises.

If a person isn't overly focused on condemnation or retribution and is even half-way gazing at someone with a gentle wonder in a larger mental space, Thin Spaces can open up and, with them comes a gift of insight for healing.

It's that hard over-focus that holds so much tension, demand or judgment, that says healing is not an option yet. But in that softer place, when we are "looking" from a safe distance—and not too hard—we relax our eyes into a gaze, the light shines in, and can give both parties a place with peace.

Now then, it's those moments that prepare the two for a divine appointment. When they just so happen to run into each other and the regret is obvious, reconciliation is spontaneous because forgiveness has already been granted to them.

Grace comes in quietly, tender like small cat's feet and gentles two people back into warmer regard. That's the hidden kindness of God. He "happens" in and with us. God helps the two contain their grief and heal in love. Hurt is not an issue anymore. As big of a deal as it was, or seemed, it wasn't bigger than the Love that swallowed them—whole.

Many times though, suffering is not just between two and it feels entirely destructive and impossible to navigate when the pain exceeds the love one has to cover the bill. Additionally, when others become identified with the injury, support for reconciliation may be lost. Even if Grace would miraculously mend the hurt, the observers may still so identify with vengeance that they keep a division alive. No one will allow for it. The compounded losses make healing appear worthless. When there are no supporting resources, there seems to be no way to recover.

Compounded Grief

There are magnitudes of hurts shared vicariously where there are witnesses. In the compounded injuries, the unhealed divide grows, people fall in the holes, and opportunities for larger conflicts in families, communities, cultures and nations grow until war emerges. It's piled on. Everybody knows. Everybody is talking about it. National discourse explodes. Afterwards, or when it seems like it is all said and done, the "victor"—whoever that seems to be—writes a slanted story but not the whole story. Forgetting that there are another dozen sides to consider and that we are living in systems upon systems, ages upon ages, a string of epochs and the whole truth is lost from history. We are not well informed yet. We are missing the greater number of details of an injury. And now we don't even want to hear from the other side, they've been silenced. So, how do we even begin to enter into the larger story of any story of suffering?

I could say we practice. I might say we determine to open our heart to see and hear more than twelve sides of a situation, but that's a tall order. I'd like to say we develop an interest in things we do not yet know that we don't know, and we include mystery as potentially knowable. Or I could insist that we begin gathering everyone up, listening to more voices, and though we assume our roster is complete, we keep the gate open for a bigger revelation because at any time, some secret could come out and change the entire story. Widening the lens is much of what I have already discussed in the first eight chapters of this book. However we still have a problem. Our relationships are little micro stories in the greater cosmos. In the micro all of our entanglements, no matter how straight we get our lines, they are still a house of cards unless the greater field has a quantum change. And it has but if we can't connect to it, we are without some needed glue. We can and we absolutely should set up our stories and everyone else's no matter how traumatic they are, until we find life altering insights and reformations. But at the end of the day, as I said at the first, Love is not a thing. Love is the person of God. And until our spirits come online with His spiritually, the fruit of the Holy Spirit of Love can not grow big enough in the realm of the soul to swallow up the whole of us. Love grows into us. So we don't simply need our micro house put in order, we also need our spirit to awake and hold our house of cards in an indestructible place. How do we get there? A cosmic lens helps swallow death.

There is that one ultimately important story of greatest suffering to which we will now give our attention. We will survey that suffering from multiple points of view, not directly as we most often have, but indirectly in the round of witnesses. How was it for "the others?"

There is no suffering so extreme, neither in holocausts nor earthquakes, that rivals or exceeds what transpired at a place called The Skull. None. It is there that we discover a champion who shows us himself as the ultimate victim of Adam's judgment, and it is there in those dialogs that we have a way to come to see ourselves and others in some unexpected ways.

We can even find slivers of our own determination to perpetrate judgment if we dare to explore a few relevant slants other than our personal point of view of the central sufferer. We have it on good report as to what He thought about His judges. So I am venturing to widen the frame into a larger gaze at the suffering all around Him. This will not be done with graphs, but through a fictional narrative.

So at a risk of doing violence to something exponentially grander than Michelangelo's sculpture of David, I am daring to present a partial piece of fiction. Scripture provides a roster of people. But what those people were thinking and feeling in the hours of Jesus's death and in the hours between Friday and the resurrection are undisclosed.

Students of Scripture will quickly recognize where I have paired quotes and people into new arrangements. But readers unfamiliar with the stories may not know just how far I went when I added to the text by creating a scene during the hours between Friday and Sunday. In going this far, I've fictionalized some very real sacred saints of faith. I trust the readers to prayerfully reference the Gospel records for themselves in personal study in order to come to their own convictions about the relationships of the people in this story.

Here is where we transcend the "me" and move towards an expansive "we." Suffering is not forever, but for a season it displays faith like nothing else—and this is not even our own faith, actually, but God's. And God had faith. He had faith in His Son and His Son had faith in His Father and this is where we find faith and define it as a gift offered to us.

A suffering heart is a risky place to tuck in an entire kingdom, but if we cannot meet Him there, meeting Him anywhere else doesn't count for as much. We have to give everything a place, especially suffering and be sanctified by the faith that comes through it.

Suffering is what puts God on trial along with everyone else. His is the only trial that counts. Everything else, as it turns out, is about this gift. This is the foundation that holds our house of cards secure. Without it, no order matters. Orders don't exist outside of the Love that is expressed in them.

Welcome to the Field of Grief.

Mary's Wish:

Two men who were about the same age met eye-to-eye in the strangest of conditions, almost mirrors of one another. Each was a representative of his homeland. One man stood as a representative of the strength of the Roman Empire, hand-picked by Caesar for his military success, for his mind, and for his allegiance.

The other man was also a representative, He represented the strength of the unknown power of the universe. He was not only hand-picked, but He was the hand itself.

One stood with the symbols of dominance; the other stood with the symbols of sacrifice. One stood to take life, and the other to give it. Both wore their symbols of allegiance on their backs.

The centurion was in command of many soldiers, and at the moment, one small squad was obediently at his side. Today though, was the first day he had to face his allegiance to the survival of the fittest. The company that surrounded him on all sides was closing in on him like four walls with only one door. Each breath felt more and more labored as the scales began to fall off his own eyes.

It had taken a lifetime to get to where he was, and now he was confronted with someone who represented an entirely different source of life. Having heard from colleagues the personal stories of inconceivable miracles attributed to a man now condemned, he was increasingly disturbed by the whole situation.

As a Roman, he was an outsider to the religious thought life of Jews. Watching this man of holy reputation suffer a crucifixion which he now had to execute, turned his stomach, and this was a new disturbance. The two representatives made repeated eye contact. Something inside the centurion wanted to stare hard at the man who displayed to him an entirely alien set of values in hopes of gaining one glimpse by which he might begin to understand the dark.

Surveying the terrain, it was obvious that the religious elite who had called for this execution had much more in common with the other two criminals who were being crucified. And they all had everything in common with Rome.

He looked at his own hands, studying them for a moment. They were trimmed clean, but suddenly all the blood he'd spilled flashed in his mind's eye as the familiar sound of hammers now began to drive him out of his identified place in this world.

Two of the three convicted men writhed, fought, resisted, and required tie-downs. The middle man laid still to receive the nails. Although some did this once they had given up and wanted it to be over, none ever prayed for the people surrounding them. The man's voice of mourning seemed painfully loud in the Roman's head. He tried to avoid hearing Him by focusing on the mockery being hurled at Him by the Jewish nobility who'd gone to great lengths to have Him destroyed. But that avoidance only drove him back to face the representative. It was hard to understand the Jewish people. The only resting place for his attention was the woman, and that was another agony.

It was especially difficult to watch the man's own mother bear witness to the vitriol. But pity for her felt like the only honest emotion he could consider in this incredible situation. Regardless of a man's guilt or innocence, it is a horror for all families, but to observe the mother of innocence tenderly was the one meditation he could offer to Jesus, who was gaining his respect by the second. The Roman wondered from what kind of family Jesus came. It was a surprise to see a woman of no clear means.

Mary followed Him, step by step, as Jesus had weakly climbed the hill with the help of another man. It was a strain for the Roman to hear her pray under her breath. She whispered verses that held her as the iron was hammered. The pitiable woman fell onto the ground as soon as her son was lifted up. Once in place, she crawled on her hands and knees to grasp onto the stake herself and wept under the weight of the unthinkable as His blood dripped onto her head and back. Sorrow beat upon her in every drop. After the sounds of hammers were over, the weeping, groaning, the heckling, and the mockery of bystanders and the elders were a swirl of madness.

The centurion wondered if she would let go of reality as she rocked back and forth in a child's position. Both the untried as well as the condemned criminals all around had one choral demand, 'If you are the son of God, save yourself!' and 'Save us as well!' The woman was pummeled by their anthems.

The Roman was unnerved by the entire scene. He'd seen people killed for a lot of things, but never for extreme goodness. Israel's national leadership clearly had a blind spot. They chose to put a known murderous radical back on the streets to have this do-gooder unceremoniously slaughtered.

Looking at the crucified man in the center, he got it, or at least one thing he understood. Given the chance, this is what they would love to do to him as a Roman centurion. He represented two sides in one frame. Guilty were all around. He wanted to leave—but he was held there.

When his eyes rested on her, though, he felt a still point—for His sake, he would consider her. It was one small thing, but it was mercy.

The hung representative prayed intermittently and began asking for pardon, not for Himself but for them, which also included the Romans. He wondered how the man's mother was tolerating that.

Whether he wanted to be included in the intercessions or not, he knew he was part of the "them" for whom the victim prayed. Who prays for others in the middle of their own suffering? The centurion wondered how that felt for the woman.

Mary seemed to be here alone. She had followed her son here. Now, having parted company with her other children, she'd never been so alone in her life. She was lost beneath her firstborn. Even within His own family, among His own siblings, they'd become estranged. The gap between one thing and another had widened beyond her ability to straddle it. Now, her own soul rose up and smote her with regrets. One specific memory made her want to burrow herself into the ground head first and worm her way into the dirt and hide.

In the recent years, once the crowds had grown so large, it had become hard to understand what her son had in mind for their country. Being hailed the "Son of David" by so many people yet lacking plans for military campaigns made Him an oddity politically. She believed He was King. But His large gatherings had been healing work for the body and revival work in terms of the laws of love for the soul of their people. His compassionate inclusion of the sick among the Romans suggested a union that was untenable for their country, and her other children rejected him for putting them all at risk.

But now if there was one day she wished she had done differently, it was the day when she and her other sons had tried to save Jesus by reasoning with Him regarding the growing political tension. They wanted Him to do things differently; He seemed to be going in a totally different direction than what seemed right.

He would not heed, and nor would she.

Jesus had refused to stop what He was doing to follow His mother.

He refused to follow His younger brothers as well.

And they had refused to enter into His circle.

They had remained outside.

They would not follow Him where He was going.

And this was now their worst nightmare.

This was why they had reached an impasse.

When word reached her of the previous night's events, the looks on the faces of her sons said it all. 'We told you this would happen. He is an offense to the ruling body. They'll kill Him, not crown Him.'

But what vexed her now were His words that went unheeded. It was that sorry day that she wished she could do over—He always said what He meant!

He had said, "This is my mother and my brothers. All who obey the will of my Father are my mothers and brothers and sisters."

The idea was painful then, but now it was unbearable. He chose His Father, and His Father chose this?

Bowing and broken, she felt her life become ghostly thin. Everything in her world as she knew it was over. The promise was dwarfing her. He was executed for failing to save Israel from Rome. As His mother, she had failed to save Him. He would refuse to escape this. These were the terms He embraced.

Was she actually hoping and praying the very thing the crowd mocked Him for, that He should save Himself, put on a power show, stun the crowd, and show Rome and Israel that He was the overcomer? Would He not make them all bow, or if for no other reason than her pain, would He not at least stop her suffering? "Why are you forsaking me?" she ached.

She heard Him pray for them: "Father forgive them! They do not know what they are doing."

Mary wept.

The hammering continued. Someone tacked up fresh ridicule: a sign was hung over the man's cruelly-crowned head, reading 'King of the Jews.' The centurion read it in every language and spit on the ground; everyone disowns everyone if the price is right.

Herod and Pilate were standing there together on speaking terms, and the centurion was disgusted. Sometimes, how a thing looks from an outsider's point of view offers a worthy slant for consideration. He noticed himself as an outsider now. He hardly felt the shift, but now he noticed another man staring at the broken woman.

John's soul was newly shocked by all the ways human authority could display evil under the emblem of righteousness. As his eyes fell to her pain-bound frame, he was struck in his own heart as a traitor. John's mind flashed to the same exact day over which Mary was in anguish. Staring at her brokenness, he realized how his pride had actually swelled when Jesus seemed to have chosen him and the other disciples above His own family. Was that what it meant to be chosen? To be above others, a better-than?

He raised his eyes to the Lord in regret.

Soldiers bartered for Jesus's clothes, and John's mind spun in returning fragments of Scriptures. "They will divide my clothing among them, and over my garments they will cast lots." He had never had a mind for this prophecy—no one did—but it was all happening right now. The soldiers wanted His robes. Everyone wants robes of righteousness, and no one minds bartering for them. John felt like he was one of them.

John's eyes fell to Mary again as conviction emerged all over his face. He'd wanted some nicer robes too. His own mother negotiated for her boys to have position in the Lord's Kingdom. He and his whole family had slighted the Lord's mother and her family. He saw her now in her own unspeakable shattering, and Jesus saw John see.

John wept.

Jesus spoke to his mother and His disciple together.

"Dear woman, here is your son."

And to John He said, "Here is your mother."

Dear woman? She heaved her sobs uncontrollably.

John fell to the ground and cradled her in her loss, and the blood continued to fall. John took her deeply into his heart at that moment, as a surging wave of compassion swept over him. The centurion wished he had that right.

Mockery vanished when the sky became dark. Fear drove some home. Nature expressed her grief as the rocks cried out and the earth quaked. One of the other crucified men saw the universe's allegiance and ventured a declaration of the Lord's innocence, praying to his neighbor in death, "Remember me when you come into your kingdom."

Hope hung in the dark.

The Lord heard his prayer, and answered, "Today, you will be with me in paradise."

The criminal wept.

Jesus hummed a bar right out of the soul of the Jewish hymn book, singing what all were thinking, "My God, my God, why have you forsaken me?" It was as if that song belonged to everyone at that moment: the centurion, Mary, John, and the criminal. It is every sufferer's song. Why, God? Even the earth sang the cry of the suffering heart, 'Why have you forsaken me?!'

Resonance fell and spread over everyone, quieting them into the hush of their world's own sorrow.

John drew his mother back, leaning her into himself as they bore up under the sacrificial song. They knew the tune better now. And together they rocked, and ached and eked out the song with Him, hardly noticing He was mysteriously hosting the hope of the second verse.

Numbered as the 22nd of David's psalms, and written 1,000 years prior, but for this very occasion, the prophetic song reminded the sad worshipers of one thing. This was the unspeakable, unalterable, predestined plan of the God who, in fact, in this song, promised to never leave them. The words, riddled with mystery unfolded inside them, now that they needed to hear them.

When they came to the end of the psalm, John saw Jesus more clearly. In a flash, the image of the dove rushed out at him as the very presence of the Father of Jesus. "This is my Son!" God Himself pierced His way into John's being. His addled brain recalled the Baptizer, who had told him, "Look! The Lamb of God who takes away the sin of the world!" And at the mountain where Jesus was transfigured, the words, "This is my son; listen to Him." flew through John's mind. The dove—the dove that first came at Jesus's baptism, that dove was taking flight.

Then the Lord said, "It is finished," and He left.

His body was as empty as His robes.

He vacated.

"Where I am going you can not go," Jesus had said the night before. And to the criminal, "Today, you will be with me in paradise." How can this all fit? Where was the Dove going to light next?

Soldiers broke the legs of the criminals. Seeing Jesus had died, they pierced His side instead. Blood and water fell. The centurion's new allegiance was evident now as he confessed aloud, "Surely, this was the Son of God." He took down his Lord with tenderness, surprising the soldiers as he motioned for them to back off as he raised up the stake alone to gently lower and release the body of Jesus and lay it onto the dear woman's lap. An odd chord of four appeared there together as one love: a Roman centurion, a dear woman, a Jewish son, and a dead representative.

Mary could hardly scoop him up the way she used to, but she held him one last time to rock him while seated in His own blood. She flashed back and forth to times past in his childhood when holding Him was easier.

A memory of him as a baby gripped her now with reality. She and Joseph met a prophet when they'd taken their newborn to the Temple for the ritual covenant of circumcision. Simeon had blessed her and prayed, "Now you may let your servant pass away according to your word—my Master—in peace. For my eyes have seen your salvation that you have prepared before all of the peoples: light to illuminate the eyes of the nations and the majesty of your people Israel." And then he had said to her directly, *"See, this is affixed as an obstacle and restoration for many in Israel and as a sign of contention. And a sword will pierce your soul, so that the thoughts of the hearts of many will be revealed." (Luke 2:29-35).*

Her gaping wound was laying in her lap, now circumcised completely: ribbony slices all over Him, without a patch of untorn flesh to be seen. A shadow hung over her as she wept and laid her hand across His side—the Master—of nations.

She saw the centurion differently now. She pitied him, seeing his deplorable "service" to his country in light of the suffering servant representing a Kingdom that was not of this world.

John recalled the way Jesus responded in the garden the night before, when he healed the man's ear that Peter had cut off. He had no doubt that the Lord could have called a military response of angels that no one could have imagined nor survived. He tendered to the centurion, too.

The centurion wept. Suddenly he was called away.

Gingerly Mary began to de-crown the lovely brow of wicked thorns. One by one by one she snapped the long dead needles from the broken twisted vine until the vine was free. Then she slowly and with more ease withdrew the cruel thorns until she could sweep his head unhindered with her palm, smoothing his hair, wiping his brow, washing His cheeks with her tears, kissing His nose, begging Jesus to come back to her as a baby again so she could be a better mother.

Soon though, and too soon for her liking, the centurion was back again but now with two other men. An unlikely threesome respectfully slowed their gait as they began to approach. One hung a half-step behind so as to not actually look at John nor the dear woman in the face. The other, Joseph of Arimathea, was the first to ask Pilate for the Lamb, and the centurion had confirmed Jesus was dead. It was time to retrieve Him out of his mother's hungry arms. She and the rain had rinsed his face of the spit and dirt thrown his way, and she had spread her head-covering over his nakedness and folded His arms close to His chest and swaddled him as if He were still alive and only napping.

Bowing in respect, Joseph spoke tenderly. "Dear woman, please, let me care for His body. I'll take Him to my own tomb." She recoiled, unconscious of what she was demanding in a mother's resistance. For her own wish, she might have sat there 'til the Lord returned, as if holding herself ransom in a demand of new terms. But too much love and humility surrounded her despair.

In a softer whisper that strained her ear, he continued, "I believe He will not be there long. We can trust Him. It has all been written exactly as we have seen it today. Let us both trust Him now. He knows what He is doing. This part is finished. We must look to what is next. Come, let us go take our next steps together." Joseph's eyes met John's for assistance to persuade her to move.

John gave a slight movement, and she took a deep haggard breath and burst into fresh aching tears. They waited. Finally the rain stopped. A ray of sun found its way to her bowed head as nature offered to fill her tired heart with no small wonder that she was indeed completely surrounded by representatives from all corners of estrangements. And she was held in mercy. She softened, and the second man stepped into that open moment and began rearranging his Lord's body to wrap him so that he could be easily carried.

Nicodemus's eyes met John's, and the silence was golden as the present shaft of sunlight pierced their darkness. He could barely give himself permission to stand in their shadows, let alone in their raw presence. John saw the hurt and flashed back to his own judgment of the weak, half-hearted, coward, elitist man of hours ago, who had given up a defense of the Lamb the night before, and John returned a pitifully downturned smile of condolence to his guilty brother. He then recalled the long night of questions Nicodemus had puzzled through with Jesus many months before. John went to stand beside him in compassion and solidarity with mercy, and the four men wrapped Jesus for the short walk to the garden.

Several others watching at a distance followed them to the garden tomb; most sat outside. In the shadows of the dimly-lit tomb, they worked together to clean His wounds and cover Him in myrrh and aloes. The dear woman studied His full grown feet, now so damaged. She effortlessly counted her baby's toes like the first time she held Him, while the men tended His body.

She placed a gentle touch to pause Joseph, so she could tend to Jesus's incredible opened side for a moment. Bowels of mercy were exposed, shreds of torn flesh were lose but as she and the men smoothed, cleaned, and wrapped him in ointments and fabric, the smells of all the spices took her back to Bethlehem, and she began to tilt with a bow to His destiny as she reconsidered the gifts of the wise men brought so long ago.

Nicodemus, now standing in the grace of a new company of saints, began to quote a text from Zechariah 13. He stood with a small gathering of people outside the tomb and, with a bereaved gaze, began to recite the old mysterious text with fresh timidity and hope—to faithful women.

"On that day, a fountain will be opened to the house of David and the inhabitants of Jerusalem, to cleanse them from sin and impurity. On that day, I will banish the names of the idols from the land, and they will be remembered no more, declares the Lord Almighty. I will remove both the prophets and the spirit of impurity from the land. and if anyone still prophesies, his father and mother, to whom he was born, will say to him, 'You must die because you have told lies in the Lord's name. When he prophesies, his own parents will stab him. On that day, every prophet will be ashamed of his prophetic vision. He will not put on a prophet's garment of hair in order to deceive. He will say, I am not a prophet. I am a farmer; the land has been my livelihood since my youth. If someone asks him..."

Nicodemus, now longing only to be a farmer, held back his emotions but proceeded on through the text:

"If someone asks him, 'What are these wounds on your body?' then he will answer, 'The wounds I was given at the house of my friends.'"

Nicodemus wept.

Joseph continued the recitation in a stronger voice, full of tender hope but without volume.

"Awake, O sword, against my shepherd, against the man who is close to me! declares the Lord Almighty. Strike the shepherd, and the sheep will be scattered, and I will turn my hand against the little ones. In the whole land, declares the Lord, two-thirds will be struck down, and perish; yet one-third will be left in it. This third I will bring into the fire; I will refine them like silver and test them like gold. They will call on my name, and I will answer them; I will say, 'They are my people,' and they will say, 'The Lord is our God.'"

Mary, the dear woman of God, was nearly touched. She was in the midst of His broken people. They belonged together now. In the midst of unspeakable horror and mystery, they began to see each other with weary but softer eyes. They broke company for the time being—but were together in heart.

One step at a time, their feet moved across the ground as two parted from the rest. One step at a time, the dear woman went with John to a new location for the first night of the rest of her life. The Sabbath rest was upon them. It was time to leave the Son of God to do His work in the grave, a work only God could do. This was the Sabbath to which all others referred. She did not know it yet, but this Sabbath would become to her the one and only Sabbath. The centurion and others rolled a stone over the grave.

The chaos of the town was now numb for the rest of Passover. The

Angel of Death had taken the Lamb and all He represented to that place no one else could go. The firstborn of creation was dead, and everyone else was safer than they yet knew.

His blood had been shed on the door posts of Mount Zion, the city of God, and all who yearned to live in the New Jerusalem were being processed in a transaction that was planned before the earth's creation.

The yet carnal priest, Caiaphas, was in as much need as the Egyptian Pharaoh of yesteryear, as much as the deadly Caesar in Rome. He unknowingly presided over slaughtering the Lamb of God, knowing only that it was better for one to die for the many, than the many to die for the one.

God had delivered up for humanity a scapegoat who was making His way to fill mankind's grave with Himself. Meanwhile, the deceived Caiaphas had revealed on that day, to Jew and Gentile alike, that mankind, all men everywhere, were slaves of violence, drunk with power, and sick with pride, from the least of these to the greatest. By gutting Jesus, he had bankrupted the structures of false religion, exposing their blindness. He had set the stage for a new viewing of faith in God. New wineskins were on the way, as promised.

The two weary people entered a home unfamiliar to Mary. Raw and spent, she sat down near a window sill and looked up at the dusky apricot sky, darkening again as night fell. This was like the end of that first week of creation, when God rested from His work. The rest to which all other Sabbaths referred. As stars became visible, the symbol of Abraham's children was still too sparse for her heart's affection, and they were of too little value for all this grief, torment and pain in her soul.

The dear woman blinked, not knowing that she had fallen into a deep dream.

A red dragon approached outside her window and stared at her. The quiet rage behind the fog of his breath was unmistakable. He was still hungry, un-satiated. She saw through him as if everything inside him were visible: his thoughts readable, his hardness clear as scales, and his deadness, though animated, made him seem like a ghost of a creature. The fumes in his chest emitted the dark thoughts of his appetite.

She vaguely wondered that the sky was suddenly and completely dark, but an image abruptly scalded her mind. His tail swept a third of the stars out of the sky and flung them to the earth.

An unseen hand steadied her from behind, but she couldn't turn her head to look because she was so riveted by the trance of the inflated snake. Wordless, his thoughts transferred: "I've tolerated you for well over thirty three years, and, finally—all your hope is dead. I almost had the wretch when he was little, before you slipped him out of the country; you can consider this payback for all those little boys you caused to be killed.

As you can tell, he was never destined to amount to much. And if you hadn't come for him as a lost lamb at twelve, I would have had him then, and you could have had long been done with your little crying jag. But, alas, all things work together for good for me, and it has been much more exhilarating to watch you both suffer this way.

You'll never see him again. I'm going to enjoy watching you kill yourself tonight, knowing that dead is dead is dead. And, once again, as always and forever, I have all the world under my complete dominion, and, thrill of it all: I have finally and entirely collapsed that diehard faith in Jerusalem. I've been all around the city, inside and out, and am glad to report that there is utter despair. If you could see what I see, you'd know how stunned the large majority of this place is. No one feels like praying now— hallelujah! They are fast dismissing their faith in your god."

Mary cast a look above him. The stars were all out now... shining. "Listen here, you little Jew, you don't get out much, so you don't realize that faith everywhere else in the world is a beautiful reflection of me and the freedom I give for folks to eat, drink, lust, and be entertained. My finest work is among the Romans, and your little epicenter is now on the verge of ruins—crumbling from the inside out—thank God—and I am certainly welcomed! I'm wiping it up with you."

The image of herself withering flashed into her mind, as well as an image of the city in flames. She saw where disease comes from, the belly of deception, and the wrath of one who hosted the appetite for devouring a soul.

He saw her as a work of his own distortion, a dead thing he wanted to shape with dead words. Deceit could do damage, and he wasted no time delivering his poison. The dragon of lies started painting his face onto hers as a mirror, as he launched his accusations, targeting her heart through her mind.

"You know that it really is your fault. I wouldn't have had a chance if you had been the mother you were supposed to be. You should have inspired him to take another route; perhaps you should have raised him entirely in Egypt and blended in for the love of safety and sanity. I could not help but notice he died calling you woman, not mother. He blamed you, too."

Mary felt her hand grip the wood of the sill; she felt it give a bit and wondered how it could.

The dragon continued, "It's not all your fault, of course; I tried to tell him how I could give him dominion, but he wouldn't bow. You, of all people, know how uncooperative he could be. He wouldn't follow me or you. He had this sick little fantasy that God was his father. How grandiose. And now you—his mother—are cast off as a dear woman and have lost him forever."

"Let's face it woman, be honest, truth is so important in moments like these. You didn't want a healer for a son. There is nothing glamorous about that. You knew it was a foolish notion, and for good reason. Sick people are slated for death; they're useless eaters.

You lied to yourself, you know. You have a wild imagination, and he got his from you! You imagined yourself a special pet, didn't you, visited by some super being. All that time, you wanted a child to be some powerful force of magnificence. You were both delusional. A healer for a king. Who does that? A lover of the souls of men? Woman, just say it out loud so you can hear yourself: people don't care about the sick, and they aren't supposed to care. They are supposed to let them go and move on themselves and be grand like statues.

Snap out of it. Everything is how it has always been. 'I am' the only I am, and you are always in this dominion—my world—my terms. You don't survive on delusions. I have the power to kill you right now, but I am—believe it or not—fair, and I always give folks a chance, one last chance, to follow me. So, now, if you are finally ready to accept my reality, I can still do something magnificent with you. Just bow."

He blew his smoke, and the belly of hell rumbled in emptiness.

She noticed, though, that she did not feel afraid.

He noticed it, too.

He laughed at her derisively, "Okay, you want to drag it out, and I don't mind playing with a little pet. I am—if anything—patient. I've got a lot of memories of you. I loved that quote we heard at his funeral a minute ago, which, by the way, was pure idiocy. I can't wait to get with those guys next, but I've got another few verses for you first. I watched you utterly wallow in this one, like you had everything in common with your hero, the mother of Samuel. You fancied yourself like her, the mother of—" yelling in false bravado—"the greatest prophet in Israel! And I thought I had a little pride. Baby, you are my kind of woman—and that's why I can't let you go without one more proposal!"

"I remember you delivering a tasty bit of text to Elizabeth when you were both pregnant. You were cut out of the same piece of cloth, and if it weren't for you two, her boy wouldn't have lost his head. I think one of the saddest things is the faith of Jewish women. I'm here to help you eat your words now."

Clearing his smoking grave of a throat, he mocked her in a singsong high-pitched girlish voice, imitating her perfectly in tone and inflection, reciting her favorite Scripture, verbatim.

> *"My soul lifts up HaShem, and my spirit rejoices in the God of my salvation, who has seen the humility of his handmaid. From now on, all generations will call me glad, for Shaddai has done great things for me, and his name is holy. His kindness endures for all generations to those who fear him. He has done powerful things by his arm. He has scattered the proud in the purposes of their hearts. He has torn down nobles from their thrones and raised up the lowly. He has filled the hungry with good things, but he has sent the rich away empty. He has sustained his servant Yisra'el, remembering his compassions, as he spoke to our fathers, to Avraham, and his offspring forever."*
> *(Luke 1:46-55 • 1 Samuel 2: 1-10)*

He stared at her, expressionless and dead. "Has he now?" he asked in ridicule. "Has he sustained? Your god has always been a disappointment. And that is why you are a disappointment. Now, dear, stupid woman, I bet you wish this was all a dream. It's not. Welcome to hell."

She noticed the sill again, then noticed that she wasn't afraid. She also noticed the he seemed unable to actually do anything but accuse her, like he was barred from coming any closer by some force she couldn't identify.

Then, she noticed the hand was still on her back. It was warm and steady and she could turn her attention to it. She did now, and in a streak of lightning, Gabriel snatched her up and flew away. In a flash, they were up, and in another flash, they came down in a field. Carefully, he set her down into the fields of the grace of Bethlehem.

She saw no shepherds keeping their flock, nor any heavenly hosts ready to break into song overhead, just the grass and the scattered rocks on the ground of this Thin Space. It was a silent night.

Inner stillness invited her own memory back while the fading dragon's words continued to try to mock her with all her grief. These terms were hardly expected. Surely, there was something else, hidden but in motion, working something. Maybe her baby boy would rise again. But then what?

"Host the sacred fields." The sentence rose up inside her from below her belly with a yearning. "Host the sacred fields?" What did that mean?

The ground on which she sat had been hallowed for a thousand years by the songs of a shepherd boy, David. He was a shepherd before he ruled outright as a king. His song started here. These were his fields too.

"Sing."

"Sing?" she said out loud. "I don't have a song now. My song is gone," she returned to the still, small voice.

"Sing," the yearning rose with a push. "Sing the suffering song."

She wondered for a moment if the dragon had gotten inside her, after all, and was going to drive her mad. But then a face she'd never seen came into her mind's eye, and she knew him immediately. The Son of David was in his face. He looked like her; rather, he looked like Jesus; rather, they looked like him. "We wrote that song for you."

She knew now exactly what he meant.

"That was for me?"

"Yes, at least you first, but you—everyone. We tucked you into it, remember?"

His whole young self came into view in front of her now. The strings he held were simple, and his strumming was sweet. His sound surrounded her with new chords, and all were major chords. "It's the song of humanity you carried and still carry," David said, "sing with me, daughter!"

She squinted at him for looking half her age, but, child or not, she obeyed and began to sing her lament again in a tune she barely recognized but followed along with instinctively. "My God, my God, why?" Verses poured up into her as if she were filled with the Spirit of the Song. The duet was piercingly lovely. Everything was in tune in her soul, though she had no idea how it could be.

"Here you are, dear woman. This is you; this is your part. You were never forsaken. Pay attention; see the truth and be free of the lie that you are ever alone!"

> 'Yet you brought me out of the womb; you made me trust in you
> even at my mother's breast. From birth, I was cast upon you;
> from my mother's womb, you have been my God'
> (Psalm 22: 9-10)

The child sang exactly like Jesus when He was young. She remembered Him sturdy and loud singing on a big rock, in a field at play, arms aloft, head back, mouth wide with melody. Her beautiful son was loud and uninhibited in His songs of praise.

"Do not be far from me, for trouble is near, and there is no one to help. Many bulls surround me; strong bulls of Bashan encircle me. Roaring lions tearing their prey open their mouths wide against me. I am poured out like water, and all my bones are out of joint. My heart has turned to wax; it has melted away within me. My strength is dried up like a potsherd, and my tongue sticks to the roof of my mouth; you lay me in the dust of death. Dogs have surrounded me; a band of evil men has encircled me, they have pierced my hands and my feet." (Psalm 22:11-16)

"Do you know what it means, Mother?" Jesus had once asked.

"Some things are a mystery, my dear," she had answered her small son.

"I can count all my bones; people stare and gloat over me. They divide my garments among them and cast lots for my clothing. But you, O Lord, be not far off; O my strength, come quickly to help me. Deliver my life from the sword, my precious life from the power of the dogs. Rescue me from the mouth of the lions; save me from the horns of the wild oxen."
(Psalm 22:12-21)

Sitting now with the one to first pen the words, Mary numbly said, "That's exactly what happened."

"That's exactly what I saw a long time ago—your time," said young David.

"I don't remember the rest of the song," worried Mary.

"I do. This is why I'm here. I'm here to sing to you, daughter. This is what comes next." He stood up on a large stone, strings in hand, and he bellowed out loudly with joy.

"I will declare your name to my brothers; in the congregation, I will praise you. You who fear the Lord, praise him! All you descendants of Jacob, honor Him! Revere Him, all you descendants of Israel! For He has not despised or disdained the suffering of the afflicted one; He has not hidden His face from him but has listened to his cry for help. From you comes the theme of my praise in the great assembly; before those who fear you will I fulfill my vows. The poor will eat and be satisfied; they who seek the Lord will praise Him—may your hearts live forever! All the ends of the earth will remember and turn to the Lord, and all the families of the nations will bow down before Him, for dominion belongs to the Lord, and He rules over the

nations. All the rich of the earth will feast and worship; all who go down to the dust will kneel before him—those who cannot keep themselves alive. Posterity will serve Him; future generations will be told about the Lord. They will proclaim His righteousness to a people yet unborn—
for He has done it."
(Psalm 22:22-31)

Mary looked at David for a moment, speechless. He jumped back down next to her, breathless and happy.

David said, "I suppose you wonder what is real and what is a dream. What is a vision and what is a prophecy, what is a song, what is faith, what is life, and what is death. The great house is God's building. I had to learn that; so do you. This is how He builds. Daughter, ask yourself about this mystery; does He build a thing not to move into it?"

Then, he was gone.

Startled, she felt for the ground beneath her. It was responsive to her touch, awake to her, coming into sync with her, movable as if she were Eve and could direct it with her thoughts. It was at her service now.

Noticing, she thought she could burrow if she wanted to disappear in the dust and wait until something better came along to wake her up. So, aware of her thoughts, the ground started to move under her, cradle her, and rock her like the tiny thing that she was. It sang as it tucked her into the dark, just as she wanted. Mother Earth sang as a hostess of thousands upon thousands of souls, and the dust began to stir with the sounds of choirs.

"The Lord is my shepherd; I shall not be in want. He makes me lie down in green pastures. He leads me beside quiet waters; he restores my soul. He guides me in paths of righteousness for his name's sake. Even though I walk through the valley of the shadow of death, I will fear no evil, for you are with me; your rod and your staff, they comfort me. You prepare a table before me in the presence of my enemies. You anoint my head with oil; my cup overflows. Surely goodness and love will follow me all the days of my life, and I will dwell in the house of the Lord forever."
(Psalm 23)

Adam was made from the dust and received the breath of the Lord. Dust to dust to dust. Who is alive today in the paradise Jesus promised His condemned neighbor? Who has their breath when dust returns to dust? She wondered this as she sank, hoping her breath would soon stop.

The wind began to blow gently, warmly and tenderly unearthing her and standing her up on her feet again. She could not leave; she could not wake herself up; she could do nothing but stand in the wind that swirled her up and out of her own control.

"Dear woman..." said the voice of the wind.

"Oh!" she gasped. And now for the first time in her life, she felt fear. Pure fear was a new sensation of essential smallness facing essential largeness. The dragon had nothing in common with true fear. This was pure and perfect terror. False fear is a dead fear. It mocks for control that it can never have. Pure fear didn't have to manipulate through deception. Pure fear was not dead. Pure fear was Life. Mary was afraid in the most wonderful way a person can be afraid. She was officially out of control, and she would have to get used to this kind of happiness.

"Dear woman..." repeated the owner of her breath.

She had to answer and could not answer for herself.

"Dear woman."

With recognition, she thought with a mind afire, recalculating everything, she said, "You, you are His Father."

"I am."

"You did all of this!" Half accusation, half revelation.

"I did."

You tore; you left, she thought in disapproval.

"Adam left. I stayed. And I promised I would come. And I came," said Breath.

"Then, you are my Father, too, but you did not crush the serpent's head."

"My dear girl, I am and know that even now I am. I am your true Father. I have been working with dust for a very long time." The wind grasped her like swaddling clothes, and she was deliriously undone as a single verse rose.

> *"The Lord says to my Lord. . . sit at my right hand until*
> *I make your enemies a footstool for your feet."*
> *(Psalm 110:1)*

There was an opening in the night sky, as clouds and stars rolled away before her. Only a dot remained. The small dot grew until it became a door appearing far overhead, perfectly in focus. It grew larger and larger, and the longer she studied it, the more apparent the grain of the wood was to her eye, though the door remained at a significant distance.

Next, the frame of it came into focus, and the hinges followed. The door was rounded at the top, and the frame had sketches that moved her heart, but her mind could not yet interpret them.

The door was marked also with the same sketches, and she yearned to reach out and rise upwards but could not. She'd not seen such a door, but by the feel of her heart, it must have had 'home' written all over it. The sketches must have meant something like an address. The yearning was so strong, she wanted to burst into tears for there was no way to go there.

In contrast to her, now, it seemed that the field in which she found herself was not enough life for her. She wanted that which was behind the door, and she didn't know what it was or how to go there, and she felt suddenly like an empty shell. She reached out her hand for the ground below her, but it too was out of reach. She hung, it seemed, in the balance between one life and another.

And though she felt as if she were hanging in between two places, it was all so beautiful. The kind ground below had been willing to cover her despair, as if it knew as well as she did that she was painfully lost here. Studying the desirable door, she asked her breath, "Did I leave, too?"

The answer came as a loud resounding knocking that was heard in the great beyond; out in the distance, something rushed the other side of the door—but the feeling inside her was like it was all happening inwardly. The inward pounding didn't feel strong on the inside; in fact, it was barely discernible except that something was making the connection for her.

Every knock on the outside door felt like a small pulse of a heartbeat inside, as if she had another heart beneath her belly with which she was not in perfect sync. But in the distance, it was quite aggressive in sound, and the reverberation was universal. The ground was pulsating and quaking.

A rattling, pounding, banging, ringing, iron-pounding force was slamming the backside of the door, which looked as if it was about to give way and shatter into pieces. The bulging sight of it was evident.

She recorded every frame as if frozen in motion. Whatever it was that was on the other side was about to take over this place. Time stood completely still as, frame by frame by frame, something was breaking.

It had seemed as if the door would become completely unhinged, but the strength of the hinges matched the strength of the force. One force on the other side did its best to break the door entirely, but there was another force at work inside the door that was connected to the frame in an indissolvable link. The door absorbed the pounding in every cell, and then, when it was finished, finally with a sudden splattering of crimson across what was clearly the doorposts of the universe, it swung opened.

She watched it in slow motion, giving way and slowly felt her own gasp at what would break in and break up inside.

The force of aggression had nowhere else to go and dissipated. Nothing was left in the pounding. Light had broken in and filled the atmosphere. It was exponentially brighter than any light she'd seen before as it went all the way through her and the ground and the rocks; she could see the depths of the ground as if looking at a crystal clear ocean of soil. Everything was subject to the light, just exactly as the door was related to the hinge and frame. All things were a part of the light that was home.

The same wind that held her swept her up higher, to cover her from another wind infusing the light, and together, it swept the fields, the rocks, and the depths below. All the treasure deep beneath the surface was visible in the powerful sweeping light. Light beneath was coming to life, emerging from the dark and fiercely shooting upward.

Surrounding her all around was what looked like a gathering of souls ascending up from Mother Earth. They were shooting up in the direction of the door like luminous souls of many colored lights. Her deep heart leaped up so full and hard into her in delight, she would have followed them were she not held still. Again, she felt that gentle force inside pulsing in her own depths, but it was now in perfect sync with her own heart.

All the souls were on a luminous path spiraling upward carried by the cross-currents of the winds toward the door home. She stared in clean terror through the breath of wind that enfolded her like fingers, through which she could safely watch.

The souls were visible upon focusing. She could see them in their essence of being. Watching was like touching; seeing was palpable, and her sight was felt even at a great distance. In seeing them as a singular being, one would return her gaze. Even if she didn't know them, with a look, she knew they knew her.

The procession of Abraham's luminous children of light from time immemorial past and present, was shooting through the night as if in the streams of a meteor shower. Some deep part of a place outside and inside was being emptied of death and filled with life. There was a joy unspeakable seen on the faces of the souls.

Heart in sync now, her eyes started scanning effortlessly. It was as if she was looking for someone who was also looking for her. Their eyes met. Joseph! Then she saw her parents, her grandparents; they were all alive and beautiful! Others wanted her to see them see her too. Reaching with their eager eyes of love for her were her great grandparents and great greats. There were so many living souls!

Then there were people she'd learned about almost as an idea, who turned out to be real. Esther and her companions were drawing her attention to them by waving as if they knew she could see them now. She wondered at it all.

Further back in the line that was surging emerged the shepherd who had just sung to her with his companions. She reached out her arm, stretching, wanting desperately to join the parade, but he shook his head and threw his thoughts into her belly which rose up in her with a strong gust of love: "You're not done yet!"

And then one sweet creature separated from the cosmic soaring lights, and she came so close to Mary that they could almost touch.

The woman bowed to Mary and said, "Dearest girl, I love you so. You won! I'm so proud! Of all the people you could have chosen to support you, I'm so honored you thought of me." Then, Hannah, the mother of Samuel, was swept back into the streaming flow of home while a mist in the wind was felt as solace.

The earth shifted beneath her and spun to another part of the sky, and she saw many other souls; she heard tongues and tunes of deep resonances while there was a joy erupting in the universe as everything was drawing to a center in the door, and, in literally no time, the parade was complete.

There was one last group trailing at the end. Of that group, one last woman came out of the trail of joy and stood in front of Mary in all her luminosity. The wind stopped and released Mary to the ground in stillness. She stood in honor of the approaching light. They were allowed to touch, up close.

Eve took Mary's hand and placed it on her own heart; Mary took Eve's and held it to her own heart. Speechless, they stared. Mary found simple words, "Mother. Thank you for agreeing to send forth my life."

Through her tears, Eve replied, "Thank you for agreeing to send forth God's."

They both turned to the door and bowed down completely to the ground. Soon, the breath drew Eve up on two feet again and then swept her homeward in the same sweet breath that had previously held Mary. Mary rolled over onto her back and watched the rainbow of lights go home.

The door became smaller but drew closer until it hung before her, small but now close enough to touch. She touched it with her fingers. It was soft as a curtain, and it rolled up like a tiny scroll. Gabriel took the small scroll and placed it in her hand. Then he withdrew a small string of light from her own skin, tied the scroll in light, closed her hand around it, and placed it over her heart. And looking at her in the face, he said, "Dear girl, you were absent from one of the lessons when your son, the Savior, said, 'Your Father is pleased to give you the Kingdom.'" Then Gabriel bowed to her and was gone.

Above the dear girl, floating like a white leaf wafting slowing on a guiding exhale of air, was a flake of brightest light. Falling perfectly, it landed on her lips. When she opened her lips for the flake of manna, her hand opened as well. The manna was sweetly absorbed, and the scroll burrowed into her heart.

Her two hearts connected inside.

"Oh! I Am! Yes! I agree! I'll follow!"

Immediately, her eyes opened to another sky, rosy with the dawn flooding the room through the window. With the living dream still present to her, she stayed motionless, pondering the images, frame by frame, all the way back to the accuser.

She drew a blanket up close to her chest and noticed that something smelled lovely: sweet like incense. She drew in deep breaths and closed her eyes again to keep her face in the morning rays and feel the warmth of the light. She soaked in the light for as long as it rose upwards in the window. Birds, breezes, passersby, stirrings in the house, all floated around her like light music.

Slowly, she rose for the last day of the week, the Sabbath. Stretching up and removing the blanket, she looked down and released a startled gasp to see how completely covered in His blood and ointments she still was. She remembered again that she was nearly sleepwalking when they arrived last night and apparently no one could bear to disturb her and just covered her with a blanket.

Fresh tears fell silently, releasing the scent again that was such a comfort in the night. His blood had dried soft on the fabric, and it had kept the same live color. Smoothing the folds of her garments, she stroked His bright blood. She knelt and prayed wordless prayers of deep slow breaths and recited the Shepherd's songs with new peace.

Something moved outside the window. She felt eyes and turned to see. Someone had been watching her and had pulled back. Rising, she filled the window to look into the streets outside, which seemed unusually quiet for a Sabbath morning. Up ahead, she could have sworn she saw Gabriel turn a corner and then check back to see if she was watching. He saw her see him and that was enough. She followed. She couldn't be sure it was him, but she felt impressed to go. Now, she was a follower. She left in a hurry to go outside, and the newly-protective son John was on her heels.

She was not easily missed. The Lord's blood on her fabric transformed the material itself, turning it into something closer to silk. She moved like the wind and left a scent that smelled like rubies that had come to life: no trace of iron, just the waft of heavenly wine full of pure sweetness.

As she moved quickly, her brain re-engaged. She began to remember things from yesteryear, how sweetly He smelled as a little boy, leaving the fields and running to her, feet pounding hard and neck sweaty when He charged her with an eager hug. She remembered the honest scent of her little boy.

She could hear Joseph's teasing voice in her head, and see again his wink. "That boy's clean as a whistle. He doesn't need to rinse off for dinner." She remembered her own voice chiding, "Yeshua! Look at your hands, all full of frogs; I'm not feeding the frogs for dinner!"

And ever wide-eyed in surprise when His mother didn't see what he was doing, he had said, "I Am!"

Now Mary began to smile again. "That's exactly what he's been doing."

Sweet memories returned as she found Him again in her mind's eye as a son to her. "Oh, my sweet lamb, my sweet little lamb. Thank you, Father. Thank you for coming for the frogs! May the royal prince of peace rise in us all, oh rise. Oh Yeshua, tomorrow, tomorrow; oh, I can't wait for tomorrow. Father, help me live today well."

She scooped up her garments closer to draw in the scent of him like the scent of His baby blanket. While re-wrapping her head in the cloth she'd covered him with for a moment in time, it occurred to her now that she was the one wrapped in his swaddling clothes, as a chrysalis.

She smelled the notes individually, the lingering spices mixed with his grand essence of life. She could feel life in the blood that could not and would not stay still for very much longer. His faith in His Father was her own confidence now, and His blood had His presence; His faith was awakening her.

She was completely owned by the priceless blood in which she was enrobed, the finest garment in all of creation. But where might she be going with Gabriel? All she could do was trust and eagerly follow the mystery; she was in rest now. It was Sabbath. Free from her own plans, it didn't matter if she knew the next step before she reached it. She'd stand in it when she arrived, and God would do the rest.

"Mother," John called out, racing to catch up, "where are we going today?"

"I'm following, son." But making a guess, she pointed to the high place on a hill in the center of town, glistening gold in the morning light. "It's the Sabbath. I bet we're going to hear the Words of the Scroll." John's eyes widened with a shock of horrible thoughts, knowing threats were always waiting in the Temple. Seeing his slack jaw, she tipped it shut, "Let's just try to keep up. Whatever happens next… we don't want to miss it."

Nearly two million people had entered the city for Passover, and the large majority knew the unspeakable had happened. Streets were nearly as thin again as if they were in ordinary times. No one was leaving town on the Sabbath, but few were interested in the Temple now.

Regardless, neither the Red Sea nor the Jordan River's parting were as effortless as the parting of meandering people at the sight of her coming. Between the elegance of obedience, and the festivity of her array, she was not hard to make room for, nor hard to follow. And some began to do so.

The broken Temple of Jerusalem was in sore need of the blood of the Lamb. Mary was moving with the speed of someone who had finally rested in a deep faith, and she knew she had one small window of a few hours to "mean it" before her faith would be turned into fact.

Did she have a single thing to lose by arriving in her finery? She had far more to lose by not coming. She wasn't interested in losing God's chosen people to despair or unbelief. Her brain was lit with the Words of the prophets she'd pushed back against in His ascent to the throne of mercy.

The Holy City of David felt like it had been gutted. But it was so solid beneath her feet, and with the deceit of the dragon crushed, she was alive in hope. She fell in line behind an angel's distant lead to a stretch of a path that let her retrace a few of His blood-drizzled steps as her robe swept up the dust of it all.

Most broken-hearted people had stayed home, and she found Torah lessons poorly attended. Few could stomach hearing the voice of Caiaphas. Only a small fraction of the ruling body was even present. No doubt others likely congregated today in the home of Nicodemus, or sat in their own houses and prayed.

Never having seen such thin spaces at the grand temple, she thought of the threat of the accuser, and a flame burned in her belly. God Our Father Himself had exposed the emptiness of human treachery by fully drawing our determination to judge and condemn all into Himself. As one of us, His Son, Our Son, the Son of Man, agreed to represent man's rejection of God, and, in doing so, demonstrated His Father's undying faithfulness inside our own skin. And though He had said it was finished, He was still on the way. She knew He'd stay out long enough for us to know He meant it. And today, sitting in pools of blood guilt, she knew all were dying of thirst. With Gabriel as her guardian, God escorted her silently, carrying her, changed from the inside out, for the sake of water.

How many recognized her today as His mother was hard to gauge but avoiding her garments with their gazes was a sign of the guilt of those who saw her coming. It brought an instant flash of yesterday's destruction. But not since Eden had anyone ever been so beautifully visible.

She arrived and stopped first at the court of women. Sight seen, some people bowed their heads in respect, while others shamefully left her presence. She could easily meander through the several temple courts and make her way to the Sheep Gate. There, she bent to scribble her own name on the dusty ground in front of a woman seated there, still bravely attending services in the house of prayer with her friends.

Rising, she sweetly touched the woman's head and was instantly recognized, though they'd never met. The woman gasped at the meaning of her dress and then leaned in to hug her around her legs, embracing her tightly from where she sat on the ground.

An unrestrained gulp of anguish escaped as the woman wept for Jerusalem while basking in the solace of her head being stroked. The fresh tears brightened a streak of blood alive again with fresh color and infused the air with fragrance. Water and new wine were on the way.

Next, Mary waltzed around the pool of Siloam, slowly coming to a still spot, she waited, hoping for the sick to also touch her. There was power in His blood. Slowly, the hum and buzz of concern was growing, though no one approached her yet.

Temple guards recognized her and spoke in hushed tones to one another, plotting only to defend her from any shard of rudeness. They'd made up their minds already, even though they knew not what she was thinking. One uprising of hope could sway them to drink living water.

One crippled woman by the pool reached to touch Mary. She immediately rose up strong and able-bodied. Another stretched out, and then one more. The rest just stared, dumbfounded, lost in unbelief. "Are you seeing this?", whispered an onlooker to another. "Now the mother is in here healing on the Sabbath. You have to wonder what these people are drinking."

"Mercy," the other observer replied. "She's a lovely mess."

John was wary but protective until he noticed that the Temple guards had all but welcomed her into that space.

Mary moved on to finally make herself seen in the court of men who were attempting to have a pitiful prayerful meeting. She entered, listened quietly, unnoticed by many with heavy heads, and she waited for the reading from the Torah. They'd not yet unrolled the scroll. They were late, or stuck, or perhaps they had lost interest without a sufficient audience.

She sat down. It was as if she was invisible. She thought, "Open the scroll!"

Then they opened the scroll to the place where the death angel passed over them. She saw Gabriel beside them, staring at her, and she knew they did not know he was there. Nor did they notice the large company of fierce heavenly hosts gathering to surround the room.

As soon as Caiaphas finished the reading, Gabriel pointed his unseen hand at Mary, subtly directing the man to recognize her in their midst. He paused, looked up, and turned white. Heads began to turn in the direction of what held his attention. When they saw her there, present in what they had assumed was their space, they all froze. Gabriel's wings extended from wall to wall in Mary's eyes. She was safe.

She could hear the silent thoughts of Caiaphas: "No one is available to remove her. Someone else will have to touch her, but then that person will be considered unclean. No one can lay their hands on her to throw her out." They would risk being defiled by the blood of their Lamb. Caiaphas was entangled and stuck.

One single person said it in a whisper that spread faster than an open loud announcement. "That's her!" Everyone became completely still and silent. "Who?"

"Her!"

"It's the mother."

"Oh, the dear woman. What a mess. She's mad."

A quick reference to her companion connected them both to the crucified.

They looked at her. She look at them. They looked at one another. It was all happening very deeply in waves of an undertowing current.

Caiaphas had a subtle tremble. Mary was serene and full of heart.

The reduced and diminished ruling body felt her presence a bit differently than they had yesterday at the execution stake where they mocked her son in front of her with no pity at all. Gabriel repeated their words to their minds which only Mary could hear aloud. "If you are the son of God, come down from that cross." Their own words accused them. Caiaphas dropped his head.

Then she heard the voice of her son again, "Father, forgive them."

The storm had broken over their own heads, and with their aggression spent, they had to find a place to rest as well. The hangover of hate left a dull ache that tried to cover up the question, "What have we done?"

It's one thing to be tempted; it's another thing to embrace the dark passion and then feel the threat of your death creep into your soul. Though the mind will not readily bow in admission of guilt, the body cannot acquit the guilt of the soul in the depths of a man. New grooves had deepened in his brow, his hair had grayed overnight; his vitals were out of rhythm.

She stood and approached him. He saw her in the full detail of her robes. It was just a flash of pain, but she saw his guilt register when he raised his eyes to face her. He was struck as she rose, to see that she was enrobed in the blood he had on his hands. She saw that he saw it. She dropped her eyes to kindly release him first. He was afraid of his own darkness.

The Temple had a crack in the floor. It seemed to gape as a chasm into which the sin of the world had fallen. This gaping hole offered a question to the institutionalized men who fancied themselves as God, rather than simply representing Him like a child of the Father. Now, their souls hung on the precipice. The division was a gap that offered no security. But alas, as institutional judges, they had sadly embodied the loss and only managed to exclude themselves from Home instead of Rome. But the Blood would bridge the gap!

Humiliation was palpable. If only God's grace in her could be seen through the fog of their guilt, Mary would almost have been welcomed. Had there been an ounce of faith in anything but the law of demand and performance, they might have taken a step to weep in her presence.

The law as they executed it became their own death march. They had politicized Israel on their terms. Now on this the "morning after" their hideous villainy was more acutely felt in facing her and facing her there. How well everyone knew, as the centurion had known yesterday, this tribe had bankrupted themselves. The rocky faith had gone completely hard.

Apart from faith, Rome's hardness was utterly seeded in them now as an alliance with death. No one could fathom where that harvest would lead in a few short decades. Soon, Rome would judge them as they had judged their Messiah. The dead race of the fallen was the representative only of the first Adam, not the second. They were just like everyone else. And everyone was free only to be slaves of guilt.

Mary, free among the bankrupt, crossed the cracked gap on the floor as easily as if she was being carried across it. She paused to look at many wide-eyed faces and then journeyed further, cascading upwards. Like a waterfall in an ascent, she was liberated to flow up, up, up the stairs. Against all sense of gravity, she landed at the threshold of the Holy of Holies.

Once there, she innocently peered into the empty space behind the torn veil, which was eagerly being attended to by a novice. The Ark of the Covenant had been absent for hundreds of years, but the sacred scrolls were still here, and she pondered these earthly things she had never seen up close until now. When she imagined the ark of the covenant, physically absent, she was struck that it was the mercy seat which had always and ever only been a representation of the real. She knew what the scroll in her dream had meant and she hosted this truth of the promise of reconciliation in her heart and soul.

Now, as if He was present to her as a mercy seat on which she could offer herself, she, by the blood on her robe, re-presented Him to them as she took a seat upon Gabriel's invisible knee. She, being so small, and he so tall, when she seated herself on his knee there was practically no change in her height. With a new clarity of the intention behind the universe, she took a deep, deep breath and, exhaling, reconciled herself to her son's prayer. She needed it. She referenced John, standing in the back, who watched her with reverence, and she saw that his eyes were brimming.

As she looked upon the unusually small group, a rising tide of mercy began to flow from her toward her Son's executioners. The Dear Woman, leveled man's guilt, a guilt she shared, born of the determination to usurp instead of follow God's lead, with the prayer of her son on the cross. "Father forgive them" rose in her as her own prayer now and allowed her to gently hold them in her gaze with soft eyes. His blood was their common ground. He owned them all in their guilt. They were all snake bitten. And just as Moses lifted the serpent in the wilderness, the Lord had been lifted as the Lamb on the threshold of Jerusalem, and on the door posts of heaven and earth.

The first public sounds to come from her mouth since she screamed at the strike of the hammer driving iron into Jesus's flesh were like warm, rich, milky, deep music, the voice of a solid woman. Momentarily, John closed his eyes to focus only on the sound of a voice stripped of terror; only a small trace of fatigue was evident. The tenderness was clear as Mary gingerly began in the common style of study dialogue, to offer some questions for them all to ponder together.

Confident in her previous night's vision, she believed the Father had extended an answer to the blessed intercession on the cross for the forgiveness of the sins of the world. "Caiaphas," she said without a hint of bite, "is this the actual place where The Blood of the Lamb is required?" In one single question, she proposed the true meaning of everything Israel.

A fresh and holy fear of a new but very old kind rose up in the eerie quiet of the room. A breeze caught up her head-covering, and it fell, revealing her blood matted hair. Some men pulled their robes closer beneath their chins but inclined themselves forward to make out her speech.

Again, she asked softly, directing her attention to the whole room with one sweep of her gaze, "Is this the very place where we come to ask for mercy and burn incense for prayers?"

They all stared and began to acquaint themselves fully with the vision of the Dear Woman dressed in all that blood. It was still streaked across her face and her hands, which were pointing to the Holy Place. The wind carried her scent back and forth across the gallery. She was a new carrier of incense.

She was a sight. The blood mixed with spices became so pronounced on her face that she looked like she was covered in new birthmarks. She and her robes were well-matched with the same markings.

Ironically the marks of war and violence, which were so much a part of the nation that they nearly embodied the darkness that they longed to expel, dimly reminded the audience of something innocent at the sight of her. But they couldn't fully imagine the idea. A snake bitten person has trouble thinking straight until the venom is removed.

She perched there like a special child of God who had no better sense than to seat herself between the golden angel's wings embroidered on the fabric of the torn veil. She was an image that could have convinced the room that she had cracked like the floor around them. But her eyes did not seem crazed, nor her voice, nor her manner, and the soul before them though broken, was on the mend to being made new, fresh and piercing with hope. She invoked a mystery in the midst of catastrophic shame and pain.

Caiaphas, who said nothing, rolled up the scroll, left it, and moved to sit with the audience, granting her the space to question and testify. The breeze held them all captive to the scent of prayer. In rapt attention, without rebuke, while a trail of women peered in from the edges, stillness filled them all.

Mary had pondered so many things and for so long that she unfolded her heart in this way. "My husband, who you might think is dead, nevertheless lives. My eldest is clearly consumed with His work for us, but as for myself, I could not imagine what reason I had for coming here of all places—today. But I was lead and so I followed, and in doing so something occurred to me while I warmed to the idea and walked here in the sunshine this morning. It's like that you know, sometimes you have to obey to begin to understand a thing. So when it finally began to dawn on me, I wondered whether or not anyone thought to bring a drop of His blood here." A strange delight was clear in her eyes. "I know there is a place back there behind the veil where the blood is applied, but I realize that the mercy seat is gone now and hasn't been there for years. Still this place is about where it used to rest."

"I wondered if there was a collection taken by anyone, or if a small sample, even just one small wet drop from his body and soul, or some blood-soaked soil perhaps where the earth may have been alarmed at having to drink Him in, was brought here?"

The men were speechless. The women stared with wide eyes in the back and John was almost holding his breath trying to calculate what moves he could make to deliver her should the need become apparent.

"Holy dirt would even suffice," she continued. "A cup of dirt perhaps? Did anyone besides me think to bring His loveliness here to this place, near this veil? This is where the precious blood is to be poured out for mercy, isn't it? Or is it? Does anyone here know for sure? He is of course the real Lamb to which all others pointed, but my question is, is this a real place for the offering? If however it is not, then where is the seat of mercy, and where is the real door-post? It does seem to appear that now as in the past, we find ourselves right back in Egypt, captives again to another fellow who thinks he is God just like Pharaoh did."

John noticed the emotional temperature of the room shift in some indistinct manner. There was no open hostility, just a tender breeze wafting with comfort. Defensiveness and suspicion were awake beneath their momentary tolerance, but she stood disarmingly vulnerable and soft. Instinctively, she knew there was only a small window of freedom to speak for a brief moment. And like a cross current in the souls of men, something hungry was moving, and just how much they wished to hear from her was beginning to surface. She was uninterested in shame, and like the breeze, she was easy and gentle.

With outstretched arms, she continued in a steady voice. "Didn't Moses say something about all of these things being shadows? The things here that we've always treasured, even if some items are now missing — like Moses glory in a law that was fading — wasn't the true idea veiled in mystery, and objects a mere shadow cast by the real? But did we forget they were symbols of the real things, gifts pointing to the real things of heaven from which we are clearly separated? Tell me now, shall I seat myself here to deliver The True Blood of The True Lamb? Or, is there some other seat to which Moses referred and some other Temple to which this one speaks and might represent?"

"I wonder would it be too inconvenient for you to watch me sit here forever? I carried him once, of course on the inside. And I now carry His insides on my outside. Would you prefer, I leave my stained garments here, as I trust someone can surely find another garment for me to wear home?"

"I don't mind changing, I'm just asking you, where do you believe the blood of the Lamb should be applied? You read from the Torah, the Lamb's blood goes on the door-post of a house; where is that house now? Is it still in Egypt? Is it in Rome, perhaps, or maybe here in Israel? Are we still slaves to a false god? Are we slaves in our own houses, or of Moses, or of you Caiaphas? Will you kill us all if we disobey? Maybe the place of application is even closer. Maybe it's inside me and inside you, in our hearts; maybe we are disconnected from our true heart because we don't follow the real God? Should I dilute the blood on this cloth that veils me with water and sprinkle it over all of your heads?"

"Caiaphas, I heard that you, the High Priest, had said, 'Better that one man die for the people than the people for one man.' " It was as gently as she could quote him without condemning the man outright. "I am only his mother, but we all have the same Father as Jesus. And though He was born to die, it was you that called for His sacrifice. And it was written. And it has happened as it was written." There, she stated the facts much like the old patriarch Joseph would have, in a tone of, "what man meant for evil, God meant for good."

She bowed her head, and then bowed at her waist, and then down she went to her knees right below him. And in humility, looking up at him and others seated close by, she said, "My name is Mary. I am glad to meet all of you who called for our son's sacrifice. It was better, as you said, that one die for all, then for all die for one. It was written ages ago. I should like to meet Herod of course, and Pilate, if they would see me. I met the dear centurion yesterday. He let me hold my darling again, lifting him off the cross and over onto my lap. You were all gone by then, frightened I suppose of the dark that fell at noon, so you did not see how kind the Roman was to me."

Looking up at him now a little above eye level as she readjusted and raised up to her height, she continued, "Caiaphas dear, you could perhaps help us in our mutual dilemma. You, being you and only you, could go draw some water from the pool and come back and pour it over my face and my stained hands and hair, while I sit still. Together, we could leave every single drop I have brought here exactly where it belongs in the Holy of Holies. That is if you really, really think this is where the blood is being represented.

But, of course, if this entire place itself is all just another representation of a true reality somewhere else in heaven perhaps—on some other plain of reckoning—if that is the case, then we'll have to decide what this place means now that the Lamb of God has been offered. Yesterday I heard Jesus say, 'It is finished,' so, without His true meaning, this place is just another building that costs our country enormously, both in taxes and in blood."

She stood up taller now after a long pause and began to smooth her garments, and as she did, she began to cry the quiet tears no one could hear but all could see. Her face glistened and her lips trembled. She took a swatch of her hanging head-covering, precariously draped it back up on her head, and wiped her face but the whole thing fell again revealing her long, peppered, messy hair. Without of a hint of becoming indecent, she continued.

"Honestly, even with nothing to wear, I really shouldn't mind going out from here just as naked as our son hung yesterday on the cross publicly in front of us all. We all saw the essence of His heart completely opened for us. His body and soul were naked, and we saw His innocence."

Gasping for her own air for a moment, she said, "You might have missed how He bore up under all that hate with never a dark word, and with constant intercession and even promises from the Psalms. He expressed the clearest image of the grace and favor of God, not an ounce of retribution, vengeance, or rejection. He acted like His God."

She cast a glance at the surrounding angels. "He could have destroyed us all. But were any of you still there to hear him tell that other dying man, an honest criminal, that he would be with Him in paradise? A man who was just as hateful as anyone else. He promised that man paradise. It was not too late for the condemned to follow Him to the Father."

She rested a beat.

"None of us followed Him. I include myself, dear men. I am guilty. I held back. You didn't know Him, and so you don't know yourselves. You did not know what you were doing. I thought I knew him, but I didn't know myself. I didn't understand what He was doing because I had my own terms. I wanted my way. I held back when He didn't go where I wanted Him to go. But He is still the life of all of our souls. He is the glory of Israel, as God's pure mercy, and that is the true glory of Israel! God's mercy triumphs over our judgments.

To see him stripped and beaten and crowned in our thorns actually demonstrated a trust in God that we could not fathom. He wore our crown of resistance. He showed us—us—and showed us His faith in His Father. Our refusal is what set Him up to testify in our court and in the courts of heaven. Poor Judas thought he could push him and shove Him into being king on our terms. But Jesus responded and showed us God's terms of surrender.

The sky was dark, the earth quaked, and the rain came, and the God of Jacob wept. God's tears were for Him and for us. He could absolutely have called on the powers of Heaven to represent the side of God that we covet. That is a place he bars us from. We want God to execute fierce torrents of vengeance on Rome, not considering that He could have done that to Israel yesterday.

But what did God do? He wept. Even the earth was outraged. It quaked. But what did God do? Just this," she said pointing to the veil. He tore this curtain, starting at the top, apparently, and for what? For us to take a look at what is missing. The Holy of Holies is empty of the ark and the law that brings us condemnation and death. What does that mean? Is that what Jesus meant by saying 'It is finished?' The law is satisfied, by the perfect spotless Lamb? The separation between man and God is over. We may come in now and have peace! Our judgment is finished.

I know you did not want Pilate to post that sign, but I believe he knew it was true, or at least his wife did. It bothered you all for good reason. Hear me now. Jesus is the Christ. And that makes Him the King. But His Kingdom is bigger than ours. It's bigger than our families and our tribes; it's bigger than Israel, and it's bigger than Rome, and it's bigger than this world. It's bigger than time and space. He is God. His Kingdom is bigger than death. This might be the near end of Israel as we've known her, but it is not the end of His Kingdom.

His promise is certain. If you've studied the Scriptures, and no doubt some of you have been earnestly doing just that, then you know this is not over. His death is not the end. These are the blessed hours of our death. This is the only Sabbath there has ever been. Things will be new tomorrow.

So, what I came here to ask is, what shall we do with all this blood? He is the Lamb of God who came and took our judgment. Caiaphas, He came for this, He is our scapegoat. It is all in the Scriptures; unroll the scroll. Who would be willing to unroll the scroll and ask for the witness of the prophet Isaiah?"

Nicodemus sheepishly stepped out of the shadows, "I will, if you don't mind hearing the Words from my weak tongue." He approached, and Caiaphas did not control the scroll. Within moments, he began to read on her point precisely with a humble voice, tendered with water.

> *"He was despised and rejected by men, a man of sorrows, familiar with suffering. Like one from whom men hide their faces, he was despised, and we esteemed him not. Surely, he took up our infirmities and carried our sorrow, yet we considered him stricken by God, smitten by him and afflicted. But he was pierced for our transgressions; He was crushed for our iniquities; the punishment that brought us peace was upon Him, and by His wounds, we are healed. We all, like sheep, have gone astray; each of us has turned to his own way, and the Lord has laid on Him the iniquity of us all. He was oppressed and afflicted, yet He did not open his mouth; He was led like a lamb to the slaughter. As a sheep before her shearers is silent, so He did not open His mouth... and yet, it was the Lord's will to crush Him and cause Him to suffer, and though the Lord makes His life a guilt offering, He will see His offspring and prolong His days and the will of the Lord will prosper in His hand. After the suffering of His soul, He will see the light of life and be satisfied by His knowledge. My righteous servant will justify many, and He will bear their iniquities. Therefore, I will give him a portion among the great, and He will divide the spoils with the strong because He poured out his life unto death and was numbered with the transgressors. For He bore the sin of many and made intercession for the transgressors."*
> *(Isaiah 53:7-12)*

The scroll was rolled back, and Nicodemus sat next to Caiaphas.

"Yes exactly. You see, dear men, He did not fight like Adam's race. He meant it when He prayed, 'Father forgive them; they do not know what they are doing.' "

Some were dumbstruck, some sat in rapt attention; some were scared that she was going to undress, some wanted to run away, a few wondered if she was enlightened, and one was beginning to feel shattered that the Mother of the crucified could stand before them and speak with a civil tongue. All in all they were well aware of their previous night's anxieties.

No one was comfortable with what had happened the previous day. Apparently, neither was Jerusalem. No clothes were torn, but all were beginning to feel naked and untethered yet with a faint relief if not hope stirring in her testimony of God. The political surface upon which they rivaled had lost value on some unspoken level. Some were secretly praying she'd never stop speaking, however unworthy each of them was to hear a word of her northern-accented speech. No one moved a single inch so as to not break the flow in her dialogue.

"The shadows are over. Just as there is no more tabernacle, this can no more been seen as the real Temple—it is empty now. This system of sacrifices is complete and whether or not we dare to make this a house of prayer is yet to be seen. But the question remains, did you think this place was the real seat of judgment? If Moses was right, and I know you preferred Moses to the Son, if these things are shadows, are we also shadows? Are you a shadow? You seem shadowy, love."

"Dear man," she said to Caiaphas, barely above a whisper, "are you the real high priest, or do you represent Him? Do you own the office in which you stand, or are you a steward of the interests of Heaven? None of this work is about Rome. This is about Heaven on Earth—in us—for the sake of the nations. They need to see the light of redemption. You have performed your duty. You have made the eternal sacrifice; did you know it was for the whole world? This blood I wear is for me and you and everyone everywhere."

Men wept. She nodded as she walked and touched them, tearing up with them and for them.

"Now, the question is, what will you do with yourselves tomorrow? I saw guards posted at the tomb as I passed this morning. It was a point of contention when Jesus said, 'Tear down this Temple, and I will rebuild it in three days.' He was speaking about yesterday and tomorrow.

Tomorrow, when Our Father who is in Heaven vindicates His Lamb — as our only Temple — what will you do with yourself? The guards at the tomb will have no power over an indestructible life. You aren't going to keep this seamstress on the payroll, twisting cords to bind up this torn veil, are you? The true veil was torn to ribbons yesterday, and there is no point in closing this one again. Your job, as you have practiced it, is obsolete. Will it suit you to de-robe yourself of unbelief?"

Silence was full of stillness as she directed her comments to everyone, scanning the room back and forth, like a painter working with a large easel.

"Well, I'll tell you what I'll do. I'll content myself to wear my beautiful robes until I see his face in the morning. I believe He knows what to do with His own blood. Until then, I'm glad to be covered in it. I hope to always be."

With that, she left them with God's love.

Deep, haggard breaths were taken all over the room as more heads dropped and waterfalls of tears began to fall into place. John instinctively stepped forward to offer Mary his hand and began to escort her out of the place, casting a glance at the woman whom Jesus had spared from a stoning, the woman whose head Mary had smoothed minutes before breeching the men's court. She stood at the threshold, beaming with sparkling eyes and a wet face.

Some of the dry-eyed watched her leave, having made her peace, surprised she released them from any hint of her own judgment, and glad she didn't start screaming at them all. Those eyes may have followed her out and perhaps noticed the adulterous woman, and they may have recalled how many had dropped their stones when Jesus questioned them regarding their own innocence.

It is hard to part ways with a dead conscience and allow mystery to take over. Losing the agendas, the plans of control, of being one's own king takes faith in God. But Mary demonstrated that if one can not keep the law, and no one can — it is best to approach the guilty party by standing with them, as one of them, and not over them. It takes something more than judgment to open a heart; it takes faith in mercy.

Judgment had a place. Judgment had taken His place and made room for Mercy to take the first place. The verdict was still several hours away.

She represented faith in Him as best she could in the in-between time, on the Sabbath. Women seem to take on the attitude of the clothes they wear. The Dear Woman could not yet afford to take off her robe until the shadow had fully passed. She wore the blood home and held Him close on through the day and into the setting sun of the new day.

A small fellowship decided to leave the old structures and to follow the odd growing group to where they were staying. Some found a way to reach the disciples in the Upper Room. The accompanying breeze was mild, and birds spotted the sky as Mary and John ambled along in blessed assurance.

A new kind of prayer meeting was held late into the day as the sun began to set, and night seemed to be in a hurry to bring in the first half of the new day of a brand new week. Conversations ended early in the evening. Mary took her seat at the window again, welcoming the moonscape as clouds made happy faces at her. She drifted with them in her quiet thoughts and covered up under the blanket. She took a deep breath and inhaled the scent of perfect Love as she stroked the soft garment.

Just when she blinked into rest, she saw Him.

He walked into her rest with His glory, brilliant like the disciples had seen Him when God revealed Jesus to them as His Son in radiance. He made his way speedily to the dear woman in her dream and touched her face, saying, "Mother." She heard Him, clear as a bell, bright as a pure soul. She reached out to touch Him and startled herself awake.

It was a dream. The sky outside was black, and the night was deep now.

But someone was there. She could feel the sense of being stared at. She was motionless, but unafraid. The room was starting to glow. She turned and smiled, "Hello, Gabriel."

Standing in his own glow, Gabriel was suited up for something regal. She just took him in for a moment, sat up, and then reached over to touch the window sill. Solid, it didn't give. She still wondered if she was dreaming and then wondered if she was dead. She tried to feel her heart, and it was racing.

Gabriel extended his hand saying, "Highly Favored One, it is time to go." This was not a dream.

As soon as she rose, they were there. Angel Michael rolled away the stone. Gabriel and Michael escorted her inside. They each then took their places: one stood at the head and the other at the foot of The Son of God. Bowing their heads, they raised their many, many wings to cover their faces, their bodies, and their feet in salute to their Master and her Redeemer.

Whatever would happen next was not of their doing, not theirs to see, to hear, to even observe. They were only to serve. The blessed mystery was not of their keeping. The wind was already present there, waiting for her. The hand of God held her again as it had in her dream; her heart filled with Joy unspeakable while Hope surged.

In the glow of angel's wings, she stared as His face. She took hold of the cloth, removing the veil from His beautiful face that was radiating with a beaming light mending and closing cuts. Savoring every moment, frame by frame, her hands instinctively folded the veil, setting it aside effortlessly just as she had folded so many of His clothes as a boy. His whole body was full of light, bright as the sun.

"Dear Daughter," said the Father, "this is my Son in whom I am always well pleased." Our Father filled Him with His breath, and He rose again as the linens transformed into our robes of righteousness.

Mary was speechless but not breathless.

The streams of light and breath met in the everlasting life of Christ, and she saw all the humanity that was swirling into Him. He was the door. Small rumblings were moving beneath the ground as many other graves were opening throughout the city beyond her sight.

The Tree of Life exhaled. As Christ breathed once again, His mother felt new in an indescribable way. She'd seen His innocence all of her life, never knowing her own guilt. She'd held him, the Living Word, the Door, the Living Water, Path of Life in the wrong way, as if she had been above, and now she began to want to bow, and find refuge under the tree of His Life. His breath permeated her every cell as well as His own. Mary found the ground and would have fallen hard had she not been held by the breath. She wept new tears of life and was gently lowered, and down she went softly.

The Son of God King of the Universe stood up, and then knelt down as a man again, ever a representative of mankind, while the radiant angels stayed at full attention. "Mother." She looked up and He wiped away her tears. "Let me take you out of the grave now. The Sabbath is finished."

Leaving the angels there, her Master escorted her out of our tomb. She felt the reality of His wounds as she squeezed his scarred hand. Raising it to her lips, she kissed him.

He said, "It was hard for you, too…but…I promise…now it is finished." As her tears flowed, she wondered again if she was dead. He answered her thought, "You were, but you didn't know it."

Through the garden they passed, where everything moved as if reaching out to them, and she wondered at so many things she'd never noticed were alive. She walked on ground that bore her as an old friend; she passed flowers that swooned at her with recognition, and the trees seemed, all in all, aware of pure presence, and even the stars were awake as part of the whole being of life.

Life was all in all, and she wondered that she had any weight at all on her feet, as if the air would always carry her along. The abundance of life was both exhilarating and profoundly reasonable, as if it were a normal she'd never known. There were so many questions and so much to ponder anew.

They returned to where she had been staying since Friday, entering a place again that was not her home. He sat with her by the window. Unwilling to let go of His hand, she reached out with her left hand to touch the sill. It was hard, and it would not give way. She was awake.

"I promise. I Am. I am here with you in this life, now and forever."

She burst into tears. "Yeshua, Yeshua, Yeshua... all this for the frogs?"

"All this for my Royal Family, for all those who do the will of My Father, and just trust me." He smiled broadly.

"I can't imagine we're worth it," she said.

"I promised a very long time ago. I am the God of My Word. I will never leave you nor forsake you. Look now, see, I have your name written in the palm of my hand, and I will never let you go."

"Yeshua." She bowed down to his feet, kissed them, and wept again. "My Lord and my God, she whispered over and over between her gasps of air. This went on for quite a while as she shook out her tears. When she was done, she looked up, "I'm so glad this part is over for you."

"It's over for you too," He leaned in close, placed His hands on her head and her heart and said, "Hear the words of our Father. He says, Dear Woman, My Life is yours; it always has been, and now you know who you are. I named you a long time ago. You are mine. I knew you before I formed you in your mother's womb. I have loved you with an everlasting love. Receive my Spirit." She felt the breeze again waft into the room as she inhaled perfect peace.

A stroke of her hair with his hand quieted her soul; Christ the Lord kissed her head, smiled an old familiar twinkling grin now and asked, "Dear Mother, would you like to know how many hairs you have, how many are black, and how many are gray?"

She burst into laughter, "Absolutely not!"

He picked her up off the ground and tucked her back into her napping place. "Yeshua, I never imagined this, not any of this."

"Shhhh. Rest a minute. There is another dream of the Father, waiting for you. You are not done here. You should know you are His dream come true. He always wants to speak with you. And I'm going back to wait outside the tomb. Friends are going to be looking for me. I'm going to wake them too. Enjoy your dream. I'll be back."

She agreed, knowing she would never not see Him again. As she laid her head down, she pondered the complete joy of everlasting life in the way her body felt. The complete feeling of utter peace was foreign to her but it crossed her mind how she could get use to it—God—in this proximity. She was now free from feeling forsaken, from homelessness, abandonment and fear—and pain and guilt were completely released from her every cell.

Christ knelt beside her and prayed to their Father of Lights giving thanks that nothing could ever separate us from the Love of the Father now, nothing. He laid his hand on her heart, and she recalled the dream the night before and felt anew the scroll of God's all-consuming love for humanity open and pour out into her soul by His Spirit's breath. She pondered God's love and His yearning for the world to know Him as their Father.

Her mother's heart began to grow in the same direction, for the whole world. Christ's and the Father's Love was enlarging in her a love for the world. His love for the world was now hers. "Father is pleased to give you the Kingdom. My death is your death, my life is your life, my Kingdom is yours on earth, my resurrection is your new birth, and this is where hope comes from; this is for everyone."

She said "Yes, yes, yes. My Lord and my God. I'm your Father's daughter."

He gently sent her into His mystery where she met their Father and found her new commission. He could hear her begin to pray for those she would have never been able to pray for until now. Drifting onto a sea of forgetfulness of all dread, she visited home. He smiled at His dear mother.

As it goes when one closes their eyes in having gone through such a passage, hours passed in a blink. She was awakened again nearly instantly to the high-pitched scream of another dear Mary who came bursting into her room, screeching at the top of her voice: "Mother! Wake up! He is alive! Get up! Get up! Get up! He is alive! I saw him myself! He is alive! He's alive, indeed, I tell you!" she screamed at Jesus' mother again, "He's alive!" Uncontrollable laughter erupted and rolled over them both like a flood. Mary grabbed Mary and they held onto Joy in each other until both women fell to the floor, where they laughed and laughed and laughed until they cried. The deep well of water had risen up in their vessels of clay and turned into wine.

"The Son of God suffered unto the death, not that men might not suffer,
but that their sufferings might be like His."
—George MacDonald, (Unspoken Sermons, Series I)

Chapter 12: God's Wish

"It's the glory of God to hide a thing and the glory of a king to find it."
—Solomon

God's Wish

We've seen dozens of images by now to consider and reconsider. We've visually placed relationships outside, on the table so to speak, where we can examine the arrangements and configurations and their implications. With the previous fictional presentation, we've had the opportunity to view an entire rearrangement between Mary, her Creator God, her Son Savior, and her enemies. Jesus reconciled her to God as Father, and in the ministry of that reconciliation, He opened her heart to the work of God in humanity. So we now come to a need to see the whole of the work of creation and redemption and attempt to discern exactly what that looks like through orders.

Trying to orient one's soul by the terms of the spirit is the most important integration in life. In this chapter we will consider a synthesis of the whole matter of parts one and two, and yield the soul to the spirit.

Now, we started out in this book defining our relationship wishes and we spent nine chapters viewing those arrangements through a Biblical framework. We explored the realities through the vehicle of clarifying a wish as a first step of detangling from a system that has limitations. As we come to the spiritual realm, we naturally have to yield and notice that God has a wish. These two—the soul and the spirit—come into agreement in this chapter.

People have all wanted Love in some human relationship. In the introduction, we defined Love as God, and it is He Himself that acts to resource us. As we saw in the last chapter, God's wish is redemption (Life.) And Life is the root and the offshoot of Love. Love Himself, wants to us to have His Life. So we can assume there is a way to come into agreement with God's wishes if we can figure out what that looks like and how it is that Learning to "Just Bow" can be a really superb way to merge.

Just as we clarified the definition of love, we clarify that definition of life. We can not have love without life.

According to a fractured world view, we define life as having a pulse. This is a physical definition. Jesus didn't speak on these terms. He spoke of waking people others referred to as dead, such as Lazarus, and Jairsus's daughter. What's more, He introduced three of his disciples to Moses and

Elijah, long since dead, but revealed as alive. These aren't parables. This is reality according to the Lord of Life.

If we have a pulse but are not spiritually alive, if we only exist in a physical space, we are terminal, or dead on arrival, without hope. Many people living in that false reality have a legitimately powerful fear of death which prohibits their freedom in life. Others, depending on their disposition, have no fear, and perhaps are not justified in that fearless reality. Just as we erred in defining love in a physical and singular "self"plane, we have also naturally mistaken life.

Point being, one can not Love well if one is spiritually dead. If Love is a product of the Holy Spirit, and if Jesus is the Life, then the indwelling presence is our source of both Love and Life.

The typical world view and world system of the survival of the fittest —is a dead system. It implies self-dependency and promotes getting for the taking. Although there is a psychological idea in the hierarchy of needs which theorizes that once one has all their needs met, they become altruistic, we don't have many demonstrations of it. Jesus asked what did it matter if a person gained the whole world and lost their soul?

I have seen people put their whole household of relationships into a fresh workable arrangement and not maintained harmony because they had no living spirit to sustain their soul. It seems like "it" didn't work. Love depends upon Life. Life is the presence of the Spirit of God who fills us with all we need for life and godliness.

I have also seen people with more professional experience than mine in facilitating this kind of work, who've gone on to make blind blunders in significant relationships as if they learned nothing, as if the structures were merely good ideas easily forgotten. Without an allegiance to someone higher than the gift of the work, work is only work and people don't really keep working at it when another option tempts them elsewhere. The futility serves to demonstrate the scripture *"unless the Lord builds the house the laborers labor in vain." (Psalm 127:1)*

The plan for the souls of men in dealing with each other relationally, is to Love well. We wish to do so. There is also will for the spirits of men to be conformed to Christ. God wishes to impart spiritual life to us. Life supports Love to bear fruit in relationships to become fellowships and light for the world.

We need a single eye, a single sight, a single organizing principle— which is Life Himself. This single union integrates us body, soul and spirit and protects us from being swallowed up by the broken systems all around us. This single unifying Spirit makes our spiritual life practical in our relations. This is why we are here.

We will give our attention to visualizing that single rule of Life now as we look at John 17 as a cosmic reality that overcomes the counterfeits of many world systems. Following that reality piece, we will synthesize the work of integration between the soul and spirit by reviewing some earlier stories and examining a final story from both a systems view and a spiritual life view. Together these will help us merge the wishes and find the bow.

The World Lost Inside the System

In an embodied study on John 17, the High Priestly prayer of Jesus, a little boy of twelve represented God. By the end of the reading, the entire room of representatives had all migrated, coming together to form a straight line. "God" was standing on a chair at the bottom of the room, Jesus was facing God, behind Him was the Spirit, next were the disciples, then the believers who were destined to come to faith through their testimony, and at the very top of the line was the world. God was at the bottom of a straight line to the world.

God leaned over so he could see the end of the line.

"Hey World!" called out the twelve year old standing on the chair.

The representative for world leaned over likewise so as to see God, "Yes God?" answered the world. They were mirroring each other's behaviors.

The Godly-boy said, "I noticed you have been quiet all night and haven't said anything yet. But I want you to know I see you back there." And stretching out his arm displaying the work of the eternal line he said, "and I'm doing all of this, for you!"

The World, taken aback, grabbed her heart, deeply touched, smiled and said "Oh thank you God."

Of course the whole room of representatives melted. People knew next to nothing about that little twelve year old boy nor the hardships in his life, only that he perfectly embodied God's Word—God's wish—for all of us.

To look at it visually speaking, it seemed initially like the World had no business being at the top of the room nor God at the bottom. The world-system was out of order. The first image, like an initial family set up, was out of order. And that's the exact problem into which God incarnated. God has incarnated into humanity to destroy the works of the devil, the flesh, and the world system in order to deliver mankind. He straightened it out but we need to see that image — now — by faith in order to come into agreement with the finished work and take our place in it.

But this is a little sketchy. We can easily set up relationship figures relative to the soul. But everything in the Spirit is spiritually discerned and requires faith to see into the realm of faith. This kind of "show and tell" is an opening to a revelation. This is the work of the Holy Spirit. The Spirit shows us what we don't naturally see.

If in our mind's eye we flip the line to reverse it, then the world would be on the bottom staring up at the light of the world beaming through each representative. Being filled with back supporting light from the Father they would be facing forward at the World and all would stand on a chair with a welcome home sign for those stuck in the limited systems. This is what's happening in heaven. May it be on earth as it is in heaven. The response? The world would not be on a chair, but in a bow, and in bowing, enter in and rise up. That rise is what happens after a bow.

To see true alignment clearly enough, I encourage the reader to make a careful study of John 17 with no hurry, just open hearted eyes to let the truth rise. The 17th chapter allows us to see how God puts the cosmos into order—where Life is, and where death is in relation to life.

In this prayer, Jesus specifically states that He is—not—praying for the world. We need to—see—what he meant and what he did not mean. Fears of exclusion and suspicion of doubt can easily creep in here and good doctrine can go bad.

Our first hint of hope though is that Jesus prayed for his disciples to be protected from the evil one. Recall that the tempter's aim is to deceive Adam's race into not keeping God's word as Life. Jesus knows the aim. His report is that the disciples have kept God's Word as Life.

Evil is a rejection of God's word.

Jesus as Life, Logos, the Word made flesh—embodied—asked that nothing change or be lost in His departure but rather only that fellowship would increase so Joy would be full.

Recall too, that in His temptation, Jesus was offered the kingdoms of this world if He would worship the devil. This would be a total rejection of Life. It is an evil thing to do, and make no mistake, worship of any kind, is currency. What is purchased is either life or death. Paul tells us our warfare in this life is not physical but spiritual—demonic powers in high places.

Jesus was not praying for the world, he was setting Himself apart from the pride of a dead system to kill it by dying unto it—for us and our salvation. He was praying to separate all humanity from a rogue system of idol worship. The captives of the world systems were being bought, not prayed for, but purchased. The deal was being struck. He prayed for those who had received and would receive the Word of Life. As for the world, He was sanctifying Himself for sacrifice. Through all of this surrender, sacrifice, and deep bowing, He purchased our salvation. God's way was through benevolence for the world not dependence on it. I love this God of Jesus. Rest assured we are all Loved. Let that light shine.

See this. He prayed for complete unity with God and with His disciples as well as all those who would come to God through their testimony. His interests were union through faith. And why? So that the world will believe. Indeed it is a straight line. Even if for a moment God is at the bottom of the room He is still on a throne. Jesus prays for union — so the world will believe.

Eugene Peterson paraphrased Paul's letter to the Ephesians in chapter 1, saying that the world is peripheral to the Church—not the other way around. Let that visual expand in your mind's eye. This locates and orients the Church which is His body in a higher order than the captives in the world system. There is a system, but there is an eternal Kingdom. God's wish is to bring dead humanity to Life through faith in the One raised from death for us and our Salvation. For now, we are in the world but not of the world. Jesus didn't pray that we'd be taken out of the world, but protected from the evil one while journeying through it.

We are all God's children in terms of His claim on us, He excludes no one in His wish. But the disciples are not at liberty to change the words of Life nor presume to 'include' others into God's will on other's terms. The terms are Life, the terms are declared in the Word of Life. These Words are Light and Life.

This is His world, His Salvation and His terms have been predetermined and completed by Him, thus "It is Finished." To His terms we bow. In them we rise. In rising we embody light for those in dark to see the way home. For man to be whole, he needs ultimate order, life in the Spirit.

"Come to me, all who labor and are heavy-laden, and I will give you rest. Take my yoke upon you and learn from me, for I am gentle and lowly in heart, and you will find rest for your souls. For my yoke is easy, and my burden is light."
(Matthew 11: 28-30)

This is not survival of the fittest, but survival of the resting.

"Every time we reverse the divine order, the result is disaster. The Lord

Jesus has done everything for us, and our need now is to rest confidently in Him. He is seated on the throne, so we are carried through in His strength. It cannot be too strongly emphasized that all true spiritual experience begins from rest." —Watchman Nee, Sit Walk Stand.

Rising to merge

Jesus having risen, is betrothed to the believers in chronological earth time, while the Spirit is drawing believers up out of the earthly systems, into that heavenly reality. This is the work of reconciliation. As Eve was returned to Adam, humanity is returning to Christ and the Father of us all.

When He ascended, His Spirit fell giving gifts to men to establish the Family of God. The Church soon came to be called Christ-followers, or Christians. This is the eternal race made up of every tribe of people groups —not at all an Aryan exclusivity—but a benevolent inclusivity born of faith in His sacrifice. The growth chart of the Church has been interesting.

As mentioned earlier, according to the book of Acts, the Spirit was quite protective of this new bride and did not allow posers to set up as leaders in the new family fellowship. This was part of the answer of Jesus prayer for protection in John 17. The 'leave and cleave' was non-negotiable. Although it is painful today to see men and women presumably Christians become exposed as insincere when their crimes make front line news, exposure is still an answer to prayer for protection from evil. Every time a minister is seen as a pedophile, we have an answer to prayer. The purge has to happen for the sake of redemption for the world.

Few worked harder for the testimony of Life than Paul. He was so heavily imprinted by the Lord's ferocious affection for him, he sincerely mirrored sacrifice for the sake of the message. He delighted in the chance to mean it. The thorn of persecution that Jesus wore on His brow, Paul also wore on his back in frequent persecutions. The Church has to mean it as well.

Jesus was flogged, which is to be beaten with a skin-shredding, multi-layered whip of straps and shards of bone: 39 lashes. Likewise, Paul survived various "thorns" of persecution. He survived being flogged five times, stoned three times, and beaten with rods as well. That was his cost for transcending his tribe. Every time he was arrested for evangelism, he owned imprisonment as a platform to preach to the judicial systems. Even in jail, while hand-cuffed to his jailer, he considered the warden as a captive audience. Persecution was the price he paid for transcending his tribal system.

He was truly free from every lesser mind and allegiance. Freedom enabled him to fearlessly fulfill his call as he constantly asked for prayer for receptivity. Clearly those prayers were answered. When Paul was arrested and tried in Jerusalem by the same political group that called for the execution of Jesus, he was free from fear; he was inspired to take another chance to explain that Abraham was indeed and at last a Father to many nations — this was the new age for an old promise of God to reconcile all men to himself. He wasn't betraying his tribe on earth, though many saw it that way, he was aligning with the fulfillment of the wish of God.

All the apostles transcended their own earthly view of their destiny and were willing to suffer for the sake of others being informed. In transcending the earthly conscience, they conformed their minds to Christ's, and, in doing so, they became an offense to some of their own. (leave and cleave.) This explains the wonder that Jesus said unless one hates their family they can not be His disciple. That 'world system' is infected with a survivalist amoral conscience.

Early Jewish Christians understood that the heart behind the law was the ministry of death, demonstrating our need for a new life. The presence of Love incarnate was Logos Himself, Jesus manifested an indestructible Life. Love meant it. Love did the heavy lifting. Love is the law. Love is the resource of faith. Love brings life more abundantly on Love's terms.

Their consciences were completely changed. They understood that cutting the skin off the end of a male sex organ never kept that body part out of mischief. It was a shadow of the covenant making God who could change a heart. The Gentiles could never improve their morality by cutting, but by faith. By faith, they reconciled their whole dead lives from the first Adam through the sacrifice of the second Adam.

The record in Acts details how they all—Jews and Gentiles together —had to work all the details of this out in their minds and come to new conclusions about old shadows. It was not easy. The old mind doesn't just lay down and die easily, the new man has to build a new mind in Christ and take every old rogue thought captive to the obedience of Christ.

It was a miraculous and messy time. The first couple of years of a new union often are. But Christians were beautifully increasing in liberty to love one another. The fellowships were multicultural—the kosher ate with the non-kosher. Racism was muted by faith. Where the Jews had trouble with liberty to eat 'shrimp,' the Gentiles had worried consciences over meat sacrificed to idols. Troubled by the old laws that had nothing to do with Love, they put up with and hurdled weak/tribal consciences for the sake of knowing God in Christ.

There are several "hall of fame" lists in the New Testament which honor those testimonies of change makers. The most familiar is the book of Hebrews which spans the whole Bible of faithful witnesses. There are several others at the ends of Paul's letters, the longest being in Romans 16. Paul remembered them and greeted them with his esteem and thanks for their work in the Gospel. Top of the list in Romans is, Phoebe, a Gentle woman, and Priscilla and Aquilla, a Gentile couple that refreshed Paul from burnout when he tried once to do the work alone. He also sent love to his family of origin who dispersed to Rome; no doubt those family members prayed Saul/Paul into faith. These lists are remarkable as a study. But point is the harmony of Gentiles and Jews in Christ.

Synagogue by synagogue, house church by house church, those who meant it took the faith all the way through Europe into the west, and north in what would become Russia and east to India, and south by way of Alexandria in Africa. Gloriously, the good news reached us! Two thousand years of the movements of the Gospel has had its share of insincerity, but it has also had the sincerity of the "one new man" as a force of heaven on earth.

In our chronological time line, we now stand on the verge of a new age. We are in the 500 hundred year shift. The nation of Israel has been resurrected signaling the end of the Church age, and the Lord is in the threshold! How, then, do we live into His Life as our own now? We live and love—Spirit first—not body first, not soul first, not tribe first, Christ as Life first.

To that end, we just bow—daily. We bow to the blood of Christ whose great mercy cleanses us from sin. And in bowing, we receive the blessing of Our Father. We bow in honor of our Heavenly Father who Adam sinned against in believing Satan, who assigned God a place beneath His rightful station.

We celebrate an incredible rearrangement whereby God bowed to the incarnation, ministry, death, burial and resurrection. He entered into Adam's terms of death, as a servant representative and won us through the hideous cross, exposing our error and forgiving us so we could see what we were made of and what He was made of — mercy. Of course we bow and agree to His eternal terms. We bow into our divine place as smaller, to be seated in the Father's lap.

Paul taught the early churches to present themselves as living sacrifices to God. (Romans 12) There was no need for a scapegoat now that the Lamb of God was provided. Just bow, as a living sacrifice, emptied of self, to embody the Life of God's mercy. No longer living a dead life according the nature of sin (which shall not be our master - Romans 6) but in bowing, we are set free to know the Living God who has given His Whole self to us, meaning it entirely.

So, here we are now, in this space where we walk in two places at once, bringing realities of heaven to our small parts on the earth. This is the bow of a Father/Child relationship. We need to see it in someone other than Jesus and the Christians. We need to see it in the shadows. Because we are still all so shadowy, we need to see it back there again for contrast. I want to discuss two Old Testament individuals whose lives give us a way to see heaven take over earth by faith back there.

We will briefly return to discuss Abraham's family system. When we discussed it earlier we looked at the rival tangle that had held them all captive in each generation. We will take a look now at their faith.

Next we will apply that same filter to King David. We've not discussed him yet, but "The Key of David" which is spoken of in Revelation 3:7, is a nice mystery to explore. *"And to the angel of the church in Philadelphia write: 'The words of the holy one, the true one, who has the key of David, who opens and no one will shut, who shuts, and no one opens.'"* No mystery should be left a mystery once we get an interest in it. These stories are stunners.

Joseph

In Genesis, Abraham's unfinished family business was carried on to future generations. The sins of the Fathers were handed down. The ancestral unfinished business was a live wire, an evil reaking havoc in the family. Competitive rivalry was older than the flood and as ancestral as Cain and Abel. But in Abraham's family, though the sins were unresolved, the subjects of their judgments were now, by faith, finding a mercy. Where God intervened, all things began to work together for the good of a larger plan, a plan much larger than the injuries. Joseph's faith allowed him to see and declare, "what man meant for evil, God meant for good."

It is a mystery that God can take anything and work with it to not only heal the victim but use the injury for a higher purpose, in this case to save many nations. It is an attribute of His grace that He is so compelled.

The evil that had taken an earlier foothold in one famine in the lives of Abraham, Sarah and Hagar the Egyptian, came full circle four generations later in another famine in the lives of Jacob and his twelve sons. In this famine the world was saved by the bread distributed in Egypt by an anointed Hebrew.

Genesis opened bringing order out of chaos in the first week of creation. Paradise was quickly lost when a man chose to trump God instead of govern God's creation.

Genesis is where a mankind-do-over through a flood demonstrated we needed more than a second chance. Man needed to put his faith in a Life other than his own.

In Abram we see the promised planted seed bloom into a family and a nation of faith as a light to the world. Slavery and exile had also been seeded into the family through Hagar. These would leave their mark. But Faith would leave a bigger mark.

Let's look again at Jacob, son of Isaac, grandson of Abraham, and now father of Joseph. Let's look with an eye for holy patterns.

Remember Jacob had been in his own version of exile, estranged from his family for 21 years as he raised his twelve sons in his uncle's land. He was also estranged about that same number of years from his son Joseph. Joseph was the son of his favorite wife, Rachel. Jacob's favoritism provoked the sons of Leah to sell Joseph to the Ishmaelites—sons of Hagar. After their reconciliation brought them together in famine, before Jacob died, he placed a blessing on Joseph's two sons, half Hebrew and half Egyptian Manasseh and Ephraim.

It should be obvious by now that earthly favoritism had been nothing but a family plague of exclusion. But what of spiritual favor? Is that exclusion? No, it is a gift of homecoming to our Father, also known as "The Blessing."

When Jacob gave Joseph a coat of many colors it had been a near death sentence. Jacob wanted to give a blessing to the children of Joseph and Asenath. He took those two grandchildren, reared outside the sight of their grandfather, blessed them and reconciled them as his very own. He declared their destiny of tribal belonging in the nation of the Israel that was still a dream of faith. He did not destine Joseph as a tribe, but each of his two sons would become included in the whole.

Notice that in the blessing, Genesis 48, Jacob deliberately reversed the order in giving the blessing. It was intentional. Had he learned nothing? Or had he learned everything?

Joseph tried to correct his father. But Jacob assured him that he knew what he was doing. Jacob gave the blessing of the firstborn to the second-born and the blessing of the second-born to the first. Why?

I believe he understood and prophetically announced the revelation of the relationship between the first Adam and the second, mainly that the second Adam (the Messiah Himself) would assume the responsibilities of the first. By faith Jacob saw the promise.

Over epochs of time, this pattern would be confirmed. Below is a chart of what followed historically in the ages to come. Notice the patterns of the first and second in Abraham's family, and then notice what happened in the 500 year spans.

The wisdom of the second Adam is a blessing of redemption for the first Adam.

First Adam: Captive of death	Second Adam: Conqueror of death
Ishmael: Born of slavery	Isaac: Born of promise
Esau: Forfeited birthright	Jacob: Lived out Esau's curse
Children of Israel: 12 tribes	Joseph: Given Ishmael's blessing
Manasseh: Firstborn (included)	Ephraim: Founding tribe of Bethlehem

500 years after these blessings of Jacob, the sons had become a nation of slaves in Egypt, whom Moses set free—leading them out through the Red Sea. They were introduced to the laws of their God. Rule number one —God first! After the first generation died for unbelief, Joshua, the second leader, led the nation to the land that had been promised to Abraham. Moses freed them from slavery to Egypt, but Joshua led them to their own place. There was a first leader, and a there was a second leader. Moses gave them the law, Joshua led them to their own place.

500 years later, having been led by priests, prophets and judges, they rejected a theocracy and asked for a king. Saul, their first monarch, poorly represented God. David, their second was a man after God's own heart.

After 500 years of monarchies and bouts of unbelief and infidelity, the nation was repeatedly warned by the major and minor prophets, and Israel, divided into two kingdoms, was conquered. First Israel, then Judah, and together they were dispersed into exile and only a remnant returned to Israel. God was quiet for seventy years and then sent a remnant to return under the leadership of Ezra and Nehemiah. But alas, Israel, under the law, was unfaithful. God was quiet for 400 years...

Then The Word of the Lord came to a priest Zechariah, through Gabriel. There was going to be a prophet—John—who would be prophet of the Lord Most High. And the same angel, Gabriel, announced the news of a redeemer secondly, to a girl, Mary. Her baby's name would be Jesus.

"First and Second" patterns persist.

Jesus came, first to Israel, and next to the Gentiles. And all those synagogues scattered throughout the entire empire were beacons of good news which was for all people.

And for the past two thousand years, while Israel has been exile throughout the world... a Kingdom without end has been rooting and spreading all over the globe.

The first time the Lord came, it was as a sacrifice. The second time the Lord returns in triumph. There is a first coming and a second. Just Bow, and buckle up. Genesis is a template for families and for nations.

Let's return to Jacob's story. After he blessed the half tribes of Ephraim and Manasseh, the scriptures from then on always refer to the two tribes in the order of the blessing, as Ephraim and Manasseh. The "second" is not a less-than station, as we might think of in favoritism, nor is the first a first-place blue ribbon position. Rather, the first born is often bearing a burden that the second born helps to carry.

God doesn't play favorites; He redeems the beloved. The Second Adam is a servant who serves to redeem the first that was lost, and to bear his burden.

Similarly, we are first born as a soul in a body. But our second birth is of the spirit. Thus, we come to the movement in the spirit realm that can subjugate the curse in us and the burden of our first birth in the earthly realm. We must be born again, born of water and the Spirit.

David

Let us now examine the earthly burden again in King David. This tale is always told forward and never backward. But this is how we unearth captivity. The burden of sin has a gravity and power, and the hold it had in the lives of Saul and David, amplify the fact that one can not escape without mercy. In their relationship, the pattern of captivity is better understood once we look at the roots. Lest we think we can escape without grace, their battles demonstrate the cruelty of captivity that was bigger than each of them.

Captivity is an issue we all have to face with the Holy Spirit. Ironically, as these men will show us, the issue shows up after our hard battles when we venture to rest in our own successes, and in our own attempts at doing good. These two kings will show us how "Do-gooding" can be a most slippery business if we remain unconscious of our family soul tangles. The soul can never accomplish the work of the Spirit. The soul must be saved in order to bow unto the Spirit.

A short review of highlights from the book of First Samuel will be contextualized by a relevant back story from the book of Judges. The two are rarely connected as one whole story. Generally, when people explore the back story of David, they reference the lovely story of Ruth. But there is an ugly story in Judges that explains a few things. After we appreciate the power of unfinished business, we will come forward again to the ascent of David. That is where we will see David almost forget how to be the right size with God. This is the key we need. This is where he found his bow. This is an incredible story. This is the most beautiful heart to heart talk between God and a man I've ever seen in the scriptures.

The Man After God's Own Heart: 1 Samuel

David was anointed as the King of Israel by the prophet Samuel when he was a teenager. In his own family, he was seemingly of no consequence: forgotten by his father and considered an annoyance to his brothers. God chose David to lead the nation after the first king, Saul, demonstrated that he "didn't mean it." Initially Saul was small in his own eyes and had to grow into leadership. However, once he was big in his own eyes, he usurped the role of prophet during war time. Unwilling to wait on the Lord, he defied God's war directions by playing priest and sparing a wicked nation's king whom God had slated for death. God replaced Saul for the sake of His people, by anointing David as king.

Although David did not formally take the ruling throne until he was thirty, his service as a shepherd began immediately. The first sheep the Shepherd was to tend was Saul. This is a dramatic picture of the long suffering of grace. Saul had become tormented by spirits. David was known and summoned for his musical skill. The praise of God became the king's only comfort. God knows us and what we need. There was trouble in Saul's veins. David was not only a comfort to the soul, he was a warrior for the people.

The nation was taunted by the various tribes that had not been fully routed from the land during the 500 year epoch of the Judges. The Philistines were a continual threat among others. Their warrior Goliath, by measurements a giant, made an offer to fight man against man instead of army against army. Goliath offered to let Israel live as their slaves if he killed their best warrior. This, of course, would strike a nerve with Israel who had been emancipated from slavery in a previous age.

David had a bigger vision and a courageous faith to support it. The text below shows the David's intent and motive.

Then David said to the Philistine, "You come to me with a sword and with a spear and with a javelin, but I come to you in the name of the Lord of hosts, (meaning God of angel armies) the God of Israel, whom you have defied. This day, the Lord will deliver you into my hand, and I will strike you down and cut off your head. And I will give the dead bodies of the host of the Philistines this day to the birds of the air and to the wild beasts of the earth, that all the earth may know that there is a God in Israel, and that all this assembly may know that the Lord saves not with sword and spear. For the battle is the Lord's, and he will give you into our hand." (1 Samuel 17:45).

David was young and wasn't actually even supposed to be on the battle front at all. He'd gone there on an information gathering errand for his father. But he was stirred up by the anointing. And in the Spirit's larger motive David decreed the highest motivation of the Holy Spirit, "so that all men will know there is a God in Israel."

In that wish, God's wish, David was empowered to defend Israel against a threat of enslavement. He did as he declared. He killed Goliath with a rock and a sling and then cut off his head and gave it to Saul. The people loved David for it. Then Saul's jealousy was aroused, consuming him with hatred for David thereafter, but why? Is this simply ego? He went to great lengths to hunt him.

First, he tried to kill David by sending him on a war game, setting his daughter Michal up as a bride-prize if David would bring back 100 Philistine foreskins. David brought him 200, winning not only the king's daughter but also the respect of her brother Jonathan. Jonathan soon became so aware of the anointing of God on David that he entirely divested himself of all his princely effects, basically surrendering his claim to his father's throne. This could have been in honor of David's anointing or fear of being killed.

Interestingly, when David's new wife Michal sent him out in the night to escape her father's latest hate hunt, neither following him nor his God, she placed her life-size idol in their bed as a decoy. The daughter of Saul was an idol-worshiper.

On the run, David had several opportunities to kill Saul, which he refused. In each test he put his trust in God and believed God would take Saul's life at the appropriate time and he would wait until then. Eventually, Saul's hostility sent David to seek refuge in exile—of course. But despair did not affect his faith. Even from a foreign land, while serving a foreign king in foreign wars against shared hostiles, David and his mighty men continued to defend and protect Israel from outside. (That will preach about Jesus)

Years passed, and finally an Amalekite killed Saul and reported the event to David as if the Amalekite could garner favor and perhaps make an alliance. David, ever-faithful, was shocked and filled with grief. He mourned Saul and Jonathan who had both died in battle, and killed the Amalekite. Had David agreed to an alliance, he would have made the same fatal mistake that Saul had made, and like Saul, would have lost the anointing in a moment of pride.

With the death of Saul, David was now safe to return to his homeland, and what he did next is curious. He taught his tribe, Judah, to mourn and lament the loss of their nation's king. The lament is one of record in 2 Samuel. It is set apart from the many Psalms he wrote, which remain the hymnal of the Scriptures.

David's own tribe immediately coronated him as their king while the rest of the tribes in Israel conferred the king's throne to another of Saul's sons, Ishbosheth. Under Saul's military appointment of Abner, it would appear their country was divided.

Military, wars, strategy, all make me yawn. And here is where we must wake up. This is where we might ask a serious question. Why and how? The whole country loved David and the whole country knew he was anointed and that was very evident. What is this about, really? Who cares?

We do.

Why is the nation divided? The prophet Samuel is long since dead and we haven't heard a peep out of any other spiritual advisor. Why does Abner seem to be in charge of Israel through Ishboseth?

Where, we should ask, did that kind of division come from?

Has this ever happened to Israel before?

Hadn't God chosen David to shepherd all of his people Israel?

Here is where we look into the rear-view mirror of history and see something sobering.

Recall that the people, prior to having asked for a king, had been ruled for 500 years as a theocracy. We must go back one generation or more to find a back story.

Once upon a time, at the end of one 500-year epoch and near the dawn of another, when tribes were led by Judges, there was a faithless priest. (Whenever priests are faithless, the country is slated for trying times.)

One priest, unworthy of his call, had a concubine; a practice that did not please the Lord, especially among priests. The woman with whom he role-played, and with whom, we could say, he did not "mean it," was unfaithful to him. Eventually she went back home to her father.

After some time, the priest decided to go fetch her. It wasn't easy. It took days for her father to concede for her to leave with the faithless priest.

It finally happened, and the two set out for home.

Traveling late and on into the evening to avoid stopping in Jebus (later called Jerusalem, the City of David) the couple made it to the tribe in Benjamin. In this tribe we get a hint about the spiritual temperature of the nation. The townsmen were as ruthless as pagan men were during the days of Abraham when he first entered the land then called Canaan. In Abraham's time, 1000 years earlier, Sodom and Gomorrah, were torched by God's wrath for debauchery. Benjamin was like Sodom had been.

Here is where the faithless priest decided to stop for the night. They waited in the town square for someone to offer them refuge, and a man finally did so out of concern for their safety. That night, the townsmen demanded that the master of the house turn over the priest for their perverted sexual pleasure.

The master refused. They would not relent. The master of the house offered them his virgin daughters as well as the priest's concubine. The men insisted on having the priest. The master tossed the priest's concubine outside, and the Benjamites gang-raped her to death.

In the morning, the priest found her lying on the ground, with her hands on the threshold of the door, dead. The priest kicked her to wake her and finding her dead, loaded her body on his donkey and headed for home. There he proceeded to cut her body into twelve pieces and send them throughout the tribes of Israel (Judges 19).

Israel was appalled. Delegates gathered together before the Lord utterly at a loss over the evil in their country. And God gave orders to cleanse the land.

God raised up the tribe of the concubines birth, to attack the tribe of the perpetrators. There was no mention of the priest's rebuke yet.

So in obedience, Judah attacked Benjamin. Judah lost over 20,000 men in the first battle. After inquiring of the Lord again, in obedience, they attacked Benjamin, and again they lost more avenging warriors. It seemed like Judah was getting the wrong end of the stick. Requesting clarity once more, they were told by God to go into battle a third time, and in this attack, they slaughtered over 25,000 men of Benjamin and destroyed their cities, nearly decimating the entire tribe.

Israel's delegates came to Bethel, where the ark was, to sit before the Lord's prophets and inquire. The civil war was not stomached well by the nation. There they grieved that they were on the verge of losing one of their tribes. Benjamin was devastated.

Now, we might ask God, "Well, Lord, what about that faithless priest?" Did he, as a member of the Levitical landless tribe, escape rebuke?

It would at first seem so, but only for the time being. Meanwhile the priests certainly did not improve in devotion. The first story in 1st Samuel is of Eli the priest and his horrible sons Hophni and Phineas. It details how dark the faith landscape remained by describing the ways these men treated the nation's attempt to seek the Lord.

At that time a barren woman named Hannah prayed for a child, she accurately represented the spiritual barrenness of the land. She sought the priest in Shiloh for intercession. Eli the priest thought she was drunk. But upon hearing her better, Eli mercifully made a declaration which she believed, and God granted her a son, Samuel. Samuel grew up in the priest's house but was faithful to God his whole life. He is the one who anointed Saul and David as kings, because the country no longer wanted a theocracy. This broke Samuel's heart, but the larger priesthood in the land had long since left their first love, and the people followed suit.

Now, let's fast-forward past the end of the book of Judges and move further into 1st Samuel to one of Saul's hunts for David. During one hunt, Saul came upon some priests who he believed had aided David in his escape. In a rage, Saul slaughtered eighty priests.

In that move, we might say God purged the land for the sake of His people. Still, the question we started with was why Saul so brutally hunted David. Was it just about the throne, the ego, the jealousy?

Why did David have to wait so long for a promise to be fulfilled?

Why was Saul so full of anxiety and vitriol?

Why was the nation divided after Saul died?

Was their battle in their histories? Did it belong to their systems?

Does the earlier civil war story, born of apostasy and unbelieving priests, have much to do with these men?

Indeed. David is from the tribe of Judah. Saul was from the tribe of Benjamin. A Benjamite had no respect for the priests, nor had they in times past.

Isn't it interesting that the first king God gave Israel in answer to their desire for a king was from the tribe of Benjamin? He was initially hesitant to take the position, and even tried to hide. He was small in his own eyes. Eventually though, he lost his humility, and forfeited his chance to restore dignity to the tribe of Benjamin.

God chose another man, one after his own heart, from the tribe of Judah. This was a stinging reminder that God commands faithfulness from His priests and his people.

The tribe of Judah was also chosen to host the lineage of the Messiah. But David, who was in the line of succession, had to be more deeply converted. His particular prayer of communion is unlike any other. It's all about the bow. We will arrive there shortly.

At the time that David came into his formal kingship, Israel had forgotten the basic commands of God. Worse, they were dismissive in their view of the Ark of the Covenant, treating it like a lucky charm. The stories about it being stolen and set up in the temple of Dagon are remarkable.

The Ten Commandments from Exodus 20:5 in Moses day stated, in regards to idolatry:

"You shall not bow down to them or serve them, for I the Lord your God am a jealous God, visiting the iniquity of the fathers on the children to the third and the fourth generation of those who hate me, but showing steadfast love to thousands of those who love me and keep my commandments" (ESV).

Saul's daughter, an idol-worshiper, showcased a lost spiritual appetite. But, in David, we see a steadfast love and mercy at work. God knows what influences have preceded our birth. He knows what has happened to tilt a tree to grow in one direction or another. He knows what has been set up in our genetic inheritance through trauma and family memory, stored in our DNA and ancestry. Though the die has been cast systemically, according to the law mentioned above, mercy triumphs over judgment for those who will bow and seek God.

The civil war was mercifully reduced down to a final two people, but structurally speaking, those two were representative of the whole nation. Instead of 100,000 warring against each other, we have two. As for the slaughter of priests, we might wonder if it was the last of God's vindications for the nameless concubine, unworthy of a priests commitment.

The state of the priesthood spiritually mediated the state of the nation. Saul had lost his appetite for God's law and he did not care for the words of the prophet. After Samuel the prophet died, in another desperate war situation, Saul sought out a witch to force the soul of the prophet Samuel up from the grave to demand comfort and direction. We see his arrogance in thinking he could force the soul of Samuel to mediate and still serve him from the grave where he was at rest. It appears that Samuel came, but he simply rebuked Saul's rebellion. There was a hidden mercy: Samuel told him that on the morrow Saul would be with him. The next day an Amalekite killed Saul.

Only the mercy of God can alter one's course. He is the willing savior, if a person can assume the position of trust. The family train of tribal influences comes barreling down a track, slating a soul to follow suit. No one can oppose this force in their own strength. Only mercy stops a train, and that is a spiritual task that calls for a bow.

Communion comes from being the right size and in the right place.

David found mercy in the eyes of God. When he taught Judah to mourn, he demonstrated grace, and this brought a little more peace to the tribes with such a history. Seven years into his reign as King of Judah, David was coronated King of all of Israel. The soul of the nation was mending.

At this point, we might think that matters of the family and national soul were settled, and things would finally be smooth for David. But this is where David nearly forfeited his life by getting out of place with God— just like everyone does when they become comfortable or wise in their own eyes. We need help everyday.

Adam lost interest in God's Words.

Priests lost interest in God's Words.

Israel lost interest in God's Words.

Saul lost interest in God's Words.

And, soon enough, after David had peace, he did something that appeared innocent. If trials can't ruin a person, success just might.

David became well-established in Mount Zion after he took the city from the Jebusites. There, he was pondering his own palatial situation when he decided he wanted to bring the Ark of the Covenant to be near him where he lived, in what was now Israel's capital city, the City of David. The ark was generally kept with priests in Shiloh. He made a search for it, and in finding the ark, he made a capricious plan to bring it to Zion.

Finding it, David presumed to lead the way, literally, without the priests, whose business it was to tend to the ark. Years earlier, when the ark had been stolen by the Philistines and set up in their temple to Dagon, the effect was the dismembering their idol's head, hands, and feet, as well as giving the Philistines tumors. They sent the ark back to Israel.

Now with the ark in David's possession, in route, it nearly tumbled from the carrier, and a man presumed to "help" support it by reaching out to keep it from falling. He was instantly struck by God and died. David was rightfully terrified. In fear, he abandoned the ark, leaving it in the safe keeping of the nearby Levitical priestly family of Obed-Edom. Three months later it was reported that a great blessing had come to this priestly family, and David decided to pursue the ark again.

This time however, a thorough search in the Scriptures was applied, and the priests were reinstated to their national duties. The priests had a place of spiritual leadership and they were necessary for mediated blessing. In the battles past, prior to the monarchs, it was the priests who went forward into battle with the Ark, leading worship and singing praises to God. This was part of the battle plan because they believed the battle belonged to the Lord. Now, David recruited them to do their part in transporting the ark and to take their place together with the ark in the City of David, to make sacrifices and offerings of praise. David reinstated the function of the priesthood.

He was learning to keep things in order, and the ark was brought to a resting place to bless the nation.

Peace, like love and joy, is spiritual. It does not come from the soul, but is a gift for the soul. Spiritual life has to be managed and integrated by faith, and though David was on a spiritual quest, he was pursuing the Spirit on the terms of the soul.

The soul of man has to be subject to the spirit, the Spirit of God. This "ordering" task is where David nearly fell out of spiritual step in his position with God. This dis-orderly approach to God is a key pattern in Adam. We see it here again in David.

Read the text below very carefully with an eye for order. Recall the orders we've seen in many relationship placements throughout this book. Remember the various kinds of love that are at work in the different relationships over a lifetime: benevolence, justice, fidelity, sacrifice and what they indicate about the positions. Notice the position from which David was acting and the placement he seemed to assign to God, and indirectly to himself.

At this point, David had been through many trials in family, in marriage, in battles for country, threats with tribesmen, and missteps with priests and the ark. Each of these human relationships in the realm of the soul illustrated how he inherited the unfinished business of his family and country. But now the key issue for David, was the disposition of his heart toward God. This was a spiritual relationship. He was human, he was a soul, and God is a Spirit that David was engaging with on his own terms.

This is likely the most astounding conversation between a man and God in the entire Old Testament. This is the crossroads between spirit and soul, heaven and earth. Here we examine the positions David applied to himself and to God. Visualize this.

After the king was settled in his palace, and the Lord had given him rest from all his enemies around him, he said to Nathan the prophet,

"Here I am, living in a palace of cedar, while the ark of God remains in a tent." (2 Samuel 7:1-2)

The prophet Nathan assumed that whatever David thought or wanted was good. He neglected to inquire of the Lord for David. David got it in his mind to build God a dwelling place.

He's the provider now. He's becoming benevolent.

How might David set up this issue?

When we set this story up to explore it in our Tuesday Grace study group, we used only a small roster. But it gave us some things to ponder.

Initially, Nathan the prophet was stationed above the Ark, God sat to the Ark's left, locating the ark "at God's right hand," David was below them, and Israel below David.

According to the text, the prophet Nathan prematurely gave his own approval and support for whatever David had in his own mind for God's Ark. He did not inquire of God. That was out of order.

But then God spoke for Himself in order—through the prophet. In our study, the God representative told Nathan, "You need to get this straight; I give the message through you."

The scripture below is profoundly relevant. Notice how God questions the wish/issue of David, and how God declares his own benevolent deeds and acts of kindnesses to David. God was the sole provider. Again, emphasis is mine.

In 2 Samuel 7:5, God said, *"Go and tell my servant David, this is what the Lord says: Are you the one to build me a house to dwell in? I have not dwelt in a house from the day I brought the Israelites up out of Egypt to this day. I have been moving from place to place with a tent as my dwelling. Wherever I have moved with all the Israelites, did I ever say to any of their rulers whom I commanded to shepherd my people Israel, Why have you not built me a house of cedar?*

Now then, tell my servant David, This is what the Lord Almighty says:

I took you from the pasture and from following the flock to be ruler over my people Israel. I have been with you wherever you have gone, and I have cut off all your enemies from before you. Now, I will make your name great, like the names of the greatest men of the earth. And I will provide a place for my people Israel and will plant them so that they can have a home of their own and no longer be disturbed. Wicked people will not oppress them anymore, as they did at the beginning and have done ever since the time I appointed leaders over my people Israel. I will also give you rest from all your enemies.

The Lord declares to you that the Lord himself will establish a house for you. When your days are over, and you rest with your fathers, I will raise up your offspring to succeed you, who will come from your own body, and I will establish his kingdom. He is the one who will build a house for my Name, and I will establish the throne of his kingdom forever. I will be his father, and he will be my son. When he does wrong, I will punish him with the rod of men and with floggings inflicted by men. But my love will never be taken away from him, as I took it away from Saul, whom I removed from before you. Your house and your kingdom will endure forever before me; your throne will be established forever."

God is always in order and always a good Father. He made the soul saving shift in the spiritual realm.

In 2 Samuel 7:17, Nathan reported to David all the words of this entire revelation. Then King David went in and sat before the Lord, and he said:

"Who am I, O Sovereign Lord, and what is my family, that you have brought me this far? And as if this were not enough in your sight, O Sovereign Lord, you have also spoken about the future of the house of your servant. Is this your usual way of dealing with man, O Sovereign Lord?"

This is the key of David: Humility, order, dependency born of trust.

...Who am I and who is my family that you have brought me this far?

...Is this your usual way of dealing with man, O Sovereign Lord?

He and his family are now small in his eyes and high in his eyes is the true Sovereign of Israel and the world. This doesn't sound like a formal prayer of redemption, as though we are trying to fill in blanks on a questionnaire or check off ritualistic codes of salvation. But clearly, this is the key of David's faith. He is seeing who God is and what God has planned, which is salvation. And in seeing, he is bowing with the deepest respect for the Great I Am and His undeserved grace. God has announced His plan for a great salvation and a great house of God.

David had previously learned to wait on the Lord for movements in his next steps in life. Now, he learned to sit before the Lord and receive the point of all life, which is the Father/Son relationship. The door was being opened to life on God's terms. God was the builder of the houses: both the one that David's soul was in, and the larger one he was growing into by the Spirit, the house of God.

Jesus, 1,000 years later, promised that in His Father's house there were many mansions, and that He was going to prepare us a place so that where He is, we are. This is the key. Eternal life is knowing God and His ways. And as such, it requires a birth in the Spirit. We then live in His Spirit first, and this life transcends the limitations of our soul and its tangled conscience.

David as a man wasn't perfect thereafter. His mistakes in the soul are on record. But as a spirit, his trust in the Lord as his "Life" was larger. He knew God and His son Christ by faith. The evidence of his knowing the Lord one thousand years before the birth of Christ is evident in many Psalms. His faith allowed him to transcend earthly bounds.

What might we learn by hearing him sing the truth? The way a melancholy note can serve to interpret a word is not to be dismissed but rather, better understood. Music is the pulse of a poem bringing it to life and mercifully awakening every ear. What a magical way to fellowship. What David did for king Saul to comfort his afflicted soul, he also did for the nation, and led them to worship. Slaying the giants of fear in our hearts is still the Father's ongoing gift to us who've made our move into the House of God. But who can help but long to hear David himself sing his heart out to the Lord. One day we will. The shepherd David knew the Good Shepherd, and together they comfort us still. David sat before the Lord. That's where communion has a chance to happen. Seeing it in my mind's eye, I circle around his reverence as God's presence dawns on him. "Is this your usual way of dealing with man, O Sovereign Lord?"

Is it? It is, and it happens in *the bow.*

Just bow and come into the House of God.

Our study group spent a little time reflecting on some of the questions we had with the text. A careful reading raises questions. One of the earthly sons of David, Solomon, son of Bathsheba, was the one who built the first earthly Temple. Upon its completion, he had a remarkable experience together with the priests and the people when they asked God to fill it with His presence. It is a truly transcendent story.

But as a man, Solomon was later unfaithful. In his rebellion, he was never beaten with rods as the above prophetic text of David's prophecy described. Now, consider this, Solomon was not actually the one to build the true temple, as we noticed in the story in the last chapter. The house of God was built by God who is the builder. In fact, God never asked for a permanent material structure to represent Him.

The Temple of God is not made of cedar, marble, stones or gold. One thousand years later, a son of David was beaten with rods. Jesus, who is also called The Son of David, was beaten and crucified, although He was never unfaithful. Does the above text reflect this? It does.

God in Christ is building the Spiritual house of God. Jesus referred to His body as the temple, and told the pharisees to tear down this temple and that He would rebuild it in three days. They thought He was referring to Herod's temple, but He was referring to himself.

To the pharisees, it sounded ridiculous that a body could be the temple of God. But to the God of David, it was ridiculous to think that men could house Him in a building of any kind! He asks to be enthroned in our hearts as our Life and Breath.

There is always an earthly soul story and an overarching heavenly spiritual one. Paul said that our bodies are the Tents in which our souls are being conformed to the Spirit of Christ. Collectively in the communion of worshipers, we are the body of Christ, the Temple of God, and a light in the world.

This is the truth and grace given to Jesus who is seated in his Father's lap, and we have been invited into this fellowship. We like David, Mary, and so many others, must come home and sit at the feet of the Lord.

Exile.

500 years after David, when Israel had lost their way again, God sent many prophets to call them home. This is the definition of repentance: coming home to the Father. The prophet Micah explained holy orders this way:

"With what shall I come before the Lord and bow down before the exalted God? Shall I come before him with burnt offerings, with calves a year old? Will the Lord be pleased with thousands of rams, with ten-thousand rivers of oil? Shall I offer my firstborn for my transgression, the fruit of my body for the sin of my soul?

He has showed you, O man, what is good. And what does the Lord require of you? To act justly and to love mercy and to walk humbly with your God." (Micah 6:6-8)

500 years after Israel's exile, the true high priest and king, Jesus, prayed for reconciliation in His House just before He offered up his body and soul and surrendered His Spirit to God. We return again to John 17:1-11, and read the high priestly prayer. (ESV) Notice the wish of the prayer.

"Father, the hour has come; glorify your Son that the Son may glorify you, since you have given him authority over all flesh, to give eternal life to all whom you have given him. And this is eternal life, that they know you, the one true God, and Jesus Christ whom you have sent. I have glorified you on earth, having accomplished the work that you gave me to do.

And now, Father, glorify me in your own presence with the glory that I had with you before the world existed. I have manifested your name to the people whom you gave me out of the world. Yours they were, and you gave them to me, and they have kept your Word. Now they know that everything that you have given me is from you. For I have given them the Words that you gave me, and they have received them and have come to know in truth that I came from you; and they have believed that you sent me.

I am praying for them. I am not praying for the world but for those who you have given me, for they are yours. All mine are yours, and yours are mine; and I am glorified in them. And I am no longer in the world, but they are in the world, and I am coming to you. Holy Father, keep them in your name, which you have given me that they may be one, even as we are one."

What is God's name? It is Our Father.
What a wish.
What a House.
What an invitation to just bow.

He is the light of the world. He has kept a light on for us all to come home. There wasn't room for him in Bethlehem as a babe, but there is plenty of room for us all in His House. Come home to faith. This is His usual way of dealing with man.

This is the key of David.

Epilogue: Kiss, and Just Bow

"I am with you always."
- Jesus Christ
(Matthew 28:20)

A little boy of about four years sat with his mother and sister in the back of an unfamiliar church, listening to his three older brothers play music for a mission fundraising concert. His father, a musician, stood near the front, helping out with sound and equipment.

The child listened to the first band finish a set, then he listened to his brothers play a second set, but once the third band began, he became antsy and noticed that other children were in the large entry playing a game. He asked for permission to go play.

Soon, however, the migraine-inducing decibels drove the boy's mother to hunt for him. Interrupting the hide-and-seek game, she told him they were leaving and that their dad would bring his brothers home later. During the car ride, the boy sat perfectly still and was quiet with his older sister, obeying their mom, who informed them that everyone—including herself— was going to be on a "mouth-time-out." After they arrived home, his mother, still out of sorts with stimulation overload, told them not to turn the lights on when they went inside.

"Mommy, how can we see where we are going?" the boy's sister asked.

"Honey, just feel your way across the room, and go lay down in front of the sliding glass door and be very quiet; we're just going to lay down and look at the stars," she explained.

The small boy and his sister obeyed their mother, and the three of them went to the floor, laid down and stared at the stars. The night was cold, the sky was clear, and the stars were sparkling white. As the three of them laid quietly, the comfort of stillness grew. A star shot across the sky.

"Mommy," the boy said, "I remember when we laid on the trampoline at the rental house and saw a shooting star. That's when I prayed for God to fix you and Daddy. He did it."

The mother agreed, "Yes, he did. He fixed us."

The children were quiet again for a while until the boy's sister, older by two years, asked their mom to sing the garden song. Feeling more relaxed now and relieved, she began to sing the old familiar hymn she used to sing when she rocked them to sleep. The girl knew the words and sang with her mother:

"I come to the garden alone, while the dew is still on the roses, and the voice I hear falling on my ear, the son of God discloses...

When they came to the place the boy knew, he sang along slowly. *"And He walks with me and He talks with me, and He tells me I am His own. And the joy we share as we tarry there, none other has ever known."*
His sister couldn't remember the second verse but wanted their mother to keep singing. So she continued softly:

"He speaks, and the sound of his voice is so sweet, the birds hush their singing. And the melody that he gave to me within my heart is ringing."
The children joined again in the chorus

"And He walks with me and He talks with me, and He tells me I am His own. And the joy we share as we tarry there, none other has ever known."
The three were all very still. Their breathing had slowed, and there was peace and quiet. After a while in stillness, the little boy said, "Mommy, I want to give God a kiss."

"Go ahead," she said. "Give God a kiss."

He rearranged himself, coming up off his back from the floor, to his knees. He turned to face the window of sparkling lights in the darkness, stretched his arms out wide and upward, reaching around the big God he imagined was up above and in front of him. He saw Him there in his heart. Then he puckered up and kissed the kind, good God he felt there present with him, near him; not only far off in the sky with the stars answering his prayers, but there in the room, close enough to touch and real enough to kiss. He kissed God.

And that's when it happened.

The four-year-old boy fell face-down on the floor, hard.

Instantly, he began sobbing uncontrollably and freely.

He was completely undone. Head on the floor, chest folded over his knees, hands and arms heavy on the ground beneath him in a child's pose, he wept and wept and wept.

A mom generally knows which kinds of cries mean what, but this was a new cry to her. He was heaving unlike anything she'd ever heard from her little boy. On and on he sobbed. His sister and mother were stunned. Cautiously, his mother sat up. His sister looked at their mother for some direction with a frightened look that begged her mother to help her weeping brother.

But his mother hesitated to invade what might possibly be very sacred territory. What if her son was having a "thin space experience?" What if, for him, the veil was open, and he was in heaven on earth, experiencing God directly?

On and on he heaved.

Slowly, his mother risked interruption to rub his back tenderly, and then she whispered, "Honey, is this a good cry or a bad cry?"

He could only stutter out his words in broken gasps, "G-g-good."

"Oh, okay," she whispered. He was in a thin space, she concluded, and respected the deep movement of God in his young, dear soul.

There came no break in sobbing. This was not his manner; he was a very easy-going boy, cheerful, and not at all prone to drama. After several moments more of his unabated tears, and a bit more concern from his worried big sister, who continued staring hard in her mother's direction, their mother asked. "Honey, can you tell me what's going on now?"

He pushed himself up so she could hear him try to answer.

In broken sobs, he squeaked out, "I keep hearing God in my head over and over and over, saying "I love you, I love you, I love you."

He was marked by a heavenly kiss.

It has always been the desire of God to mark his people with His name of Blessing. His people are called to be blessed and to be a blessing. It was the job of the High Priest to receive the people's offering and confer a blessing of reconciliation. When Jesus ascended from the Mount of Olives, it is believed by some that he raised His hands to confer the same blessing.

I leave my reader with the blessing found in Numbers 6:24-27. This was what was despised by the priests who had abandoned "naming" the children of Israel as God's beloved, which later led to their captivity in a foreign nation.

Read it out loud, and consider that this is the Lord's usual way with people who bow.

"May the Lord bless you and keep you.

May the Lord make His face shine upon you and be gracious to you.

May the Lord lift His countenance upon you and give you peace.

...So they will put my name on the Israelites, and I will bless them."

In Hebrew, the word blessing means "to bow." It's how we receive His love. It is what God had to do to give it to us. He bowed; He condescended to us, but even in doing so, He remained big, and with Him, we are small.

Be blessed. You belong. Just bow.

Acknowledgements

I'm enormously indebted to Tuesday Grace Group for the blessings of taking weekly trips into fields of grace in scripture study. I thank these saints for treasure hunting and excavating countless gifts of insights. Thank you for trusting the Spirit to teach us together. The ways you've cared for one another during beastly life experiences, as well as celestial moments of joy, have shown to me again and again that God is with us. Thanks for tending to each other with His Love. Special thanks to those who asked for me to write this book, and for exercising the patience of waiting for it. This book is in part your work of fellowship.

To clients who've generously allowed me to share their experiences of soul healings from workshops and private practice, I give my heartfelt thank you. Your stories are miracles and they continue to inspire me each time I think of them.

I also want to express warm appreciation to friends and colleagues who've read and discussed concepts, and referred clients with full faith that these tools cut to the chase in record time. Thank you to: Vo Payne, Patricia Cone, Karen Strange, and also Kim Ballard for reading, and encouraging this work and for prayers and abiding friendships. I want to thank Claire Boor for early edits. Thanks to Sheila Saunders for providing the initial courses for Mountain Area Health and Education Center that brought me back to, and expanded my graduate school roots in family systems. Thanks for introducing me to the work of Bert Hellinger, Stephan Hausner, Bertold Ulsamer, and referring me to the German Intensive. I appreciate the many who have facilitated my healing: Saunders, Mahr, Hellinger, Hausner, Hemming, Schneider and Webber. Thanks also to the New England colleagues: Ed Lynch and Bill Mannle for bringing facilitators from across the pond. And special thanks to Susan Pogue, Linda Lockspeiser, Bethany Bryant, Margaret Opaterny for being game to explore the Bible set ups with me and see the value of this door to spiritual reconciliation. I appreciate your open-heartedness and cheers for where I've gone with this work. All of these have enhanced my understanding of family systems, even though many do not share my world view.

Finally, Thank You Father God, for allowing any of us to participate in your ministry of reconciliation, to see with your eyes of the heart, to sense your movements and flashes of light in the darkness of suffering. You do so solely out of the generosity of your mercy—whether we even recognized it was you all along or not—I give thanks. Your sacred presence, hidden among the least of these, is Love. Help us all to abide in Christ and believe. To you I most sincerely just bow.

Resources

Having a wide base of resources related to family systems as well as faith expressions is desirable, simply because no two practitioners are alike, just as no two Christian denominations are alike. The idea of the body of Christ having many different parts in one whole, where Christ is the head, applies to learning. Different parts of the body tend to different needs in different ways and not all are suitable to all others, yet they may fit in a grander scheme. Below is a short list of resources. My own favorite author is George MacDonald whoes fairy tales, romantic fiction, unspoken sermons draw us into a simple mysticism. Everyone should sit down with *The Curate* for general spiritual well being. I agree with C. S. Lewis, G.K. Chesterton and J.R. Tolkien regarding the Victorian writer, "George is the master." He inspires me like no one else outside the scriptures, simply because he loves Jesus for His very self. And that is where all healing comes from, the ever living Christ. Grace loves and heals us.

Faith Based:

Christian Mystics: 108 Seers, Saints and Sages., Carl McColman, 2016, Hampton Roads Publishing Co.

Healing the Family Tree: Kenneth Hall, M.D., 1982,1984, 1986, 2013, Society for Promoting Christian Knowledge. www.spckpublishing.co.uk

Healing Generational Wounds, Restoring Families, Churches and Communities: Douglas W Schoeninger, Ph.D., Judith Allen Shelly, DMin. Xulon Press, 2015.

General Education:

Even If It Costs Me My Life: Systemic Constellations and Serious Illness Stephan Hausner, 2015

The Healing Power of the Past: a New Approach to Healing Family Wounds Bertold Ulsamer, Ph.D., 2005

It Didn't Start With You: How Inherited Family Trauma Shapes Who We Are and How to End the Cycle, Mark Wolynn, 2017.

Looking Into the Souls of Children: The Hellinger Pedagogy in Action, Bert Hellinger and Suzi Tucker, 2014

My Wish:

JUST
BOW

CPSIA information can be obtained
at www.ICGtesting.com
Printed in the USA
FSHW021452120819
60950FS

9 780578 512228